YOUNG MAN BLUES
Notes on a Nervous Adolescence

JAMES HOWARD KUNSTLER

Young Man Blues
Notes on a Nervous Adolescence

First edition, published 2023

Copyright © 2023 by James Howard Kunstler

Written by James Howard Kunstler
Edited by Donald Kennison
Cover Design by Allen Crawford
Cover Photo Credit: Jody Uttal

Paperback ISBN-13: 978-1-952685-77-4

All rights reserved. No part of this book may be reproduced or transmitted in any form or by any means, electronic or mechanical, including photocopying, recording or by any information storage and retrieval system, without written permission from the author, except for the inclusion of brief quotations in a review.
Special discounts for bulk sales are available.
Please contact publishing@reprospace.com

Library of Congress Cataloging-in-Publication Data

Published by Kitsap Publishing
Poulsbo, WA 968370
www.KitsapPublishing.com

BY JAMES HOWARD KUNSTLER

FICTION

The World Made by Hand Series
The Harrows of Spring
A History of the Future
The Witch of Hebron
World Made by Hand

A Safe and Happy Place
Maggie Darling, a Modern Romance
Thunder Island
The Halloween Ball
The Hunt
Blood Solstice
An Embarrassment of Riches
The Life of Byron Jaynes
A Clown in the Moonlight
The Wampanaki Tales

NONFICTION

Young Man Blues
CrazyLand
Beauty and Catastrophe
Living in the Long Emergency
Too Much Magic
The Long Emergency
The City in Mind
Home From Nowhere
The Geography of Nowhere

THIS BOOK IS FOR ALL THE BOYS WHO HAD TO RAISE THEMSELVES.

Fore Note

This is not a sob story. It's a story about the difficulties of growing into manhood and my own particular struggle with disabling anxiety that came along with it, and how I managed to find my way. That was more than fifty years ago. American life was more comfortable and comprehensible than it is now as we face the discords of what I call *the long emergency*. I still had a hard time. I observe that boys today are up against a whole lot more in their quest to become fully functional adult men.

Strife comes at them now in every direction these days. Family life is more rickety. Fathers are more absent or damaged. College, if they get that far, exposes them to a lifetime of debt serfdom and a cargo of ideology at odds with how the world actually functions. Whole lines of work have vanished, and with them the chance for a secure existence in what was broadly conceived to be the middle class. The latest iteration of feminism literally mocks them for being men, for acting like men, and for wanting to develop into men.

I don't want to talk out of my ass about things I don't know. I do know what it's like to feel lost and terrified, and I would like to help other boys learn how not to be terrified as they pass through the archetypal struggle to grow up. I've learned a thing or two about navigating these latitudes. One is that life is difficult for everybody, forever and always, including the people who seem to be privileged, who seem to have it made. Another is that out of every room with a hundred people in it, ninety-nine of them think they are the only one who doesn't have his or her shit together. That is, just about everybody is insecure — and the single standout may be a sociopath.

My life has been fortunate. I was not called to my generation's war, in Vietnam. I was able to make a living in a vocation of my own choosing, writing about things that interested me. Since my twenties, I've hardly been bossed around — except in my bohemian years when I took short-term scut jobs to pay the light bill. I found my way to live in a tranquil and beautiful corner of the country. I made it to my seventies, with a few medical misadventures that I lived to tell about. I did not have any children, though I was married more than once. Perhaps what I have to say here is a message to the son I never had. To some degree, I was forced by circumstances to become my own father.

So I'm going to tell my story, thinking that young men who are struggling with despair, anxiety, and hopelessness will find enough encouragement in it to keep going, to become a full-grown someone who can cope with the tragedies of existence, and find meaning and joy in the journey — because those things are there for you. I'm going to jump around a bit chronologically in the telling, because the meanings of each episode in my life did not reveal themselves to me in exact linear order, but in patches, bursts, and sideward glances. I view a lot of this as comedy now, so don't be surprised if you find yourself laughing here and there. Samuel Beckett was right when he said, "Nothing is funnier than unhappiness."

PART ONE

CHRISTMASTIME 1965

New York City

One night sometime in the week before Christmas, which fell on a Saturday, I lost my mind. It was the last school day before the holiday vacation, so I'm guessing it was Wednesday, December 22. I'd just turned seventeen years old. I was on my way to a party off Riverside Drive with two friends, and something scary happened inside my brain while we were standing in a Carvel frozen custard shop on Broadway, up in the West 70s. It was like walking through an open elevator door where there is no elevator. I was never the same person after that. I don't know whether it subtracted or added something to my life. It felt like death might feel if you lived through it.

I went to the High School of Music and Art, a "specialized" public school established for so-called gifted children under Mayor Fiorello La Guardia back in the 1930s. I enrolled in it because my parents had split up rancorously eight years earlier and they liked to bludgeon each other about money, so private school was out of the question. (My fondest wish was to be sent far away from the city, and them to boarding school, but that was not to be.) By the mid-1960s the city's public schools had degenerated into a de facto dual system: the hundreds of regular high schools, which operated in the *Blackboard Jungle* mode, and four selective schools: Music and Art, the Bronx High School of Science, Brooklyn Tech, and Stuyvesant High School, where learning actually took place.

I made the arrangements to get into M & A on my own. My parents were preoccupied with their own affairs. I don't think we ever had a conversation about it. You had to pass a musical audition or submit an art portfolio. I got in as an art student. I'd already been painting a lot by age fourteen and had enough to show. I was coming out of a middle school where every day was like *Riot in Cell Block 11*. This was Junior High School Number 167, named after Senator Robert F. Wagner (1877–1953), whose son, RFW Jr., was then mayor. Though it was in the heart of Manhattan's "silk stocking" district, the Upper East Side, Wagner was a very disorderly place with shakedowns and beatdowns every day if you were careless. The school district was like a long fuse a few blocks wide that ran uptown and exploded in Harlem. By the end of my three years in that hellhole, I was desperate to *not* go on to one of the "regular" city high schools. We heard vivid stories about the mayhem in them and were warned to stay out by any means available.

M & A was about 80 percent white and the rest black and Puerto Rican, all of us there on merit. Most of the white kids were Jewish. They came from households like mine where books were part of the decor. Many were the offspring of arts professionals, a few even in showbiz, political lefties who believed in public education. And then there were some like me, whose parents were self-involved, distracted, or uninterested, so M & A represented a default safe haven in the absence of a better alternative. It was strictly a public amenity and there was no tuition charge. To be fair, M & A was a good school in its day, and it was still very much in its day when I went there. The daily routine was a regular academic load as prescribed by the State Board of Regents, with an extra two hours of music or studio art instruction tacked on, so it made for a very long day. Most students were highly motivated and well behaved. I was well behaved but not very motivated.

The art zeitgeist was at least a part of my bad attitude. The 1960s was the high tide of modernism and I was against it. Growing up in Manhattan, I was exposed to plenty of art early on, and knew a lot about it. My primary school had been PS 6 on 82nd and Madison, a block from the Metropolitan Museum of Art. They actually released us little inmates to the streets at noon, and I spent many lunch hours wandering the great halls and galleries of the Met. This was before art had become just another branch of the financial world. On a weekday afternoon the museum was quite empty because New York was still a middle-class city and most people were at work. There was no shakedown to get in the place either. It was free, another public amenity. Nor was there a security check. You just walked in. To be nearly alone in a place like that felt glorious, as if you owned it.

After I started at M & A, I became a regular at the Museum of Modern Art, the Guggenheim, and the Whitney too. Many class assignments required us to go. Our apartment on East 68th Street and Second Avenue was only a few blocks from the holy mile of art galleries up and down Madison Avenue. I saw the work of the art superstars of the day when it was fresh and hot: Roy Lichtenstein,

Young Man Blues

Robert Rauschenberg, Franz Kline, Robert Motherwell, Lee Krasner, Willem de Kooning, Bridget Riley, Jasper Johns, Marisol Escobar, the inevitable Andy Warhol, and many more. There were no pickup ball games or bike rides for me in those years. And I always went around the city by myself for reasons I'll explain shortly.

Modern art didn't move me. Even as a fourteen-year-old, the work struck me as little more than marketing stunts for a cynical age. It felt to me like the tale of the *Emperor's New Clothes*, a con that the public fell for and didn't dare oppose. I didn't buy my teachers' spiel that it was all about the paint itself on the flat surface, about the brushwork, about advancing *the cutting edge*, and the other bullshit they proffered. Edward Hopper was my idea of a painter, but by the mid-1960s anything that tried to represent the observed world was under suspicion of unseriousness, beyond the pale, retrograde, *square*! The sense of personal loneliness Hopper portrayed really moved me. That was the kind of painting that I wanted to do, and you didn't get a whole lot of support for that from the M & A faculty. I wish I'd known about Fairfield Porter, a figurative painter at the top of his form when I was in high school, who struggled to get attention then. Porter's work would become my ideal for painting much later in midlife. I still paint.

The teachers at M & A were almost entirely of a type: second-generation Jewish working-class lefty bohemian intellectuals who had been traumatized by the Depression and the war and who found a refuge on the New York Board of Ed payroll, with all its job security, pension benefits, and the stupendous amenity of summers off. Their slant on modernist art aside, my teachers were smart, well educated, and cultured. Many of them were products of the college campus that

M & A was geographically embedded in: City College of New York (CCNY), which, for decades, was tuition-free for city residents. If any of my teachers were successful artists in their own right, I did not know about it — I suppose they might not have had to teach.

The CCNY campus was way up in Harlem on 135th Street, over on the far upper west side near the Hudson River. Our apartment was way down and across town from there. The daily journey back and forth was tedious and depressing. By subway it was quite indirect. First, you'd have to go downtown on the Lexington Ave line to 42nd Street, transfer to the Times Square Shuttle across town, and then catch the Seventh Avenue uptown train to 135th and St. Nicholas Avenue. It was even more of a schlep for the many students who came from the outer boroughs of the city, Brooklyn, Queens, and the Bronx. One kid in my homeroom attended the school illegally, coming in from beyond the Nassau County line on the Long Island Rail Road (and then the subway from Penn Station). Some of these kids had to lug cellos, French horns, and other awkward items with them. But being highly motivated, they soldiered through it.

The disintegration of the subway system was already advanced in those days. Crime was on the rise. We heard plenty of stories about kids getting robbed, mugged, set upon by gangs on the subway. The rational transportation choice for me was the Number 3 Fifth Avenue bus, which at least ran above ground in daylight. The Number 3 followed an eccentric route, first north up Fifth Avenue, then west across 110th Street, and then it rambled uptown along Morningside Avenue through the slums, past the storefront churches, dive bars, and sorry tenements and finally to Convent Avenue. I often had to wait a good long time for it to arrive, stuck out on Fifth Avenue waiting in the icy wind. The trip took an hour each way on a good day.

Three other kids rode that bus from the East Side, two girls and a boy. We were all friendly, but I never saw them outside the school day and the journey up and back. Nobody else lived in my part of the city. Everybody else just lived too far away. At M & A, there were almost no extracurricular activities besides seasonal art shows and concerts, no sports teams, no dances, and when the time came not even a senior prom. Away from school I led a solitary existence. I went to Yankee Stadium now and then. You could get a decent seat for two and a half bucks. The bleachers were just fifty cents. The stadium was a straight shot up the Lexington Avenue subway line just over the Harlem River to 163rd Street in the Bronx, the cars stuffed with fans.

I did not hang out in Greenwich Village much because it reminded me of the people I went to school with. I did not identify with 1960s bohemianism. I didn't yearn to be a beatnik and hippiedom had not quite been born yet, at least not on the east coast. What I yearned for was to go bass fishing, ride motorcycles, play varsity baseball, and have romantic adventures with girls named Alice and Polly, and none of that was available in the city. I did skulk around Chinatown, though, eating in odd, filthy dim sum parlors and then inquiring among the herb dealers and knickknack vendors of Mott Street for fireworks, which they were rumored to traffic in. (I never found any.) I went to the movies incessantly and made many visits after school, near closing time when the crowds were gone, to the Central Park Zoo, which was also free in those days. I identified with the large, sad mammals held prisoner in their jail-like quarters: the gorillas, the lions, and a black panther who had developed the neurotic habit of banging his head against the wall of his cage.

By my senior year of high school I had developed an avid interest in drinking, and despite the fact that I was a very young-looking seventeen I was able to buy drinks in bars. The legal age for buying alcohol was eighteen in New York State then. Among the artistic skills I developed at M & A was a knack for forgery. Documents were not computerized in 1965, and none besides passports even included photographs. I turned out all kinds of meticulously handcrafted fake identification cards using India ink and watercolor and sold them to my fellow students. Bus and subway passes, which allowed students to ride free, were my stock in trade. They were sold only one day a month in the school cafeteria, and if you missed buying yours that day you would have to shell out a lot more money than I charged for a forgery. So my services became known and kids would come to me. Bus passes were easy to make, since it was the custom to just flash the darn things at the bus driver or the subway token vendor, who couldn't be bothered to look closely. I could make ten, twenty bucks a week easy, and beers cost only fifty cents then.

Forgery was my chief evening occupation at home that fall on school nights. It almost looked like I was doing homework in my room — though I worked while listening to "Cousin" Bruce Morrow's Top Ten countdown on WABC radio during the emergent golden age of rock and roll music. The fake driver's licenses I crafted under a magnifying lamp were from obscure states such as North Dakota and Missouri — my logic being that few New York bartenders would know what a real one looked like. Nor did I. To me, they were just little artworks. That was my version of modernism. A *genuine* con. The final touch, plastic lamination, made them even more impressive. You could buy laminate sheets at any stationery shop. I did not have a New York driver's license and nobody I knew at school had one, since everybody traveled by bus or subway, and few New York City parents had cars then either, let alone their teen children.

I also ventured into other bizarre, made-up forms of fake ID just for fun. For example, a conjured-up document I called an "Interstate Immigration" card, which purported to allow a US citizen to move from one state to another. It was very official-looking, with seals and stamps and, of course, the date of birth very clearly displayed. Though it was total nonsense, I never encountered a bartender who would not accept it as legit. I loved seeing how credulous adults could be.

My main watering hole in the fall of 1965 was an establishment called P. J. McCabe's on 70th Street and Second Avenue, two blocks away from the apartment I lived in with my mother and stepfather. Earlier on it had been one of those old beer and steam table corner saloons out of *The Lost Weekend* but the owner was buffing it up, turning it into more of a hangout for people who worked in advertising, television, and the press. The crowd were not arty people, per se, which was fine with me given my disdain for beatniks, but most were clever, cynical, and humorous young professionals who gave me some inkling as to a persona I might craft for myself. Luckily, my stepfather never dropped into McCabe's, so I didn't have to worry about getting busted. He worked in midtown, in the Seagram Building, and his after-work spot was P. J. Clarke's, on 55th Street, with its patina of glamour and prestige, where famous newspaper columnists, Mad men, TV producers, novelists, and even movie people went to schmooze. He also took turns at Toots Shor's establishment down in Rockefeller Center, which had a different mix of sports stars, journalists, and politicians.

Mr. P. J. McCabe himself was a tiny, wizened, jugeared figure nearly lost in his overcoat, who only turned up for a few minutes in the early evening with a blue money bag. He had no discernible personality, and always seemed in a hurry to get out of the place, which was actually run by a magnetic bartender/manager named Jack, who was largely responsible for improving the joint. When I first handed over my ID to Jack, he gave me a very long skeptical look that morphed into a conspiratorial smile, averring that I was a long way from North Dakota as he handed back the fake driver's license. He asked what it was like way out in Fargo. I told him things had changed there since Roger Maris broke Babe Ruth's home run record a few years earlier. It was well known that Fargo was the slugger's hometown. Then I ordered a Dewar's on the rocks because that was what my mother and stepfather always ordered when we went out to eat. Scotch was the official beverage of New York secular Jews in the media orbit. Once I established my presence at McCabe's I was never challenged. I was careful not to abuse my drinking privileges there, a hard lesson I had learned from the previous summer, to be explained presently.

I was friendly with some of my classmates at M & A during school hours, but I really had no friends, at least not in the city. When my parents divorced in 1957, our family was living in a new suburban housing development, one of the first east of old Roslyn village on Long Island's North Shore. We'd moved out there in 1954, just as the wholesale destruction of Long Island got rolling. As soon as their divorce was concluded, my father married a recently divorced woman on the other side of the subdivision. My mother moved back to Manhattan with me in tow. And so, for years, I went out to my father's house on alternate weekends, as specified in the divorce settlement, where I continued to visit with my earliest two childhood friends, Roger and Brian. Roger lived around the corner from my father's post-divorce house and Brian lived right across the street from the old house where our family broke up. We rode bikes, mostly. Roger and Brian never came to the city.

Later on, as a solitary teenager without brothers and sisters, I developed some interesting routines for occupying myself and seeking adventure in the city. I became an avid party crasher. My method was to cruise up and down the avenues on the east side on Friday and Saturday nights on the lookout for groups of teenagers and then follow them into whatever building they went into, and into the elevator, and into the party on the floor where the elevator stopped. I was never challenged for crashing parties. Even for teens, New York was cosmopolitan. We lived in a constant flow of strangers in the daily life of the city and these kids I latched on to accepted strangers showing up at their parties.

There was an inexhaustible number of teens I didn't know and a very large number of schools they went to, so I never encountered the same bunch twice, and I went to many parties, often in magnificent apartments. I was mostly interested in meeting girls, and did, and a few times ended up in makeout sessions with them that never went beyond that to actual sex. The birth control pill was not on the scene quite yet, high school girls were cautious, and anyway I was utterly without experience. I also never saw any of them again, though I wrote floridly romantic letters to one girl up in Connecticut who had been visiting her old summer camp friend in the city. I'd been reading the Andrew Turnbull biography of F. Scott Fitzgerald that fall and Scott's persona had come to replace Holden Caulfield's as my model for a plausible identity. Drinking was a big part of that, of course, along with a jejune tragic air. I felt doomed that fall, but so self-consciously and superficially that I wasn't aware of how I actually felt deep inside.

The question that loomed over me that fall was where I might go to college, or, more to the point, whether I might go to college. It was the normal programming for seniors at M & A to go to college, especially the Jewish kids. At my summer camp in New Hampshire, we were trucked over to Dartmouth to see movies at the Hopkins Center for the Arts every year, and Dartmouth was my idea of a college! The quaint small town of Hanover with its redbrick and white-trimmed buildings on Main Street, and the adjacent campus with its leafy main quadrangle, seemed enchanted to me. I wanted to go — if not Dartmouth, then somewhere like it. I had no idea how to proceed. The other kids at M & A talked about their applications incessantly. Of course, I received zero guidance from my parents. As for my school's guidance counselors, you had to at least show the initiative of asking to talk to them, and I didn't. I did my best to ignore the question.

My academic grades were submediocre. I'd flunked geometry and algebra and had to repeat both of them. My SAT exam scores would turn out disastrously, coming in under 1000 points of a combined 1600 for the math and language tests. I doubted any decent school would let me in. I also understood that generally you had to pay to go to college, unless you opted for the tuition-free City College — but the idea of spending another four years around the corner from my high school horrified me. I knew nothing at the time about New York's SUNY system of far-flung campuses all over the state and no one suggested I look into it. The truth was, I didn't know what I was doing with my life besides pretending to be tragic.

I gathered from my classmates that they expected their parents to foot the bill for college. I was afraid to ask my parents about it. They had managed to send me away to camp every summer since I was eight years old. I knew that the camp charged eight hundred dollars for the eight-week season, which was a lot back then. Since my mom had remarried in 1960, she and my stepfather had a share each summer in a big groupie house on Fire Island, a beach community, with a gang of TV writers they knew. If I'd gone there with them all summer instead of off to camp, they would have had to pay an additional share for another bedroom, plus worry about who would look after me on weekdays while they were back at work in the city, on top of just having me around on weekends. It was probably best for all concerned for me to not be around all summer. So I was sent to camp, which I loved.

In the course of things the fall of my senior year, I somehow found out that Dartmouth cost about two thousand a year, a lot of money in 1965. I assumed that we were too well-off for me to get a scholarship, but I wouldn't have known how to apply for one. I didn't inquire and nobody suggested it to me. Of course, I inferred that my mother's lack of interest meant no one had any intention of putting me through college. Though my mother never actually came out and said so, I figured she would say the same thing about college that she said about everything else I needed: *ask your father*. I was afraid to.

Even though I had heard and read the phrase "he worked his way through college" in books, movies, and adult chatter, it never occurred to me that it might be a way out of my quandary. My seventeen-year-old brain believed that autonomy began and ended with smoking cigarettes and drinking. I just did not know that I could make long-range plans and take active measures to direct my own life in a favorable direction. I felt entitled to be sent to college — it appeared that my classmates could count on that in their lives — and since it didn't look like that was going to pan out, I did nothing to help myself. It helped justify my tragic new persona: *the doomed young man*. I was dimly aware that high school would be over in six months, but I did not give a thought to what I might do. It was just a blank horizon like one of those surreal Yves Tanguy paintings in the MoMA. I suppose I assumed that some miracle would prompt my parents and eventually they'd realize that they had overlooked this matter and come to my rescue with help applying to schools and promises to foot the bill. That's where things stood around Christmastime in my senior year of high school.

That fall of 1965 I was no longer going out to my father's house on Long Island. At all. We'd been on the outs, not speaking to one another since the previous spring. Even before that, the routine twice-a-month visits had dwindled to once a month. Over the years he'd adopted the practice of putting me to work as soon as I arrived on Saturday morning. (I'd take the train from Penn Station, and he'd pick me up in Manhasset.) During the temperate months that meant mowing his lawn. If it was fall, I was detailed to rake leaves. I resented these tasks, for the obvious reason that I didn't actually live there, I was only an infrequent visitor. I generally didn't complain about it, though. I just did what I was told, resentfully, and took off as soon as I could to see my old friends.

On a spring Saturday of that year, I'd come back to the house in the afternoon from hanging out with Brian and Roger. We might have been listening to Bob Dylan's latest album, *Bringing It All Back Home*, released in March — because that was what teenage boys did in a boring suburban housing subdivision surrounded by other subdivisions. When I came in, Dad's wife, my stepmother, Pauline, asked facetiously if I was "checking in." The inference seemed pretty nasty to me. I answered with an insolent crack. My father was within earshot. He flew into a rage and began whacking me about the head, calling me "an ingrate." He was generally not a violent man, nor any kind of a habitual hitter, perhaps because of a serious neck injury he'd suffered at seventeen that I will tell you about later. But he had a temper and must have been extremely pissed off at me, and in a cumulative sense holding in his own resentments for years at having to care for a child he'd conceived with a woman he now loathed and detested. Otherwise, his rage was baffling, since he never seemed starved for my company. He only wanted me around to help with some home carpentry or yard project. He never once planned an outing, or so much as threw a ball with me. Anyway, when he ran out of steam smacking me, he ordered me to collect my stuff and then drove me back to the train station in Manhasset, a miserable fifteen-minute journey for both of us. By Christmastime 1965 I hadn't heard from him since that day, and I hadn't tried to contact him either. Over the year, I just let it slide.

I long suspected that my father just didn't like me or care about me very much. I was a chubby, unattractive pubescent at sixteen and I was deep into a phase of dressing like a slob. He was dapper, with a nice wardrobe and rather formal European manners. I wore the same blue sweatshirt all the time until it became raggedy. It was a gag sweatshirt with "Sorbonne, Paris" printed on the front, and I thought it was the last word in sophistication. It also happened to look just like the blue sweatshirt that Steve McQueen wore in *The Great Escape*, a 1963 movie that distilled my longings to get away from the places and situations I was stuck in: the city, my school, the weekends on Long Island. I wanted to ride away from it all on a motorcycle, like Steve did.

My father often complained about me being a slob. He groused that he sent child support to my mother and he was indignant that she didn't buy more clothing for me. He might have taken me shopping for clothes himself, of course, but that never seemed to occur to him, which added to my suspicion that he didn't like me. I was uncomfortable and self-conscious being a fat kid. But during the year we weren't speaking or seeing each other, I'd gone through quite a growth spurt and lost my baby fat. Suddenly, I got interested in clothes. My mother was actually delighted to lend me her charge card for Bloomingdale's department store, where I put together a *preppie* wardrobe of button-down shirts, ties, khakis, and a gray herringbone sport jacket, because that's how New York male teens dressed just before the hippie revolution changed everything. My improved appearance certainly reflected on her better. I'll go into more detail later on about my relationship with her too.

Around the Thanksgiving holiday, I had received a letter in the mail from my father's wife, Pauline. She suggested that I reunite with my father, and that she would like to facilitate it. I did not especially miss my father, though I missed *having* a father. And I did have a stepfather, my mother's husband, Bernie, who was quite a decent fellow — and you'll hear more about him, by and by. But even at seventeen I sensed it would not be a good thing for me to have permanently poisoned relations with my dad. So I wrote back accepting her offer, saying, *sure, whatever you can do*. She then went ahead and made the arrangements. The plan was for me to go down to my father's office late in the afternoon on a Friday around holiday time. Together we would take the commuter train from Penn Station out to Long Island, and I would stay overnight as I did in the old days. I didn't have any conversations with my father about the details. I was just expected to show up. That reunion was set for Friday, the week before Christmas Eve. The holiday fell on a Saturday that year.

Though I was not crazy about growing up in New York City, I always loved the air of festivity at Christmastime in the city — the crowds in the shops and department stores, the raggedy Salvation Army bands on the sidewalk playing carols off-key, the chestnut vendors with their fragrant, smoking pushcarts, the glorious fir tree in the Metropolitan Museum of Art with half the population of ancient Judea in ceramic figurines roistering around the nativity scene at its mighty base. Friday, December 10, we mercifully had a half day off from school so that we seniors could have our yearbook pictures taken. We were told to report to a commercial photo studio in midtown.

A classmate of mine, a zany kid named Bobby, was a voice student on the music side of M & A. We weren't in any classes together, but I was just getting to know him that fall from hanging out in the cafeteria on the same assigned lunch shift — there were several shifts between 11 a.m. and 1 p.m. He had a great collection of outfits from the city's thrift shops: tuxedo jackets, military tunics, a double-breasted gangster suit from the 1930s, some cool old hats. With my new interest in clothing I admired his style. He acted in school plays and was a natural comedian and was almost always switched "on," performing *schtick*, fun to be around. Halfway through my last year of high school, I felt I was making a friend. At lunch that day, he invited me to meet a third kid, his best friend Larry, who went to a different high school, and goof around with them after getting our yearbook photos shot. There was a party that night he knew about. Of course, I liked parties and was excited about going to one, and not all by myself for a change.

When school let out at midday, Bobby and I went down to his apartment to wait for Larry. Bobby lived with his mom on the West Side, behind Lincoln Center, in one of those white-brick high-rise slabs that commercial developers put up by the score around Manhattan in the 1960s. There were quite a few poor kids at M & A and clearly Bobby was not one of them. I wondered about his absent father, whether Bobby got along with him, but I didn't ask, of course. He seemed untroubled. Perhaps I seemed untroubled too.

Larry, who I hadn't met before, showed up soon in a secondhand formal tail-coat outfit. He also had a theatrical bent. The two of them apparently had been working on comic routines for years. This was back in the days when comedians came in pairs: Abbott and Costello,

Martin and Lewis. Bobby and Larry worked in that vein. They called themselves Bertram and Charlie, or Boitram and Chollie. They could both do a lot of funny dialects and foreign accents and they had a refined sense of the absurd. I think they had some notion of turning pro after high school and were trying out their act on me. (In fact, not many years later, Bobby would be cast in a TV network sitcom produced out in LA, unfortunately not a success, before giving up showbiz to become a plumber in Marin County, CA.) One of his routines was a riff on the cosmic loneliness and futility of the universe. "We're constantly traveling through endless space, *endless space*, at tremendous speed, through eternal nothingness, destination unknown," he intoned melodramatically as we made to leave the apartment. It stuck in my mind.

We took the fire stairs instead of the elevator. Larry fired up a joint there. They were obviously experienced dopers. I was not. I'd never smoked marijuana before and I warily took a couple of halfhearted tokes while they got a good buzz on. I might have experimented with marijuana sooner, but I led such a solitary existence that there was no peer pressure to do it. Anyway, I was quite satisfied with the transformative effects of alcohol, a big part of the F. Scott Fitzgerald tragic-romantic persona I was cultivating at the time. It hadn't occurred to me to seek out marijuana. I hadn't encountered it at the parties I crashed either. M & A in 1965 was a far more bohemian place than the private prep schools those kids went to, but I didn't socialize with the kids in my own school, who were scattered over all five boroughs. The pot available in those days was not as strong as the stuff you can get legally now in many states, but you could certainly get high off it if you smoked enough. Heading down to the photo studio, I really didn't notice any changes in my perception.

When we got there, Larry did card tricks for the girls waiting their turns in line while Bobby and I duly submitted to the camera. When we left the photo studio, we took the fire stairs rather than the elevator and Bobby fired up another joint. I'd been smoking cigarettes regularly since I was thirteen, so I did know how to inhale. This time I toked a little more adventurously. We had no particular itinerary in mind. Midtown was bustling with Christmas shoppers and tourists. We wended over to Rockefeller Center to watch the ice skaters under the golden statue of Prometheus. I was struck by the beauty of the scene. We were laughing a lot since Bobby and Larry had resumed their Boitram and Chollie act, and pretty soon, seized by hunger, we bustled into the Horn & Hardart automat on 57th Street.

These now defunct chain of eateries were quite grand and wonderful, all gleaming brass and chrome, with great shiny coffee urns and marble counters and magnificent high ceilings, all designed to make ordinary working folks of the mid-twentieth century feel like royalty. The crowning feature of the program was the way they displayed their menu items: in great banks of automated cubby holes behind glass windows. They'd have all the pies lined up in one vertical row, and entrees such as macaroni and cheese or potpies in another section, and side dishes in another. The cubby hole windows were coin operated and designed to take only nickels. This was, no doubt, a holdover from the decades before World War Two when nickels bought a lot more. By 1965, though, inflation was eating away at the dollar, so it took a lot more nickels to get something, and they hadn't redesigned the machines to take dimes or quarters.

So we tripped into the automat that afternoon, three laughing teenage boys, one in a strange costume, and duly changed some bills for handfuls of nickels, and, before long, I got lost psychologically in the vast selection of foodstuffs on offer behind the bewildering array of cubby hole windows. After goggling at the wall in awe for a while, I decided to get a slab of pie. There was a whole vertical row of them. It cost twenty-five cents, five nickels. I put a couple of nickels in one slot, fumbled with the coins in my hand, got distracted, and when I looked back up I had forgotten which window I put the first two nickels in. So I picked the most likely one and put in three more nickels. The door wouldn't open. I began to realize that I had the wrong window, so I put three nickels in the one just below it. But it didn't open either. Eventually, I had nickels invested in at least three cubby holes. That was the point where I broke down giggling and finally realized what being stoned was like.

Being stoned was very funny, indeed, I discovered, and not exactly like getting high on beer or vodka. The world just seemed wonderfully absurd. I brought three plates of pie back to the table where the other guys were eating what they'd bought, laughing so hard I could barely explain that I didn't mean to buy dessert for everybody. The hilarity continued for the rest of the afternoon. We eventually piled out of the automat and wandered up Fifth Avenue past Bonwit's department store windows, all tricked out with snowy glitter and Yuletide scenes, past the Pulitzer fountain and the Plaza Hotel, and the horse-drawn cabs lined up on 59th Street, the carriages festooned for Christmas, carols floating on the air from the speaker outside FAO Schwarz's toy emporium across the street, and holiday lights sparkling against the low winter solstice sun turning the panoramic scene purple at four o'clock.

We ended up at the Central Park Zoo. Boitram and Chollie's comedy routines kept us entertained all the way there, though my pot buzz was wearing off. I was probably as much intoxicated with the experience of finally having friends to goof around with after a lonely three years of high school. By and by, I wanted to go home, get some dinner, take a shower, and put on some fresh clothes for that party Bobby mentioned. It was on the West Side, he said. We all agreed to meet up again later at Bobby's apartment.

Intermezzo: The Strange Drunken Doings of the Past Summer, 1965

I think it's pertinent to pause and describe what happened a few months before the night I lost my mind so that you get a clearer idea, from another angle, of how I was struggling in my own way to enter adulthood.

For seven years, from 1959 to 1965 (age ten to seventeen), I spent my summers at a New Hampshire summer camp. I loved being away from my parents. Most of all, I loved not being in New York City. These were the years before the interstate highways were completed and New Hampshire still possessed a lot of old, rough, rural New England charm. The mills still operated in the mill towns, there were no highway strips or shopping malls, most of the roads in the vicinity of our camp were unpaved, and the country folk one encountered looked like the flinty characters out of O'Neill's *Desire Under the Elms*.

Camp Mascoma was the only establishment on our side of Crystal Lake. The woods around us were dark and deep and we were really quite cut off from civilization. It was a boys-only camp. Most of the kids who went to Camp Mascoma were New York Jews, but the operation was owned and run by a Catholic couple, Frank and Helen. Frank was a handsome, bouncy fellow, with a great head of white hair and a salesman's smile, charismatic with small children. Helen was retiring and uninvolved, a kind of spectral presence occasionally turning up in the dining hall. Frank's godlike control over things was largely an illusion. In reality, life at Camp Mascoma was anarchic, with *Lord of the Flies* overtones. Adult supervision was irregular. Our counselors often snuck off nights (when they were supposed to be on duty). We blew things up, held knife-throwing contests, persecuted the misfits, and, one memorable year, helped ourselves to the rum bottle that our counselor had stashed in the tank behind the toilet in our bunk.

But I loved all the routine camp stuff too: baseball, swimming, riflery, sailing, bass fishing — things I couldn't do in the city. The previous summer I was fifteen, in 1964, Frank elevated me to "junior counselor." I was tasked with chores like mowing the ball field, minding younger kids now and then, and bailing out the moored sailboats after rainstorms. My mother appreciated it, I'm sure, because she got a half-discount on the tuition. I was a good worker, because I loved it there, more than being home. The 1965 season, surely my last, I was going to be a junior counselor again — most of the guys I'd come up in the bunks with had moved on to other summer things, like group tours around Europe.

I went up to New Hampshire in late June, a week before camp opened, and worked hard cutting the tall spring grass, putting in the steel dock, setting up the archery targets, hauling down all the mattresses stored in a mouse-proof room in the attic of the main lodge, cleaning winter blowdown out of the rifle range, and much more. Then, when one of his hires didn't show up before opening day, at the last minute Frank promoted me to full-time counselor, with five little kids and a cabin to look after, and full adult privileges: a salary ($200 for the season), and days and nights off. I was assigned to work at the waterfront as a lifeguard and boating instructor.

The counselor in charge of the waterfront was Frank's son Timothy. Tim was twenty-two and had just graduated from Adelphi college on Long Island. Camp was in his blood, but his blood was thick with grievances and dark hostilities from being who he was in the Mascoma order of things: seemingly special, but treated as just one of sixty other campers — making him, in reality, conspicuously less than special. As a recent frat boy, he was above all an accomplished and prodigious drinker, and he enlisted me as his drinking buddy that summer. We'd established a kind of rapport during the preseason setup. It was just the two of us working together, especially the arduous days-long job of putting up the three-sided steel crib dock at the waterfront in a lake that was still pretty cold that early in the summer. We bonded doing that. This was also, you see, just a few months after my father threw me out of his house and his life, and I was quite in need of a father substitute, though not conscious of it. Tim was more like the older brother I didn't have than a father, but that was good enough, and it meant a lot to me to become his sidekick.

As the camp director's son, I think, Tim resented his duties the same way I resented working around my father's house. Tim knew the setup drill backward and forward. Frank mostly left us alone that week, at the very end of which he traveled down to New York to greet the campers and their parents in Grand Central Station and bring the kids north in a chartered Pullman train. We hardly ever saw Tim's mother, Helen, that week. She was a tippler herself and didn't get up until midday. Nights, Tim and I drove into the town of Lebanon in his beater Mercury for hamburgers at the A&W root beer stand and he'd buy a couple of six-packs to take back to camp. I kicked in a few bucks and drank as many beers as I wanted. We got loaded every night that week before the kids arrived.

Tim had a girlfriend back down on Long Island he was supposed to marry at the end of the summer, a nice Catholic girl. So hanging out with me was theoretically a way for him to avoid certain other temptations. He flat-out disliked a number of the other counselors his father hired, many of them returnees, who were not so dedicated to his primary avocation, drinking. They were more interested in chasing the student nurses who worked over at the Dartmouth hospital in Hanover, exactly what Tim was trying to avoid. And despite our age difference, Tim seemed to enjoy my company. Like Tim, I was a simmering cauldron of inchoate grievances. Like Tim, I had a dark view of the world, a sense of humor tinged with malice, and an extensive profane vocabulary. And we both could play the guitar and knew a lot of rock and roll songs.

The counselor staff was divided into two "shifts" of six counselors each. We got every other night and one full day and night per week off. Tim and I were on the same shift. We went our own way in our own world of power drinking. Typically, on a night off, we'd buy a case of cheap beer such as Narragansett ("Nasty") at the little general store on Route 4A in Enfield Center, and drive fifteen miles to White River Junction, just over the Connecticut River in Vermont, drinking in the car all the way. We generally took in a few rounds at the "Wee Tee" miniature golf course in White River. Even with my fake ID, I looked so young I could not get into bars in New Hampshire or Vermont, where the drinking age was twenty-one — unlike New York, which was eighteen — so that was out of the question.

Tim and I did most of our drinking on back roads around the camp. We'd park on some desolate stretch of the Canaan Road or the Potato Road and work our way through the case of "Nasty" yowling out classic rock and roll songs: "Twist and Shout," "Oh, Donna," "Money Honey," "Be My Baby," "Heartbreak Hotel," "Wake Up Little Susie," until after midnight. (By the way, the Rolling Stones' "Satisfaction" was released that June, and Bob Dylan's "Like a Rolling Stone" in late July, the next wave breaking.) There was nothing along those dirt back roads in those days — a few abandoned farmhouses, no other cars, no police — and nobody bothered us. What had once been hardscrabble New England farming country had gone back to forest by the mid-1960s, and nothing had taken farming's place.

Tim was not a big guy, perhaps five foot ten, but he was physically imposing. Once a superb athlete, he had nearly destroyed both knees on the high school lacrosse field and at twenty-two they bothered him constantly. I remembered him as a ferocious ballplayer when he was an older camper from my earlier years. His lifestyle since then had added some bloat to his frame. He had an odd pigeon-toed gait with short footsteps and all his weight forward that gave him the appearance of lunging at you as he approached. On our days and nights off, he put on his drinking uniform: a one-piece green jumpsuit with a Narragansett logo over the heart — a garment issued to the company's truck drivers. Since he was almost always hungover in the morning, you learned to steer clear of his glowering temper before noon. I just went about my morning business down at the waterfront, running the swim class kids through their lap routines, while Tim caught some Zs in the boathouse. By noon Tim was alert, but he was never fully restored to equilibrium until the kids in our cabins were asleep and we could steal off into the night for some "frosties."

There was a glade behind the ball field known as "Mongolia" where the counselors parked their cars. Tim and I buried a Styrofoam cooler out there and camouflaged the lid with brown paint and pine duff sprinkled on top. Nobody else knew it was there. We kept it well stocked and even iced. Mongolia was where we'd steal off those nights we were supposed to be on duty. Our mission: to get loaded. I liked getting intoxicated and smoking Pall Mall cigarettes under the summer stars. I didn't see anything not to like about it. I couldn't keep up with Tim, of course, but by early July I was waking up with hangovers too.

Our full days off, which included the nights, featured some spectacular benders. Early in the summer, we assembled a wilderness drinking kit. This included a barbecue grill and a galvanized steel trash can for mixing gigantic batches of cocktails. We kept the stuff under a one-lane-bridge that crossed a brook which formed the camp boundary. There was some room down below by the abutment for us to hang out there. The state liquor store in Lebanon sold gigantic Jeroboam bottles of booze — the kind you'd see only for display purposes in liquor shop windows in New York but never for sale. In New Hampshire you could buy them. We'd get a giant bottle of Smirnoff vodka and mix it in the trash can with several no. 10 cans of cranapple juice and Hawaiian Punch and pineapple juice and hang out under the bridge drinking all day long, with some incidental guitar plucking, steak eating, and target practice with an air pistol I'd picked up in town.

One of those afternoons, we got so wasted that I stumbled drunkenly all the way down the slippery freestone brook to where it entered the lake in a swampy delta — at least a mile — and woke up the next morning covered with lacerations. Another day, we each took out a camp sailboat (with two six-packs each) and by midafternoon I overturned mine about two miles down the lake. They were tubby little O'Day "Sprites" that could not be righted by standing on the centerboard, so I had to swim the damn thing all the way back, upside down with the mast dragging, drunk. I was lucky I didn't drown.

On another day off we'd stopped at a church rummage sale in Lebanon where I picked up a stuffed armadillo and a carton full of Santa Claus candles. That night we set up our wilderness drinking kit beside a small waterfall on the same brook at the edge of the camp property and, in our drunkenness, constructed a weird sort of shrine to the "Armadillo God" by surrounding it with dozens of flickering Santa Clauses. Sometime after midnight, we managed to drive back to Mongolia and crawl into our respective cabins. It's a wonder we didn't both die in a car wreck that summer. Late the next afternoon, Frank came tearing down to the waterfront in his pickup truck, obviously pissed off, and ordered Tim and me to come with him. He had some shovels in the back of the truck. Apparently, the Santa Claus candles had started a smoldering root fire in the piney grove at the waterfall. When we got there, it looked like some steaming geothermal glade in Yellowstone. We had to spend the next six hours digging up the hot spots where smoke was rising and put out the fire.

Apart from that episode, though, Frank left us alone all summer long. I don't know what he knew at that point about our routine boozing, but it continued at the same intense pitch until the season resolved into one endless bacchanal. It climaxed (and came to a sudden halt) on the last night of the season, which was, by tradition, a banquet for all the kiddies followed by an awards ceremony. Tim had planted a quart of vodka for us in the handyman's toolshed that adjoined the main lodge and I made enough visits to it during the dinner that I was close to falling-down drunk when the awards ceremony got underway. Frank followed me outside on the last of those excursions to the toolshed, flew into a rage when he caught me with the bottle, and sent me down to my cabin, telling me not to bother applying for a summer job next year.

I don't know exactly what the consequences were for Timothy, but I'm sure they were unpleasant. He didn't talk to me the next day when we counselors had to help the kids in our bunks pack their footlockers for shipment home and prepare them for the overnight trip in Pullman cars back to Grand Central Station. That night, I took the train down to New York with the kiddies. The trouble, of course, was that I had betrayed Tim, betrayed my sidekick, betrayed the person who had become a role model for me, more or less a father substitute, or a big brother, at least a mentor. I had disgraced myself and him and been thrown out of his world, the camp world that I loved more than my own home, just as my father had thrown me out of his world the previous spring. I was not doing well on my journey into adulthood. My guides were all ditching me. I learned years later that Tim died an alcoholic in his early fifties.

Losing It

The phantasmagoria of that two-month drinking spree made normal life back in high school seem unreal when I reentered it that fall. If Frank the camp director ratted on me, I did not hear anything about it, so I suspect he did not. Maybe he felt he'd look irresponsible for having given a sixteen-year-old adult privileges in the first place. Without a sidekick to keep up with, my drinking tailed off quite a bit. I rarely tried to buy booze at the regular retail liquor stores. The few times I tried they laughed at me. They were much more careful than bartenders, who always accepted my forged IDs. My mother and stepfather, Muriel and Bernie, had a well-stocked bar in the dining room at home and I discreetly nicked gulps of scotch or vodka or cognac now and then. They consumed a respectable amount themselves and, apparently, they didn't notice the level going down more than usual.

I hung out at P. J. McCabe's bar on 71st Street that fall, as usual, but only Fridays and Saturdays in the early evening, getting a buzz on before the main adventure of looking for parties to crash. If I was depressed about being estranged from my father, and the way things had turned out at camp, and having no idea how to proceed about going to college, I successfully cordoned off my feelings to some realm of the mind that I did not visit. *Depression*, as a psychological state, had barely entered into common parlance. It was something that movie stars like Marilyn Monroe suffered from in the newspapers, going to expensive clinics to get diagnosed and cured. Bohemian hipsters on the downtown scene talked it up, too, because it was a sophisticated way of saying that your misfortunes were due to a medical syndrome, not because your art didn't sell, or your novel was rejected for the sixth time. Teenagers used the term "depressing" flippantly, in the Holden Caulfield sense, to describe something you just didn't like. There were plenty of things I didn't like, but I wasn't conscious of having the blues that fall.

It was remarkable how few people I actually communicated with day by day. I really had no one to talk to, either my peers or adults. I wasn't close to anybody. I never saw any of my classmates outside school, except the few who rode the No. 3 Convent Avenue bus back and forth, and I didn't see them after we got off the bus. All my old camp friends were long gone. My early childhood friends on Long Island, Brian and Roger, never came to see me. I had no uncles, aunts, or cousins around — they were all in Washington and Los Angeles. I often chatted up some of the young professionals from the neighborhood who hung out at McCabe's bar, but it was purely superficial. I was capable of being precociously and entertainingly clever. I didn't talk to them about anything really important or personal. Amidst all the bustle of the nation's most densely populated city I was an adolescent lone ranger.

My family, such as it was, never had dinner together, except the infrequent occasions we all went out to a restaurant. From about age twelve on, I always made my own dinner, because I didn't want to wait for Muriel to come home from work. We had a charge account at the butcher's on Second Avenue and I always had hamburger meat in the fridge. That was all I ever ate for dinner. They were often not around in the evening anyway. At the time, Bernie was the publicist for the New York League of Theater Producers, so they were frequently out at a Broadway show or an awards dinner, or some affair at the Lambs Club or the Players.

Friday evening, December 10, 1965, I made my usual hamburger and ate it, as usual, in front of NBC's *Huntley–Brinkley Report* on the TV in my room. I took a shower and changed into a clean shirt with a tie, then went down to McCabe's to begin the evening. I eagerly anticipated having two new friends to meet up with and a party to go to. After a beer or two there, I caught the 67th Street crosstown bus to the west side and met up with Bobby and Larry again. We didn't linger in the apartment but went out to Riverside Park and smoked a couple of joints there. It was not so cheerful now in the winter darkness, with a cold wind coming off the Hudson River, and I had gone out with only a tweed sport jacket and a scarf, my usual outfit in winter. I probably didn't even have gloves because whenever I got a pair I promptly lost them, and I never wore hats.

We left the park and headed a couple of blocks east over to Broadway in the winter murk. The Christmas festivity of midtown was absent north of Lincoln Center. Broadway was a dreary smudge of lights from the stream of taxicabs and the fluorescent shop fronts of mundane businesses that dominated the neighborhood: greengrocers, dry cleaners, newsstands. Bobby and Larry wanted to stop in a Carvel ice cream shop. It was warmer in there, of course. The place was not busy. There was a big clock behind the counter and I noticed it was about eight. I didn't order anything but just stood there staring at the menu on the counter that described various flavor combos and sundaes. It was mesmerizing. I was not paying attention to the other guys. The next time I glanced at the clock it was twenty after eight. I'd been staring at the wall for about twenty minutes and I hadn't registered the passage of time at all.

That's when I realized I was very stoned, way beyond what I'd felt back in the afternoon, with all that hilarity in the automat. I didn't like it at all. I felt myself being overcome by a profound sense of unreality, like nothing I'd never experienced, a feeling of being at once outside myself and trapped inside something sinister. My hands felt numb. But at the same time my perceptions had turned uncomfortably intense. The fluorescent lighting in the Carvel store made the place look exceptionally squalid, actually dangerous. Just then, a weird pulse of electric fire ran up my spine and something seemed to explode inside my head. It was like one of the myoclonic jerks that I suffered constantly at this time in my life just before falling asleep — a sensation like stepping off a cliff, a spasm of terror — only this was much more powerful, a surge that reverberated in the depths of my brain from one hemisphere to the other. It almost knocked me out.

I lost my breath and any sense of who I was. I dashed out of the Carvel store like a frightened animal into utterly unfamiliar surroundings. The people walking by on the sidewalk — old neighborhood Jewish couples, young adults out on a Friday evening, businessmen, junkies, trannies — all seemed to glower at me menacingly. I was sure they meant to do me harm. The paranoia was vivid. I backed up to the corner of the building and then around the corner until I was cringing up against a standpipe on the side street off Broadway. Just then, Bobby and Larry came into my field of view, which was unnaturally tunnel-like as though they were at the wrong end of a telescope. I suppose they were wondering where I'd dashed off to. All I could say was, "I'm scared, I'm scared . . ." I thought I was going to die out there. I was shivering jerkily. They got on either side and sort of conducted me, stumbling, down the side street, a block or two west, toward the river, until we came to a fancy limestone town house off Riverside Drive where the party was.

I felt the same sense of panicked menace inside the house full of partying teenagers as I'd felt on the street among the strangers on Broadway. The place was jammed. The loud rock and roll terrified me. The hostess, I'd been told earlier by Bobby, was a girl named Sarah who went to New Lincoln, a small private boho school for arty kids, like M & A, only it charged tuition. Her parents were both psychiatrists who routinely went to a country house somewhere on weekends, leaving their daughter in charge of the town house off Riverside Drive.

I had no idea what was happening inside my head and could only repeat how scared I was. Bobby and Larry steered me into a small bedroom where kids had piled up their winter coats. They more or less dumped me there, saying I'd be okay in a little while, and left. I still felt waves of terror running through me, baffling sensations of desperate unwellness and alarm that I'd never felt before. That my terror had no focus was the most frightening part of it. The purity of it just buffaloed me in surge after surge of panic. I crawled off into a corner between the bed and the wall with the piled-up coats forming a mountain-like barrier between me and the next wave of arrivals, who apparently didn't notice me cringing down there when they ditched their coats. I fought off the impulse to go home, realizing I'd have to go back outside into the fearsome night streets to get there. I just remained on the floor behind the bed with my knees drawn up, imprisoned in my fear for what seemed like a long spell but might have been an hour or so, praying that I had not lost my mind.

Eventually, I was able to physically unclench my body. Whatever was going on in my adrenal system had loosened its grip and my intense fear ebbed into a sort of exhausted funk. It began to dawn on me that I'd had a bad reaction to smoking pot. My terror subsided into a fog of shame. I'd humiliated myself. I was a *feeb* who had flunked some essential test of young adulthood. My new friends hadn't checked in on me to see if I was okay. Surely, I'd embarrassed them — the jerk hiding in the coatroom.

I crawled out of the corner and sat on the edge of the bed beside the piled coats. Kids were still arriving and at least one girl asked me if I was all right. A while later, I left the room and entered the party. It was even more of a mob scene than when we got there. The kids, students from New Lincoln and other schools, were all strangers — I didn't go over to the West Side much. Their obvious high spirits only left me feeling more hollowed out. There was some liquor in the kitchen and I downed a stiff vodka, my go-to hard beverage. Before long, I felt closer to normal, but still conscious that something very disturbing had happened to me. I was in no mood to try chatting up anyone. I remember seeing Bobby and Larry across a room, but I didn't talk to them or tell them I was leaving the party. I slipped out into the dank winter night and caught a cab on Broadway back home across town. It

Young Man Blues

was still before midnight on a Friday evening. Of course, my parents were out somewhere.

A Dark Season

The plan, set up by my stepmother, Pauline, was for me to meet my father down at his office on 47th Street at the end of the workday, take the train to Long Island with him, have dinner, stay overnight at their house in Roslyn Heights, and return to the city Saturday on the train by myself. I understood that the limited parameters of the visit were designed to minimize potential conflict. The object was to just formally reestablish relations, which was probably phrased simply as "to see your father again." I appreciated Pauline's diplomatic initiative. That my father took no part in the negotiation might have informed me about his mixed feelings, or trepidations, or perhaps indifference. But at seventeen it didn't occur to me that my father had complicated feelings. I preferred to think I was just a "bad boy" who was now getting "another chance."

The date for this reunion was set for Friday, December 17, exactly a week after my bad reaction to getting stoned. Of course, what I'd experienced was a whopper of an anxiety attack, but I didn't know it at the time. I'd never heard of such a thing. That last full week of school before Christmas vacation, which was scheduled to start December 23, I went up to M & A Monday, as usual, and ran into Bobby back in the school cafeteria on our lunch shift. He was busy running his perpetual comedy act and I couldn't find a way to talk to him about what had happened that night. He didn't ask me about it either. Maybe he was afraid he'd get into trouble because pot was involved. He might just not have comprehended what I was going through. I learned later on that Bobby had skipped a grade and was actually a year younger than me, probably even more immature than I was. In any case, I never saw him outside of school after that. We did not become friends. And I never saw Larry again.

I certainly didn't tell Bernie and Muriel about what happened. And since I had nobody else to talk to, I just stewed in a nervous daze the week between my humiliating crack-up and the upcoming reunion with my father. I'd returned to that familiar globe of isolation, only now it had a darker tinge to it. I was shaken up inside and became obsessed with a sharp awareness that danger lurked unseen behind humdrum reality, as if the universe could sneak up and mug you like a thug on a late-night subway platform. Bobby's jokey riff about *traveling through endless space* had also become a morbid preoccupation for me. My world seemed weirdly empty, disorienting, and treacherous, with no compass points, no up, no down. I'd developed a sort of tunnel vision that kept me fixated on unseen cosmic malevolence. Something had really shifted in my personality, and I worried that I might have started on a journey into madness.

What I didn't do was think about my actual circumstances, the practical, on-the-ground, close-up quandaries I faced at that moment of my life. I was unmoored from all that. I didn't think about my time running out in high school and what I would do when it was over in six months. I didn't think about applying to college. I didn't try to anticipate how to act in my father's presence, or what I might say to him, or acknowledge the pain of being cast out all year, and of apparently being considered little more than a nuisance to him. What I really couldn't face was the possibility that my father didn't care whether I was in his life or not, and might have actually preferred it if I just stayed out of the picture indefinitely.

I skipped school that Friday and I went down to 59th Street to catch the first afternoon showing of a new movie, *A Thousand Clowns*. It was a heartwarming comedy about a washed-up TV comedy writer raising his sister's unwanted twelve-year-old boy. They are beset by social workers trying to separate them on account of the writer being chronically unemployed. The movie touched me in many ways, but mostly because the comedy writer, played by Jason Robards Jr., obviously cared about the kid, spent a lot of time with him, and did what a good parent does in helping the boy prepare to enter adulthood. Then I marched ten blocks home to take a shower and change, so I would look my best when I met my father.

I had my own bathroom in the apartment and, as usual, stepping out of the shower I flung up the window to let all the steam out of the small room. It was probably going on three o'clock, nearly the shortest day of the year, with the sun in the west already sunk behind the skyscrapers of midtown, and the early winter evening murk gathering over the city. Something I saw out there from the twelfth-floor window threw a switch in my head. Perhaps it was the horror of realizing I'd soon have to go out there . . . *outside into the scary world* . . . and make my way to my father's office. I was suddenly overcome by exactly the same sensations that swept over me in the Carvel ice cream store on Broadway the week before: waves of terror, a feeling of being in an altered reality, of my brain malfunctioning, along with alarming physical symptoms of a racing heart, being short of breath, numbness, and tremors. I thought I was dying. Of course, I was having another anxiety attack and didn't know it.

I stumbled out of the bathroom and ended up retreating into my closet with the door closed in the dark, with the waves of panic washing over me. It occurred to me that smoking that pot the week before must have done something to permanently injure my mind and I was now going insane for certain. This idea only provoked more waves of panic, which I endured there in the dark, sitting on pairs of shoes and breathing in the scent of mothballs, until my adrenal glands finally had enough of a workout and quit pumping the chemicals of terror into my system. Shaken, I emerged from the closet and horsed down several big gulps of vodka from the liquor stand in the dining room. It helped a bit, but I was more and more convinced that there was something really wrong with me. I called my stepfather at his office — since I didn't trust my mother to understand any of this — and told him I thought I was having a "nervous breakdown." Bernie told me to go up to the family doctor and said he would meet me there.

Doctor Bob Brown had an office on 68th Street just off Madison, a few blocks from the apartment. I managed to put on my prepster outfit and even tie my paisley necktie with trembling hands, grabbed my scarf — my sole piece of winter outerwear — and left the apartment. Everything about the four-block journey across the east side of Manhattan that day was like being in a German expressionist movie. The apartment towers seemed to teeter over the street at weird angles, threatening to topple over on me. Even the Christmas decorations in the shops seemed sinister. The people on the streets looked the like hollowed-out figures in the spooky paintings of city life by George Tooker. The whole world had suddenly taken on a new and dreadful demeanor. I was even more convinced that I was going crazy.

Like a lot of family doctors in those days, Dr. Brown had a simple practice — not like today when the average HMO is run like the motor vehicle bureau. You came into a small tranquil waiting room furnished with comfortable armchairs, oriental rugs, and some decent prints on the wall, with no receptionist or other intermediaries, perhaps another patient or two, depending on the hour. The mood was one of serenity and order. When the doctor was ready for you, he came out of the inner sanctum himself and invited you to step in.

Dr. Brown was tall, bald-headed, and deliberate, a reassuring presence. He was the brother-in-law of one of my mother's college chums. He'd never treated me for anything before besides a case of bronchitis and tetanus shots for camp, and I'm quite sure he had no conception of my inner life, nor would he have had any reason to develop one. His office was book-lined with a leather club chair for the patient to sit in. It connected to a white-tiled examination room filled with the usual array of mystifying medical equipment. I sat across the desk from him and lit up a cigarette, because that's how it worked in those days: everybody smoked cigarettes, and even doctors had ashtrays on their desks. I told him I thought I'd become mentally ill from smoking marijuana, which had done something to my brain, and now I was having weird, scary feelings even without smoking it. I doubt I said anything about the imminent reunion with my father. That's how dissociated I was from my own emotional life. It didn't seem relevant and I would have been embarrassed to go into the details of how we came to be estranged.

After a few minutes, we heard someone come in to the waiting room from outside. I said it might be my stepfather, Bernie, and Dr. Brown went out and got him. I had to explain the marijuana part all over again. Bernie was not easily ruffled and just absorbed the news placidly. He must have tried pot himself, since he had a lot of friends in showbiz and the arts and had been hanging around in Manhattan jazz clubs since right after the war. Dr. Brown asked if I took other drugs, speed or downers, he said, using lingo I might be familiar with. I said no, which was true. Alcohol? he asked. A little, I told him, now and then. He might have picked up that I'd imbibed some liquor before coming in, but he didn't press it. Where did I get it? Bernie asked. Kids have it around at parties, I said. I didn't mention anything about the two-month horror show in New Hampshire the previous summer, or my budding career back home as a barfly.

Dr. Brown invited me into the adjoining examination room and performed a few routine checks on my pulse, blood pressure, throat, eyes, pronouncing everything perfectly okay. Back in his office he wrote out a prescription and told me to take one if I felt weird again, and to come back the following week. Apparently, he didn't believe that I had lost my mind from one night of pot smoking. I don't remember the term "anxiety attack" even coming up. I was feeling normal again from being in his tranquil, plush office. The visit probably ran about ten minutes.

Out on the sidewalk I reminded Bernie that I wouldn't be home that night because I was going out to my father's house on Long Island.

He asked if I was sure I wanted to do that, considering my afternoon freakout. He'd put the two things together better than I had. I was so abstracted from my own feelings that it hadn't occurred to me they were connected. I just said I had to go, and asked him to please not tell Muriel about what happened. He was a kind man but he'd been through some of the worst times of World War Two in the Ardennes Forest, 1944, and might not have been too worried about my adolescent tribulations. He gave me $10 to fill the prescription and hailed a cab. He had a Christmas party to go to and asked if I wanted to come along and get dropped off downtown. I said I'd rather walk. My father's office was just twenty blocks away from Dr. Brown's. I had more than a half hour to get there and I wanted to hit a drugstore on the way.

I found a place to fill the prescription on my way downtown to Henry's office. The script was for Miltown (meprobamate), a primitive but effective tranquilizer of the *Mad Men* era. I took two, and by the time I walked the twenty blocks the city and its trappings looked normal again. My nerves felt cushioned. I even got back some of that old Christmas spirit making my way along Fifth Avenue past Tiffany's and St. Patrick's Cathedral, Saks department store and Rockefeller Center. It was the week of the winter solstice, the shortest day of the year. Night had fallen, but you might not even know it because the streets were bright and mobs of shoppers melded with all the people leaving work for the day. I turned west at 47th Street, past the glittering windows of the ground floor diamond sellers.

Despite the side trip to the doctor's office, I got to my father's office absolutely on time, just before five o'clock. He was on the eleventh floor of a tall, narrow building tucked into 47th Street between Fifth and Sixth Avenues, the block that comprises all of New York City's fabled diamond district. The whole building was filled with people in the trade, from diamond cutters on up. My father was a dealer, as his father was before him, a wholesaler to the jewelry trade, a middleman. In his prime (which he was then in), he flew to Antwerp, the world diamond distribution center, every six weeks with absolute routine regularity, bought "stones" there, as they called the merchandise, and then parceled them out back on 47th Street to customers further down the retail food chain who turned them into wedding rings, watches, ear clips, and other trinkets. He shared an office with his younger partner, Marty, in a suite of rooms that included a secretarial station and a conference room.(His previous partner, one Emil, had robbed all the merch from the safe one night back in the early 1960s. The NYC detectives determined that signs of an outside burglary job were faked and Emil went to prison. The business had recovered from that misfortune.) The building was unostentatious to the point of being utterly drab. Since it was full of diamonds, the last thing they wanted to do was advertise a message such as *Treasure Within*. The hallway on the eleventh floor had an ambience that brought to mind Dickensian countinghouses.

Henry's secretary, a fiftyish bottle blonde named Sylvia, buzzed me through the security door and told me to go right in. By now, the Miltown had fully kicked in and I was feeling comfortable enough to go through the ordeal. Henry and Marty's inner office was spartan, though it was a large corner room with big windows on two sides, bright during daylight hours. Now it was dark out there. My father sat behind his supernaturally tidy desk sorting through little piles of small pear-shaped or marquise cut stones on a giant white paper desk pad. You didn't want to lose valuable tiny gems in and around desk clutter, so he had none. Marty occupied a similar station on the other side facing Henry. Each of them had a delicate carat scale housed in a glass vitrine, the most interesting things in the whole office besides the view down the block toward the dazzling lights of Times Square.

My father and Marty glanced up as I came in, both visibly surprised at my appearance. Marty, more voluble, remarked that I'd grown and slimmed down since last he saw me. I avouched that this was probably so. My father smiled, perhaps registering some relief that my wardrobe had improved, that I was no longer the embarrassing slob of a year earlier. But all he said was "So . . ." and scooped the day's last batch of diamonds into a glassine envelope. The entire inventory of the office fit into a wooden case no bigger than a shoe box, though it resided in a safe the size of a walk-in refrigerator. We didn't shake hands or hug or anything. Marty, ever cheerful, always liked to engage me in badinage. He was in his thirties, tall, dark-haired. I had him pegged as a ladies' man. He asked if I had a girlfriend. I said no. We swapped Christmas salutations. Well, let's go to the station, Henry said. In the outer office, he put on his overcoat and his hat. Men still wore hats in 1965. He told me to put on my coat. I said I didn't bring one. I had on that tweed sport coat and a long scarf. Visibly annoyed, he asked, why doesn't your mother buy you a winter coat? I said I had a peacoat. He said, why don't you wear it, then, it's winter. I said, it doesn't fit over this (the sport jacket). Anyway, I said, we're just going down to the subway and onto the train and into a car to your house. He said, don't get smart. We left the office.

Young Man Blues

My father was hardly an imposing figure, physically. He was then forty-nine years old, five-foot-eight, trim, bald-headed, with a mild, owlish face and a wry smile that seemed to signify his surprise at the most common occurrences of life, like when you walked into the room he was in. He looked like Phil Silvers, the comedian who played Sergeant Bilko on TV in the fifties. Unlike Sergeant Bilko, my father never made it into the army for World War Two. In 1941, age twenty-four, he tripped and fell into one of those elevator shafts so common along the Manhattan sidewalks and broke his neck. He didn't end up paralyzed, but he was in and out of surgeries for the next few years, which kept him out of the army, after the war got underway. The injury limited his ability to turn his head without moving his whole upper body, and left him in chronic pain. He rarely complained about it.

I'd grown a bit taller than him. He dressed very carefully in fine suits he bought on those frequent trips to Europe. His hands were manicured. Come, he said, which meant *follow me*. Outside, we bustled a couple of blocks through the rush hour mobs to the 50th Street station (to avoid Times Square proper) and down into the subway. It was too noisy to say anything. Two stops later, we debauched into Penn Station. My father, being a person of exacting routines, did what he always did: bought an evening paper. After all those years, he had the timing down perfectly so we just glided onto the Long Island Rail Road train without waiting around the gate.

It was the old familiar journey from Penn Station to Manhasset, a thirty-minute ride, I'd made it a hundred times over the years. As we settled in, Henry asked if I had been "a good boy," but didn't inquire further about any details of my day-to-day existence, or my inner life, or social life, or school life, or what I had done the previous summer when we were out of touch (when I was not exactly *a good boy* up in New Hampshire). Once underway, chugging through the East River tunnel, he read, as always, the evening edition of the *New York Post*, which was a liberal Democratic party paper back then and had a big stable of lefty op-ed columnists who were good writers: Murray Kempton, Pete Hamill, Max Lerner, and their ilk. My father was conservative by nature but a default Democrat, like many Jewish New Yorkers with vivid memories of the Great Depression and Franklin Roosevelt.

Once we emerged from the East River tunnel, I just gazed out the train's scratched, filthy window at the nightmarish vistas of Queens, where the elevated tracks ran over block after block of identical bunker-like houses that stood inches apart, and the auto-repair yards with arc welding torches throwing off sparks in the gloom, and other small-time industrial vignettes along the right-of-way. The dreariness of Queens always amazed me. A lot of the kids I went to high school with lived there, including Marion E., the most astoundingly beautiful girl at M & A behind whom I sat diagonally in geometry, where I could stare longingly at her while flunking the course by slow degrees . . . Henry and I hardly spoke till it was time to get off the train.

My father kept a car at the Manhasset station, a flimsy little Opel wagon (made back in the days when foreign cars were laughable). From the station to his house in Roslyn Heights was another four miles along Northern Boulevard, Route 25A. The familiarity of the scene along the highway made me blue, provoking memories of all those unhappy visitation journeys over the years and even scrolling back further to the time before my parents' marriage fell apart and, to some extent, my sense of my life with it. Henry and Pauline's house was in the same subdivision, called Northwood, off Glen Cove Road. He'd married the lady down the street, two amoeba-shaped blocks from the house where he and Muriel and I had lived until 1957.

When we got to the house and pulled into the garage, my father lingered there by the snow blower and the tool rack and initiated the first real conversation we'd had since I met him at the office. He asked me if I'd given any thought to who would pay for my college education. The way he just came out with it kind of buffaloed me. I'd given up thinking about college and was shocked to be reminded about all that. It was a rhetorical question, of course. I said I didn't know and hadn't gotten around to applying anywhere. He said that if and when I got around to it, I'd better ask my mother and that he hoped she'd saved some of all the money he'd sent her over the years. I didn't know what to say about it, and didn't reply. I knew he was eternally aggravated over child support. I had no idea how much money my mother received each month, or what she did with it, or if she was supposed to put some aside for my college. She never spoke to me about college. She was as tuned out as I was. I was so tuned out I surely didn't realize how tuned out she was. *Come*, my father said, signaling the end of that conversation, and I followed him inside the warm house.

The evening proceeded in a spirit of odd false normality, as if the intervening months of alienation had not occurred. My father made a drink and disappeared into the bedroom to change out of his business suit. Pauline was occupied with the maid in the kitchen getting dinner ready. That left me in the company of my stepbrother, Jonathan, four years younger, an unhappy child whose own father lived down in

Florida and who ignored Jonathan and his little sister, Madge, as if they had never been born. Jonathan was an ADD case, often agitated and noisy. His behavior drove Henry crazy and Henry's obvious lack of affection only made Jonathan's ADD tics more pronounced and extreme. He got plenty of attention as a result, all of it negative. But he wasn't stupid. Now, thirteen, entering puberty, he was understandably growing resentful. His neediness and painful self-control problems took on an aggressive edge with Henry — a self-reinforcing feedback loop of disaffection that would only get worse in the years ahead.

Toward me, however, Jonathan held no grievances but rather had a kind of exaggerated reverence for an older "brother," despite the fact that I avoided him as much as possible the few weekends when I was around. This particular night in the Christmas season of 1965 he was delirious to see me again. Despite all his behavioral problems, I could tell that he'd grown up a little, too, and not just physically. He was listening to rock and roll now, and wanted to learn how to play the guitar — could I teach him, maybe, please? Mostly, though, he was exercised by the need to tell me all about the new swimming pool that was installed in the backyard the previous spring, after Henry kicked me out. That was news to me. While Henry was changing clothes, Jonathan took me downstairs to show me, throwing on the patio lights in the winter murk. Sure enough, beyond where the patio used to merge into the lawn (that I was obliged to mow all those years) lay a new in-ground pool under its protective tarpaulin, surrounded by a broad flagstone lounging area and the pool furniture draped in canvas covers. My first thought was that there would be less grass to mow. It was only when dinner got underway that I got thinking about the cost of the pool versus whatever it might cost to pony up for my college.

We all had dinner together in the formal dining room, an unheard-of happening in the old days when the maid fed us kids at the kitchen table. This was surely Pauline's well-intentioned attempt to have us act like a normal "family." However, the actual household script rolled out flawlessly to quash any semblance of theoretical normality, family élan, or holiday spirit. Jonathan's glee at having his "big brother" around sent his ADD tics into overdrive, which prompted my father to commence warning and scolding him — you're skating on thin ice! — which provoked the indignant reaction in Jonathan — I'm not doing anything . . . what am I doing? Pauline attempted to avert further escalation — the awful spectacle of her son being persecuted by her husband — by asking how things had been going with me. For some reason, I naively answered in so many words that as a result of smoking marijuana the previous week I had done something to injure my brain and was now having *kind of a nervous breakdown that the doctor had given me pills for.*

My father goggled at me across the table. Then the look in his eyes resolved into a steady glare of fury. We ate the rest of the meal in silence until Jonathan did something else and my father hollered at him and insisted he leave the table, and little Madge started to cry, and my father ended up being the one who left the table. I didn't see him again until late the following afternoon, Saturday. He did what he always did on Saturdays: attended to some home improvement chore. By the time I got up, he was off to the lumberyard and since he didn't get me to come along for the ride, as he might have years earlier, I got the message that he wasn't interested in my company. So I rang up my childhood friends Roger and Brian, and we passed the day in Roger's rec room listening to the Beatles' new album, *Rubber Soul*, and Bob Dylan, and the Byrds.

Roger and Brian had not yet started smoking pot. I told them about my recent misadventure with it, and the nervous breakdown I was currently having, and they didn't know what to make of it. To me, the pose of going insane fit nicely with the tragic young man persona I'd been cultivating under the influence of Holden Caulfield and F. Scott Fitzgerald. At this point in their lives, I doubt that either Roger or Brian had ordered a meal in a restaurant on his own, and certainly hadn't spent a whole summer getting sloshed on vodka. Roger would go to college out at UCLA the following year, and Brian, who was not much of a scholar but a good athlete, would go to the University of Toledo in Ohio. I was going nowhere, of course.

There were no further conversations about my future or anything else that weekend. My father and Pauline went out for dinner with friends Saturday night, as had ever been their usual routine. Sunday, Henry drove me to the Manhasset station to catch an early afternoon train back to the city. In the car, he warned me to straighten myself out and knock off the drug taking because he wasn't going to pay for psychiatrists to rescue me from that, and to talk to my mother about going to college. He told me to call Pauline and figure out another weekend after New Year's sometime that would be convenient to come out and visit. I was aware that the reunion was something less than a resounding success.

Not Exactly Insane, But Close Enough

Of course, I never could bring myself to have a conversation with my mother about college, or about money for college, or anything remotely connected with college. I knew what the answer would be: *ask your father*. Christmas vacation was on and I just floated. Henry sent me a check for twenty-five dollars and that gave me some dough for movies and cigarettes during the school vacation. But I could no longer avoid thinking about my college predicament and I became painfully reacquainted with the abyss that awaited me when I would graduate from high school a few months ahead. Faced with problems I had no idea how to solve, nor any plan of action, nor anyone to talk to about it, I sank into a morbid depression that had me preoccupied with death and the existential horror of being shoved into a world that I could barely navigate through.

We went to Uncle Jack's on Christmas Day. Uncle Jack was my mom's sister-in-law's brother. They had all known each other in New York before and after the war when they were young, and they were all part of the same extended social circle ever since. Uncle Jack was a TV producer. His wife was an actress and they lived in one of those glamorous rambling apartments in the East 80s with as many rooms as a Connecticut country house. Their friends were all drawn from TV, magazines, and advertising, mostly Jewish but into the Christmas spirit, as filtered, say, through the lyrics of Irving Berlin. The kids on hand, including some cousins, were all younger than me, and I was not obliged to consort with them. I liked chatting up the adults, but they kept asking me where I was going after high school and, when I said I had no idea, they seemed a little sorry for me. I managed to cadge a few drinks from the help-yourself bar without anyone noticing.

Muriel and Bernie gave me some more cash for Christmas. I bought a record album, *Turn! Turn! Turn!* by the Byrds, which had just come out in December and I played it incessantly in my room on my two-tone turquoise-and-white Decca mono record player. Something about Roger McGuinn's jangling guitar, the intricate high harmonies, and Pete Seeger's lyrics lifted from the Book of Ecclesiastes perfectly captured my troubled, yearning state of mind. I also wore out the grooves on Bob Dylan's two majestic albums of 1965, *Bringing It All Back Home* and *Highway 61 Revisited*.

Dylan had accomplished something prodigious with them: he demonstrated (probably inadvertently) that the long-playing record was destined to be the art form of our generation. (The Beatles album *Rubber Soul*, released three weeks before Christmas 1965, ratified that.) But Dylan's songs turned a key that opened up vistas of something sublime to me, something both awesome and terrifying. I could not have articulated what it was at the time because it was the very thing I was struggling so haplessly to get to, and I had a long way yet to go. Dylan's songs were the testimony of a young man moving successfully into adulthood. It became clear years later that he was not especially comfortable acting that role out in public, but he managed it intrepidly at the time and he came off as fearless. The songs were emotionally rich, complex, and bravely original, the tunes stately and beautiful, despite his middling guitar, and he delivered them in that reedy voice with utter conviction — conviction about anything being what I most lacked.

The rush of wild imagery coming out of Dylan reflected all the strange novelty of the grown-up scenes of bohemian New York he circulated in: the folk scene, the blues scene, the off-Broadway theater scene, the civil rights scene, the Andy Warhol scene. I didn't even try to penetrate those scenes, though I lived only a couple of miles uptown from it all. Dylan was going on twenty-five that winter. He'd already been famous for several years, the very years when, the neuroscientists say, young men finally develop the region in their brain devoted to judgment — knowing that you know enough about the world to act securely in it. His songs chronicled that journey, which was the mystery that I, born a little later after the war, was not yet initiated into. The songs were all about knowing: knowing the secrets of the society he had suddenly become an iconic figure in, knowing himself, and knowing the ways of the world as it acted on him. Dylan was sending me bulletins from the shore of an unknown country while I was still far out at sea.

On New Year's Day 1966, the city's transit workers union called a strike and the buses and subways stopped running. January 1 was a Saturday. We were supposed to return to school from Christmas vacation the following Monday. The Board of Education canceled school until further notice. I felt no exhilaration about the unexpected free days because, much as I detested it, school was the only thing that gave my life any structure. Bernie and Muriel didn't tell me to do anything, or even make any suggestions. They were busy with their own lives. I didn't have any friends to hang out with. Bobby and Larry had apparently written me off after my freakout, and everybody else who went to Music & Art lived far away in the other boroughs. So I followed my familiar, well-trodden paths. I went to movies. It only cost a buck and a half during the day. I made the rounds of the museums. I walked the streets. I went to the Central Park Zoo and communed with the imprisoned animals. I felt like a ghost.

Looking back from where I stand now more than fifty years later, as an adult with a very lively painting career on the side of my writing career, I can see very clearly at least one enormous opportunity I missed: I might have spent my free hours roving the city with a watercolor kit or a drawing pad or an oil painting pochade box and engaged my attention recording what I saw — like Edward Hopper surely did, and Sloan and Bellows and the other New York artists whose paintings of the life of the city thrilled me when I encountered them in the museums. Roving, drawing, and painting is exactly what I did later in life when I traveled around the USA and went to foreign countries. I derive tremendous pleasure and meaning from this.

I can only guess why I did not do this at age seventeen: I just did not understand the self-reinforcing effects of disciplined practice — that you get better at something by doing it, that you can gain pleasure and confidence as you go along, and that it generally entails a certain amount of failure you just have to blow through. Of course, these are propositions that an emotionally mature person can grasp and act on, and that is not what I was then. But then no adult in my orbit suggested it, not even my teachers at the High School of Music & Art, perhaps because pop art and abstract expressionism reigned at the time, and you never had to leave the studio to do that.

As the days went by that January of 1966, I grew more and more anxious and blue. That menacing *Doctor Caligari* feeling of moving through the schizoid city frequently came over me in the streets, and I'd have to duck into a store and pretend to be shopping for something until my heart stopped pounding and my breathing returned to normal. I took refuge in bookshops where you could easily lose yourself, especially the ones that sold used books, and I rooted out odd volumes on abnormal psychology. I bought several and pored over them at home, trying to ascertain what was wrong with me.

By the mid-twentieth century, the experts had settled on a schematic taxonomy of mental illness. There was the basic division of neurosis and psychosis: disturbances that left you merely distressed and dysfunctional and conditions that left you disabled, insane. There were long lists of phobias: fear of heights, of open spaces, closed spaces, crowds, isolation, mirrors, spiders, a thousand other things. And then there were the psychotic states, schizophrenia, paranoid schizophrenia, hebephrenia, catatonia. What I was feeling was mostly a relentless grinding sense of unease, that nothing was right with me and my relation to the world. And, of course, periodically I'd slide clear into one of those panic attacks, when it felt like I was truly losing my mind. I began to understand that this was some kind of anxiety *neurosis*, but I was worried that it was an early sign of something that could get much worse, and that I'd end up raving or catatonic like the photos of those poor souls in the 1950s abnormal psych textbooks I'd bought.

At home, when I wasn't psychoanalyzing myself, I ventured to try writing a few things. My stepfather, Bernie, had given me the 1930s Royal Model O portable typewriter that he'd takento Tufts University before the war. It was black and had glass covered keys, and it made me feel very professional. I was already using it to write papers for history and English classes. But during those two weeks off school, I turned out some Whitmanesque free verse poetry and started a novel. The novel was set in Florida, where I'd never been, in the aftermath of a national disaster, never spelled out, perhaps atomic. I was inspired by the 1959 end-of-the-world novel *Alas, Babylon*, by Pat Frank, which was also set in Florida. Apocalypse was in the air then, with the Cold War at its height.

The first line of my story was "Cigarettes were hard to get in those days." For about twenty-five double-spaced pages the first-person narrator related his misadventures trying to find smokes. Smoking cigarettes was, of course, an activity central to the persona I was cultivating, the doomed, tragic budding writer, a 1960s F. Scott Fitzgerald, with overtones of Thomas Wolfe (author of *Look Homeward, Angel* and not to be confused with the young journalist Tom Wolfe, whose dazzling pop style had already caught my attention in the *Herald Tribune*'s Sunday supplement, called *New York* magazine, and in the pages of *Esquire*).

After about two weeks on strike, the transit workers settled their beef with the city and we were called back to school. Though I had no close friends, I did have lunch in the cafeteria — we weren't allowed to leave the building — with a rotating bunch of acquaintances. They talked incessantly about the colleges they'd applied to, and one girl named Andrea, a swanlike beauty who'd been in various art studios with me for three years, was shocked to hear that I hadn't even applied anywhere. She very kindly brought in her copy of the *College Guide* one day and showed me how you looked up the addresses of the admissions office, and let me borrow it.

One evening after the subway strike was settled, Bernie came home from work and told me that a picture framing shop up on Third Avenue had a sign in the window, "Help Wanted, After School Position." He suggested I go over there and present myself. So the next day I did and I got a job making deliveries and sweeping and dusting the place before closing, from four to six in the afternoon. With tips from the deliveries, I made about twenty bucks a week. It was a lot less work than forging ID documents tediously by hand. The owner was an irascible middle-European fellow who seemed battered by the wickedness of the twentieth century. He sold some actual artwork, as well as being a framer. The art was pretty schlocky: third-rate knockoffs of Camille Pissarro's Paris street scenes, abstractions that could have been done by a monkey. But real estate was booming on the East Side. They were tearing down blocks of old brownstones and hoisting up dozens of twenty-story towers in the mid-sixties white brick mode,

The after-school job got me out of the slough of anxious depression I'd been stuck in. At home, I began to sift through the *College Guide* that Andrea lent to me and by February I managed to send in applications to three schools: Tufts, Bernie's alma mater near Boston, though I knew next to nothing else about it; Syracuse because it had a renowned football team that had featured the great running back Jim Brown, and then the tragic Ernie Davis, who died of leukemia in 1963 and never got to play in the NFL; and George Washington University because I was interested in politics and I had walked past the campus a few blocks from the White House on a trip to our nation's capital in 1964. They were all private colleges. The tuition plus room and board ran about $2,000 a year. I had no idea how I was going to come up with it, but I just let that slide.

I coasted through the last semester of high school doing the minimum that was required of me to just get through. The anxiety attacks tailed off and my preoccupations about insanity and death faded too. In April I had a disagreement with the old gent at the frame shop about working on Saturdays and went back to selling forged IDs for ready cash. I still hung out at McCabe's bar regularly and crashed parties. One of my classmates even threw a party uptown near Gracie Mansion, the mayor's residence, and I met a girl there, a sophomore named Vanessa, a very pretty, petite, redhead with a stunning figure. She became my only high school girlfriend, and only for about a month. I had no idea how to be a boyfriend. We did little besides make out in her bedroom in her parents' apartment in Stuyvesant Town, the sprawling postwar housing complex way downtown near the East River, and we never went beyond taking our shirts off, though her substantial bare breasts were amazing enough to me. I was too shy to proceed further, and dimly cognizant that I could get her pregnant and create a monumental problem for both of us. Otherwise, we never actually dated, that is, went someplace together to do something fun. We didn't break up so much as just stop meeting to make out.

The only other party thrown by a fellow M & A student those last months of my senior year was out in Brooklyn, by a black kid named

David. His father was a professional and David was a prepster who hung out with a small group of white intellectual prepsters, the kind of guys who went to obscure Japanese films and smoked unfiltered French Gauloises cigarettes. I might have joined their little clique if there'd been another year of school. One of them, also named James, died only a few years later of a heroin overdose. Brooklyn was a place as foreign and mysterious to me as Burkina Faso. I never went there, not even to the Brooklyn Museum, though it had a magnificent painting collection. Street crime was on the rise in New York in the mid-1960s and still had quite a way to go. Brooklyn was notoriously unsafe and a lone white kid could be an easy mark after dark. In my party-crashing adventures back in Manhattan, I'd gotten into the habit of carrying an ice pick around in the breast pocket of my tweed sport jacket as personal protection against muggers.

Nothing special happened at the party, just the usual teen drinking, some pot smoking, too, which I didn't join in on. I did help myself to several drinks. They inspired me to chat up some of the senior girls that I'd never spent time with outside of class. They seemed so much more grown-up than me, as girls at eighteen usually are compared to boys. At least I knew them from school, and I'd developed some flirting skills over the past year by crashing parties full of total strangers. But I didn't latch on to anyone that night, and I left the party alone. Besides, at that hour there would have been no place to take someone. New York teens didn't have automobiles, basement rec rooms, or other places of sexual opportunity — and one would hardly go back to a girl's apartment that late to make out in her room with the parents sleeping down the hall.

James Howard Kunstler

Around midnight, I was waiting for a train back to Manhattan in a decrepit subway station. There was nobody else around. The trains were running at very long intervals at that hour and, to ward off boredom, I began flinging my ice pick into an old wooden stanchion from a few feet away on the platform. I was pretty good at making it stick. An old lady happened to come down the steps just then, saw me doing that, shrieked, and rushed back upstairs. About five minutes later a couple of cops showed up and arrested me.

With half a load on from the party, I had to be a wise guy. I'd happened to notice that the squad car they took me to the station house in had a headlight out, and when we got there I joked to the desk sergeant that I wanted to make a citizen's arrest of the officers for driving with one headlight. They weren't in the mood for comedy. After a few hours in a holding cell with a bunch of actual reprobates, the cops told me to go home, minus my ice pick. I thought that was the end of it. But my mother got a notice in the mail on Tuesday from the NYPD Youth Division requesting an appearance with me downtown. Naturally, she flew into a rage and I just toughed it out until she exhausted herself. Bernie actually found it amusing when I told him what happened, the kind of story his TV-writer friends would tell about their misspent youth in the Midwest (they were all from the Midwest). I wasn't grounded or punished, though. I think they both understood why I carried a weapon, but they surely thought it was stupid of me to flaunt it like that. For a month or so I had to report to an officer downtown every Friday afternoon to confirm that I was staying out of trouble. My mother also signed me up to visit a psychiatrist once a week down at the NYU Medical Center near the Youth Division.

I'd never seen a shrink before. I wasn't against it. I came to appreciate the sessions I had with Dr. Sands, perhaps the only sympathetic adult I talked to across all those teen years, not counting my mentor Timothy at summer camp, who was only a demi-adult and often drunk when we spent time together. Dr. Sands had endured some terrible injury, perhaps a war wound (I didn't ask), that left him with a profound limp. He had to hitch his hip way up to swing his left foot forward. I would watch him struggle painfully down the long hall in the busy NYU psych center to fetch me from the waiting room and marveled at what it took for him to just get around. His injury provoked me to discard any inclination I might have had to play games and be a wise guy with him, lest I make his life even more difficult. Around him I was able to drop my experimental pose as tragic, doomed, literary youth and simply be a confused, worried teenager. He proved to be a kind and reassuring presence and prompted me to open up about what was going on in my life. I told him about my travails applying to college and, of course, filled him in on the family dynamics. It was a novelty to be listened to and taken seriously. I began to discover how alone I felt, how injured I was by my father's indifference to me and my future, and how little parental guidance I was getting about anything. We had perhaps six sessions. At the end of it, I was feeling quite a bit better, though my post–high school future remained a quandary.

I was invited to my father's house a few weekends those spring months, but we didn't connect in any way. We were just going through the motions, as in the simple fulfillment of the visitation clause from an old divorce decree. We didn't do anything together, except sit in the car for ten minutes from the Manhasset train station to the house and back again on Sunday. We had no father-son activities, no ball games, movies, walks, excursions. I didn't tell him that I'd applied to three colleges that cost two thousand bucks a year to attend. He didn't ask me anything about my life, my activities, my plans. I'd simply go out to Roslyn on a Saturday morning train, get picked up, mow the lawn as a kind of penitent ritual, and then split to go hang out with my old friends Roger and Brian.

Roger had gotten his driver's license and we'd drive over to the giant new shopping center, Roosevelt Field, in his father's train station car, a Dodge Dart with the old push-button transmission, and catch a movie or browse around the record store. In the evening, Henry and Pauline always went out, without fail. I'd go back to Roger's and we'd watch TV shows or listen to a new rock and roll album over and over again: the Blues Project, Paul Butterfield, Donovan, the Fugs, the Mamas and the Papas, the Lovin' Spoonful, the Rolling Stones, the Beatles, and most of all Bob Dylan, whose epic, intricate songs of the period were so obviously superior to everyone else's, and stood up to endless relistenings. Neither of my old friends got invited to any parties, it seemed, at least not the few weekends when I was around. They weren't into boozing or pot. Suburban teen life seemed pointless to me. I felt sorry for them, though they turned out just fine. Roger would go on to become a hippie carpenter in Colorado, and then a distinguished mountaineer. Brian became a newspaper editor in Woodstock, New York, and, on the side, an accomplished musician who played the joints in that town into his seventies.

Young Man Blues

Late in April, I received a string of letters from Tufts, George Washington, and Syracuse U: all rejections. I can't say I was surprised but I was certainly disheartened, as it deprived me of my only illusory hope for moving forward in life the same way as everyone else I knew. But it was a flimsy illusion. My high school record was abysmal. Over the years at M & A, I flunked math twice, geometry and algebra, and barely passed the foreign language requirement (Spanish). I did well enough in the sciences, biology and even chemistry — the only class I actually studied hard for to pass the final. I had high marks in history and English, and did well enough in all the art studios. But those math and Spanish grades dragged it all down and my cumulative average ended up around C-minus. My scores on the SAT exam, the so-called college boards, were a combined 700 — moron level. All three letters from the colleges noted that I had submitted my applications past the deadline, anyway.

That misfortune prompted me to go see the M & A guidance counselor for the first time. His initial reaction when I sat down in his office and explained the situation was a crabby *You're a little late, aren't you?* But then he warmed up a bit and, after sifting through my abysmal record and sighing a great deal, finally said, *Look, I know somebody out at Stony Brook . . . I'll give him a ring and see what he might be able to do.* The upshot was that I got an appointment the next week to go see an assistant dean in the admissions office at the State University of New York (SUNY) Stony Brook campus way out in eastern Long Island. I kind of liked the idea. Stony Brook in 1966 was still a remnant of the old rural Long Island that we'd moved to in 1954 — though it, too, would be completely paved over as the university expanded, a decade later. I took a day off school and rode a rickety old Long Island Rail Road train out there — a two-hour trip from the city — in beautiful May weather. The campus itself was a fairly dreadful amalgam of brutalist architecture on a dreary modernist layout, but the old village around the train station had some charm. It wasn't Dartmouth, but it would do, since I was desperate.

I found the admissions office easily enough. The assistant dean was a tall young man, probably not twenty-five, swarthy, with thick, scrunched eyebrows and a forbidding demeanor. He gave me the impression that I was keeping him from more pressing matters and came right to the point, saying he'd received my grades and SAT scores from the M & A guidance counselor and that they fell short of Stony Brook's entrance requirements. I'd brought along a photocopy of the novel I'd begun (and not continued), the one set in Florida starring the teenager searching for cigarettes. I said my grades might be perhaps less impressive than my determination to become a great American novelist, and handed over the envelope with my opus in it. He was not very good at small talk, and seemed altogether uninterested in learning more about me, and when it was clear that there was nothing more to say I left his office and hiked back to the train station, feeling gyped that I'd bothered to come all the way out there.

I got the official letter a week later informing me, regretfully, that I would not be a member of SUNY Stony Brook's incoming freshman class next fall.

Saved

The plain reality that in about a month I wouldn't have to go to high school anymore was, alone, so exhilarating, along with the fine spring weather, that I did not sink back into that anxious, death-haunted depression with those frightful panic attacks. But I desperately wanted to get out of the city for the summer, so I called old Frank, the director of Camp Mascoma, and told him I was sorry I behaved badly the summer before and pleaded for a second chance and a summer job. He invited me over to his apartment on 83rd Street off Lexington Avenue, where he lived off-season, running an organized after-school play group for kids that I'd been enrolled in back in the third grade, 1957, the year my folks split up and I moved to the city. We'd play softball in a little glade up a hill behind the Central Park Boathouse and have snowball fights in the Ramble.

Frank and Helen's apartment was a comfortable place in a "prewar" ten-story redbrick building, full of framed photos of the camp and of his two now-grown boys, Peter and Timothy, and shelves of their many sports trophies garnered in high school, college, and at camp. He asked me if I was in college yet, and I told him I was still waiting to hear from a couple of schools, which was bullshit at that point, and he seemed to detect it. He said, *Sit down, son,* and gestured at the sofa. All boys were "son" to Frank. Like the assistant dean of admissions at Stony Brook he came right to the point. He said that apart from me getting drunk at the awards dinner he'd lost several campers over the winter because I had done such a lousy job taking care of the kids in my cabin and, much as he'd liked me down through the years, and had such a long association with my family, going back to my Uncle Buddy in 1933, and thinking my mom was a peach, he couldn't risk bringing me back.

I said I understood, but remarked that it seemed he never informed my mother about what transpired the previous summer, because I'd never heard anything about it from her. *Let's just say I shouldn't have promoted you in a pinch*, he said. *My mistake. You weren't mature enough.* He was right, of course, and I guess he wanted to tell me face to face instead of over the phone. Frank knew a lot about boys and young men and habitually offered life lessons they might learn from. It was kind of a parting gift because I could see a chain of consequence emanating from my actions. But it left me feeling horribly guilty for harming the place that I loved so much.

What he left out was the part about his son recruiting me into a summer of alcoholic dissolution. I asked about Tim, who I hadn't heard from since the previous August. Tim was married now, Frank said, and had gotten *his first real job* in the sales department of IBM. I couldn't imagine Tim working in an office. To me, he'd always be in that green ratty Narragansett Beer jumpsuit, out in the woods somewhere, half in the bag. Frank said he wasn't mad at me anymore, before showing me to the door and wishing me well. I shed some tears walking back downtown toward home on 68th Street, thinking how much I'd miss New Hampshire and the camp after so many seasons there, and what a screwup I was. Years later, I heard that there was a scandal that summer of 1966 about some of the older boys selling marijuana to the younger kids, and after that the enrollment really sank. Not long after, Camp Mascoma went out of business.

As it happened, though, my mother and Bernie were invited to come out to Uncle Jack's place on Fire Island for the Memorial Day weekend, and me with them. Bernie and Muriel were frantically in search of a last-minute summer rental because their usual groupie gang fell apart for various reasons that spring (alcohol rehab, divorce, overseas assignments). So we took the train out to Bayshore and the ferry across the Great South Bay to the twenty-odd-mile sandbar off the south coast of Long Island, which, contrary to myth, is not an all-gay enclave. There were half a dozen little towns strung like pearls down the slender island, and really only one of them, Cherry Grove, was overtly gay then. The town of Ocean Beach, where Jack had a house right up behind the dunes, occupied the widest stretch of the barrier beach. You could walk across it, from bay to ocean, in under ten minutes. OB was a family enclave, almost entirely Jewish, and full of the kind of advertising and showbiz types my parents gravitated around.

One big draw of Fire Island, what it made it really special, was that cars were banned there, giving it a mellow ambience exceedingly rare in car-crazy America. Only the police, fire, and garbage departments had motor vehicles, plus a beach taxi company that ran Jeeps from town to town along the ocean. There were no proper roads otherwise, just "walks," concrete paths that ran up to the beach perpendicular to a "Midway" walk halfway between the bay and the ocean. There was an old custom on the island to never wear shoes not even in the bars and stores. Everybody went barefoot. It was a charming place.

My mother, Muriel, met my father, Henry, out there after World War Two. (I was born in 1948.) As young marrieds, they rented a house on the island every summer in the early 1950s. A season or so later, Henry got into some kind of bar fight there and he refused to go back ever again. The postwar young adults of the 1950s were heavy drinkers, and the war had reinforced that behavior. They'd all been teenagers near the tail end of Prohibition, and that social experiment had shifted American drinking habits more toward hard liquor. So the cocktail culture of the 1960s was a big thing for their generation.

The summer of 1957 I was sent to a saltwater camp called Annisquam on Cape Ann, north of Boston. When I came home, Henry and Muriel were divorced. In 1958, I was sent out to California where Henry's baby sister and her family lived in the San Fernando Valley. I spent the whole summer there with my two cousins, Kathy and Johnnie. Aunt Lenore drove us to a country club every morning where we never left the big swimming pool surrounded by ladies in cat's-eye sunglasses playing mahjong. I came back to New York with a sensational tan. In 1959 we were living in Manhattan. Muriel scraped together enough money to send me to Camp Mascoma for the first time. After Muriel met and married Bernie in 1960, she got them going back out to Fire Island in those groupie houses with their writer friends.

Through the 1960s, when I was up in New Hampshire at camp, I'd only go out to Fire Island in June and September, so I hardly knew who ran anything, or the other kids who spent their whole summer out there. But that Memorial Day weekend, in 1966, I was intent on finding a summer job at the beach. For dinner Friday night, we all went down to OB's quaint village center around the ferry dock on the bay side of the island. The grown-ups favorite joint was called Goldie's with a deck overlooking the Great South Bay and a piano bar. When Goldie stopped by the table to chat up everybody, I asked if he was still hiring for the summer. He said he was all set. Muriel seemed taken aback to learn that I was thinking of sticking around.

I peeled off as soon as I could. There were five or six other joints in the village. I went to one just opening up under new ownership called the Sea Turtle. There were many other teenagers in the bar that night including most of the OB lifeguard crew, guys a little older than me, college kids. (I wouldn't turn eighteen until October.) While waiting to get the bartender's attention, I struck up a conversation with another kid waiting at the bar, and he started telling me how stupid everything in the world was, such as bartenders who were too busy chatting up chicks to fetch you a beer. I appreciated that point of view because it was an antidote to my own rather melancholic turn of mind. His name was Chris. I asked if he knew the owner of the joint. He said, *why, do you want to complain about the lousy service?* I said, *no, I was looking for a summer job.* He said he knew of a summer job working as the slave over at the Fire Island Summer Club. The slave? I'd never heard of the place and asked what this slave was supposed to do there. He said, *mop the floors and wash dishes and do chores.* I said, *I could do that.* He said okay, *if you're on the beach tomorrow, look for this guy named Baz, he's the manager. He's always out there working on his tan.*

The next day I asked around and I found this Baz sitting in the sand among a group of eight or ten teenagers, most of them girls, kind of holding court. He was older, beyond college, a dark-haired, handsome guy in RayBan shades, apparently quite charismatic to teenagers.

Nobody was interested in going in the water because the ocean was still quite cold in May. But it was a warm day out on the sand and the girls were all test-driving their new bikinis. I just sat there in the circle watching Baz flirt up the chickies. After a while he got up and headed for the stairway over the dunes. I followed and caught up with him on the deck at the top, where the town walk started. I said I'd heard about a possible summer job as a slave at the place he managed. He lit up and told me to come over there with him. On the way, I got the lowdown on the Fire Island Summer Club. It was a real estate association, he said, started by a bunch of army pals right after the war, all Catholics, old-time islanders who wanted their own enclave apart from the Jews who were taking over OB. They bought about twenty acres a couple of hundred yards east of the OB line. There were perhaps ten houses built there now, but they still had many lots for sale. I told Baz I was a Jew and asked if that was a problem. Naw, he said. They loved to get Jews working for them, like *Shabbos goys* in reverse. He had to explain to me what a *Shabbos goy* was. Baz himself was Jewish, first name, Michael, though nobody called him that.

A big old hulking former Coast Guard station occupied the bay side of the property. This was the association's clubhouse. It had a commercial kitchen, a dining room, and an attached bar decorated with stuffed game fish on the walls. Baz explained the job to me. I had to keep the place tidy, mop the floors, clean up the suite where the real estate prospects stayed overnight, work in the kitchen assisting the chef and washing dishes on Fridays and Saturdays, and do various other chores during the week. It paid sixty bucks a week. The job came with a place to stay, a little garret room under a dormer upstairs, which was electrifying news, because it meant I wouldn't have to stay with whatever Muriel and Bernie ended up renting. Baz hired me that afternoon. I could go back to the city after the holiday weekend and get the rest of my summer clothes, but otherwise I'd just blow off the last few weeks of high school, which was fine by me. It turned out Bernie and Muriel were fine with the arrangement too. They'd found a tiny cottage to rent that was an outbuilding behind a bigger house. It had only one bedroom.

It was a great job. I worked very hard those two weekend days and nights, but during the week my duties were light. I had to clear the sand off the Midway Walk every few days, which tended to accumulate with the blowing wind and would make it difficult for the homeowners to tote all their stuff from the ferry dock with the red Radio Flyer wagons they all had for that purpose. I kept the clubhouse clean and mopped the hardwood floors. On Thursdays, I had to roll a gigantic dolly with iron wheels all the way down to the ferry landing to meet the freight boat and bring back boxes of provisions for the weekend festivities — liquor, meat, vegetables, linens from the service on the mainland. An elderly French chef named Jean came over from the mainland to cook dinners on Friday and Saturday nights and he kept me hopping. I helped him prep the food, washed all the pots and pans, and then the dishes from the dining room. I was still hosing down the kitchen long after Jean retired to his room upstairs. And then I'd go downtown with Chris and several other Summer Club teens and drink twenty-five-cent beers until two in the morning.

Chris Dunworth's large, Irish family had a house on the club's property up near the ocean. There were seven kids. They lived in Shaker

Heights, Ohio, the Cleveland suburb. Chris was third oldest. The other middle kids, Jane, Joe, and Patrick, liked to spend time hanging out in the clubhouse playing the jukebox, which was rigged so you didn't have to put quarters in to play records. Chris was exactly a year older than me. He'd been left back in school one year for being a fuckup, and would be just entering the University of Tennessee as a freshman in the coming fall. His sister Jane was fourteen, freckly, pretty, and fetching in a bikini, and I was careful not to mess around with her. Rather, I had a crush on a little cookie named Kathy, a "mother's helper," as au pair girls were called, and I hung around trying to charm her every weekday afternoon when she took her two little kids to the beach. Kathy was sixteen, blonde, wore a red and white polka-dot bikini, and looked like someone the Beach Boys might write a song about. I got nowhere with her romantically, though we got to be friends. She had a crush on a hulking lifeguard my age named Garth who, a few years later, went crazy from doing too much LSD at American University, in Washington, DC, and then committed suicide in a mental institution.

As far as I could tell, Baz had hardly any duties besides ordering supplies, keeping track of the dining room and bar expenditures, and showing building lots to the real estate prospects. He had a bedroom behind the bar and a great stereo and the entire collection of Dylan albums to date, which I played incessantly over the PA when I was working around the clubhouse. Baz was hardly ever there. He had his coterie of teenage admirers on the beach and was also rumored to be popular with the "weekday widows" of OB, mothers whose husbands went into the office on Monday mornings and didn't return until Friday. I did what he told me to do and we got along just fine.

Young Man Blues

One day near the end of June, I took an early ferry to the mainland and a train to the city to attend my high school graduation. It was held in a ballroom at the Waldorf Astoria. I wanted to say farewell to some of the seniors I'd gone through school with, even though none of them were close friends. I didn't tell Bernie and Muriel that the ceremony was even happening, and as soon as it was over I hurried back to the train station for Fire Island. What impressed me most that day was how strange it felt to walk around in shoes after going barefoot for weeks, and how awful the air was out on the city streets. I never wanted to go back there again.

The summer days went by in a rhythm of hectic weekends and leisurely weekdays. I loved my little room in the garret, the first place of my own away from the city. At night, there was no din of traffic and sirens, just the gentle lapping of the bay fifty feet from my window. I only ran into Bernie and Muriel half a dozen times that summer on the island, either on the beach or downtown when I blundered into them on my way from McGuire's bar to Hausers bar, the two spots popular with teens. I seemed to mystify them, like they were seeing a ghost. They didn't ask me about my plans for when the summer was over, and I didn't give it any thought myself.

It was altogether a happy time after a disturbing year. I made a lot of friends. Everybody called me "Slave," because that was the traditional title of my job at the club — there had been many slaves before me. I didn't take it as an insult. It was *an identity*, a special one nobody else had, comical too, and a nice break from the tragic young artiste persona I was working on before. I had no more panic attacks. Though most nights I drank some beers, my alcohol consumption didn't come close to the debauch of the previous summer keeping up with Timothy at camp. There was some pot around and I avoided it. I went to the beach virtually every day and swam in the ocean, and sometimes borrowed friends' surfboards.

I didn't get anywhere with the girls, especially Kathy, who I was nuts about. But one night in August I had my first sexual experience. I'd made friends with two college guys, David and Mark, who worked on the village garbage crew and had a crappy apartment behind a shop that sold beachwear, and I used to go over there weekday mornings when they were done with work and play rock and roll songs on the guitar with David. I was authorized to use the Summer Club charge account at the grocery store and I always brought over a box of Captain Crunch cereal. That August night, I managed to pick up a girl in McGuire's, a mother's helper whose name I've forgotten — or perhaps she picked me up — and took her over to David and Mark's apartment, because it was such a long walk back to my room at the club, and borrowed one of the bedrooms for a little while to make out with her. Things simply proceeded from there. It was a classically awkward and self-conscious initiation into the grand mystery and had not much to do with love or romance, really, just two teenagers who had been drinking, under the spell of their hormones. It didn't happen again, and we never really became acquainted in the short time that remained.

As the end of summer loomed, some of guys I hung out with, Chris and his lifeguard cohorts, a few who were well along in college, sat me down one evening in McGuire's while we were all still sober and said they heard I had no plans to go to college, and that I better get into one because the Vietnam War was revving up and I could get drafted into the army and end up over there getting my ass shot off. They were quite adamant about it, and rather surprised at how complacent I was. They helped me figure out a plan of action. I was surprised and grateful that anyone cared enough to help me out. They told me to send out letters to schools immediately and advised me how to pitch my situation. Baz had a typewriter in his quarters that I could use.

It happened that the one standardized test I scored well on was the New York State Regents Scholarship Exam, so I sent letters to three small SUNY colleges upstate, New Paltz, Oswego, and Brockport. I didn't even know where these towns were on the map, just far away from the city. I said that family trouble had kept me from applying during the regular school year, but now I was able to and would it be possible to make a late application? The next week, they all replied. New Paltz and Oswego sent me applications. Brockport sent me a letter with a dorm assignment and a housing contract.

At the first opportunity, I used the Summer Club phone to call the dean of the housing office at Brockport who had signed the letter. I told him my name and he indicated he remembered my recent letter. I said, *I'm not sure what your letter about the dorm assignment means.* He said, *Oh, that's where you're going to live when you come here.* I said, *When am I supposed to come there?* He said, *Freshman orientation starts August 30. You'll want to be here for that.* I said, *Okay, so that's when I come up and move into this place Harmon Hall?* He said, *That's right. It's a brand-new dorm. Very nice. You'll be very happy there.* He added that they had confirmed my Regents scholarship status, which awarded me $250 on the $500 tuition and fees, and that I could submit the balance any time before October first. *Welcome*, he said, *to Brockport State.* I never mentioned that no one had sent me an application, and I'd never filled one out, but I surmised that if there was some problem over that I could straighten it out later that fall.

78

Part Two

My Parents

I don't know that much about any of them, including the two stepparents who were in the picture during my childhood and adolescence, most particularly, their interior lives. Three of my grandparents did not survive my earliest years, and the fourth I never saw and did not know at all, so these transmitters of family lore were absent in my life. None of my parents spoke very much about their childhood and early adulthood. I really only knew how they were in the present time of what is now my past. But I will attempt to backfill their histories and draw accurate portraits of them, and perhaps I will discover something about them and myself in the process.

My Mother

Muriel Rose Imbrey, born 1920. Her mother's side, the Harburgers, were German Jews who came to New York in the wave of immigration that followed the European political uproars of 1848. The town of Harburg is located in Bavaria, in southern Germany, but I don't know whether the Harburgers in my family actually came from Harburg. The first of that line I know of was Julius Harburger, born 1850 in Manhattan. He entered Republican Party politics as a young man, supporting Presidents Hayes, Garfield, and Arthur, and later boosted for Theodore Roosevelt. He served in the New York State Assembly 1899 to 1901. Between 1902 and 1913, he served variously as New York City excise commissioner (that is, taxes); sheriff of New York County (which is Manhattan Island); and county coroner. He was renowned for being remarkably short, under five feet. (I am five feet and nine inches.) He lived in a brownstone row house on St. Mark's Place, off Second Avenue, and died there in 1914 at sixty-four.

Julius Harburger, 1905

Julius had four sons. (I know nothing about his wife.) This is where the family lore gets a little sketchy. His son David, a young lawyer, eloped with the daughter of the city water commissioner against the wishes of both families sometime between 1896 and 1899. Her name was Dorothy Kopf, perhaps a non-Jew. David was disowned by his father. It's likely Dorothy was spurned by her family, too, but I can only conjecture from the way things worked out. The marriage produced two children, Hazel, my grandmother, and Blanche, her younger sister. The marriage was a failure and the couple divorced around 1907–8, a relative rarity then. Dorothy remarried, to a violinist, whose name is lost to history. One day, this violinist came home and caught Dorothy in the arms of yet another man. He shot Dorothy, shot the other man, and then shot himself: a double murder / suicide. Little Hazel and Blanche supposedly witnessed the crime.

I got all this from my mother late in her life. It seemed to shame and depress her, a sordid, squalid thing she was not eager to own. Though I searched high and low through the newspaper annals of the New York Public Library nothing came up about it. It's possible that this extravaganza of criminal violence was deliberately kept out of the newspapers. Politically prominent people were able to do that in those days, when the news would embarrass them or harm their reputation — and Julius Harburger was a highly visible figure associated with law enforcement. Depending on the year it happened, it's even possible that the three dead bodies were conveyed to his place of business, the county coroner's office, which is a dramatic twist more fantastic than most crime novelists might manage. Or maybe he was county sheriff at the time.

I know nothing more about his son David Harburger, my great-grandfather, the ex-husband, who was out of the picture by then. Perhaps Hazel and Blanche were placed with their father after the murders, perhaps with other relatives. In any case, Hazel went out into the working world as soon as she could, first as a teenage shopgirl and then as a model, and before she reached twenty she found a husband, Saul Howard Imbrey, a young attorney. He was born in London in 1885 and came to the US at age six. His father, one Maurice Imbrey, was an anglicized Austrian who had changed his name from Immergluck to Imbrey. Immergluck translates as *always lucky*. Young Saul went to New York Law School, and eventually practiced corporate bankruptcy law, a brisk business in his heyday, the years of the Great Depression.

He styled himself professionally as S. Howard Imbrey. At home, he was Saul.

Muriel was born in 1920 (Hazel must have been about twenty) and her brother, my uncle Howard, known lifelong as "Buddy," came along in 1921. The Imbreys led a posh upper-middle-class life in a spacious apartment at Park Avenue and 84th Street. Muriel and Buddy both went to the Horace Mann prep school, with separate boys' and girls' divisions. Much of their later kinship and social relationships revolved around the kids they went to school with there. They were conveyed up to the Bronx campus each day in a chauffeured LaSalle sedan.

The family were nonpracticing Jews who kept Christmas trees and ate ham sandwiches. They went on steamship vacations to Europe and the Caribbean, mainly Cuba. Muriel went to Camp Hiawatha in Maine for many summers and Buddy was sent to Camp Mascoma in New Hampshire, where I later went in the 1950s and '60s. One part of her girlhood Muriel did like to talk about were her teenage dating years, which seemed glamorous and fun-filled, even in mid-Depression. She and her school chums snuck into nightclubs in Harlem, went to Broadway shows — in those days, apparently, you could walk right up to the box office the night of the performance and get tickets — and of course to movies and restaurants. New York was safe. If you had some money, it was as posh, lovely, and stirring as a new Gershwin song.

Muriel did not talk about her mother very much. I gather that Hazel was a remote and emotionally inaccessible figure, actually a classic depressive who retreated more and more to her bedroom over the years with vague neurasthenic complaints. One might surmise that Hazel never recovered from the trauma of witnessing her mother's murder.

Saul, though, was active and garrulous, very busy professionally, and liked to declaim poetry in the English accent he retained from his early childhood in London. I can imagine an aura of tension in the family between the depressed, retiring Hazel and the gregarious Saul. He was also apparently a household tyrant and was surely responsible for Muriel's primary grievance in life: he quashed her aspirations to become a dancer and actress, forcing her instead to go to a teacher's college run by the Ethical Culture Society. I'm sure she would have succeeded in showbiz. She was a good-looking brunette, five-foot-five, athletic, and graceful. Her personality was naturally and forcefully histrionic, with excellent comic timing. She also had a good head for business, and would have managed her earnings nicely. Anyway, she soon engineered her escape from the teacher's college by getting married to one of her old Horace Mann schoolmates, one Lincoln Palmer Bloomfield "of Boston and New York" — as the wedding announcement in the *New York Times* read, October 5, 1942.

At twenty-two, Muriel was a little older than Hazel was when she'd married Saul. Lincoln was an ensign in the navy. He must have appeared dashing and he was very intelligent. The war was on. Many girls were rushing into marriage with their sweethearts as the men prepared to ship out and perhaps die young, tragically, far from home. Quite a few did, actually. And perhaps because the marriage was based on that kind of wartime sentimentality it didn't work out. Lincoln survived the war and went on to serve in the State Department and then thirty years on the MIT faculty teaching political science. He wrote several books on conflict and crisis management in foreign affairs and pioneered techniques of war gaming. He lived to the ripe old age of ninety-three.

I never met him and he most likely knew nothing of my existence. I knew nothing of his until about age fourteen.

You already know that Muriel met Henry Kunstler on Fire Island around 1947, where Saul and Hazel had a summer house. Saul had a fatal heart attack in the surf there on the July Fourth weekend, 1948, some four months before I was born. He was only sixty-three. Less than a year later, in June 1949, Hazel committed suicide. The method was never disclosed to me. I suspect she cut her wrists because my father late in his life averred to the scene being "a horror show." Hazel had moved from the big apartment on Park Avenue to a more manageable one-bedroom on 72nd Street off Lexington Ave. She was barely fifty. And however their opposing personalities worked in that marriage, Saul was Hazel's rescuer and protector from her rocky start in life, and losing him unexpectedly must have been another blow. Muriel always kept a photo of Hazel in her bedroom, a slim, stately figure in a tall poufy hat, with a broad smile. You wouldn't necessarily read despair and tragedy in her face. I think Muriel felt angry ever after that her mother checked out on her so abruptly.

Muriel and Henry and I moved into that apartment on 72nd Street briefly. There was an acute housing shortage after the war. In 1950, the family moved to a brand-new two-bedroom apartment building in Rego Park, Queens. It was called the Halsey House after Admiral "Bull" Halsey, a hero of the recent war. It had a posh modernist lobby and stood across the street from a playground, but as far as Muriel was concerned it might as well have been in Uzbekistan. Except for a couple of months when she lived in Champagne, Illinois, where Lincoln did some graduate work, and those summers at camp in Maine, Muriel had never lived outside Manhattan.

JHK Fire Island, 1951

My own memory goes back to about age two. I remember digging for sand crabs on the beach at Fire Island and being taught to make angels in the sand and being fed endless bowls of Campbell's cream of tomato soup. During those years the family kept a Studebaker sedan. We made a long trip in it to Washington, where my dashing Uncle Buddy temporarily lived with his household, which included an exotic manservant he'd picked up in India after the war. He had become a CIA spook by then after serving in the OSS in Burma during the war, and later on the agency always brought him home for a year when presidential administrations changed, so that would have been 1953 when General Eisenhower came in and I was going on five. Uncle Buddy took me to the Smithsonian to see the Lindbergh's *Spirit of St. Louis*. Muriel was crazy about him. He was a terrific wit and played the piano at parties. It seems to me that Muriel was a capable mother during those years. She liked to frighten me at bathtime though by putting on foreign accents, which she was good at, and pretending that she was a stranger who had replaced my mother. I fell for the gag time after time and she seemed to enjoy bringing me to tears. She was literate and steeped me in good children's books: *The Wind in the Willows*, *A Child's Garden of Verses*, all of A. A. Milne. She became friends with a German Jewish refugee family in our building, and their younger offspring, Roger, became my lifelong friend. I spent many happy hours in their apartment, where his older brother, Danny, had a fine collection of British-made tin soldiers we were allowed to play with, and piles of World War Two comic books about grizzled, cigar-chomping machine gunners fighting the *Japs*.

After Henry had his barroom fight on Fire Island, and we quit the place, the family spent a couple of summer vacations in a rented house in Port Jefferson on the north shore of Long Island, where the beaches were stony and you couldn't make angels in the sand. Our family life seemed stable in those years. I was a happy child. I don't remember Henry and Muriel carrying on affectionately around me, but there were no histrionics. They seemed content. They did not have another child, though, a telltale sign maybe.

They must have felt they had a future together because in 1954 we moved to the suburbs, Roslyn Heights, Long Island, into a comfortable two-story ranch house in a subdivision called Northwood, one of the earliest such real estate projects in an area that had formerly been large estates of the old plutocrats. Muriel called it "the country," as she called anyplace that was not Manhattan (Fire Island was "the country"). I think she enjoyed the first couple of years there, being a fifties housewife. I sure did. I wrote a chapter about my idyllic sojourn there in *The Geography of Nowhere* (1993). For all the shortcomings of suburbia, which I have chronicled in several books, it was a very good place for children between the ages of five and eight, who don't require much contact with the adult world of shops and workplaces and public life.

My friend Brian's family moved into the house across the street. His mother, Elaine, was Muriel's chum from teacher's college. And Roger's family, from Halsey House, also moved to Northwood two streets away. Northwood was full of baby boomer kids and we played all the games of the day incessantly: flies up with our new baseball mitts; running bases; bike games like cops and robbers. There was the ruin of an old estate behind our house. It had belonged to Clarence Hungerford Mckay, who laid the first trans-Pacific cable between the US and the Far East. His daughter had married the songwriter Irving Berlin, a Jew (the horror!). Mckay died in 1938 and by 1955 his abandoned mansion was an abandoned wreck. But the 600-acre property on Harbor Hill abutted our backyard and was still threaded with lovely carriage trails lined with rhododendron, a perfectly scaled, completely safe demi-wilderness for little boys to ramble in.

We all went to the Greenvale elementary school, and walked there without adult supervision about three quarters of a mile in a group, starting at age six, exiting Northwood and crossing busy Route 25A at the corner of Glen Cove Road. Rainy days, Muriel or Elaine drove us. Old Greenvale, Long Island, was a pre-suburban village mostly of immigrants who worked on the many estates in the neighborhood, and we kids from the new postwar subdivisions were not a majority. I loved going to that school and fit in just fine with the other boys and girls. These were the most confident, hopeful years of the postwar period and Roslyn Heights was saturated with comfortable normality. Summers, my friends and I went to the Pierce Country Day Camp in Mineola, which was an alternative wilderness of ball fields and swimming pools —now, all hemmed in by suburban houses.

Life at home in Northwood seemed happy and predictable. My father commuted to Manhattan weekdays, like every other father in Northwood. We had dinner together most nights at the dining room table that Muriel inherited from Hazel. Henry and Muriel had friends who came over regularly, including a bohemian couple from the city who played recorders (that is, wooden flutes). I endured the usual battery of childhood diseases in rapid succession: mumps, chickenpox, measles. I had a tank full of tropical fish in my room. I watched *King Kong* on WOR-TVs "Million Dollar Movie." Henry built me a layout of Lionel trains on a big table in the basement, with switches and grade crossings and buildings that lit up. We got a standard poodle named Kelly and a black cat named Tarbaby. Muriel seemed to thrive out there, away from Manhattan — but what did I know?

What I did know was that in early 1957 the fighting began. I would wake up in my room late at night to the sound of Muriel shrieking at my father and Henry replying, but not quite matching her in volume. I especially remember her mocking tone, though not what was said. These fights continued through a period of weeks. I sensed that something was very wrong, and grew frightened and ashamed, and had no one to talk to about the bewildering developments in my home, not even Roger and Brian. I started to urinate at night in a large basket of toys in my room — where I kept my Prince Valiant helmet and other enchanted objects — and soon it began to smell. Obviously, this is the kind of thing that a distressed child will do, and parents will notice, which Muriel eventually did. There was some imputation that I had something physically wrong with me to do that. But I knew she knew why, and she knew I knew, and, anyway, the shrieking stopped.

Next, Henry started working on the second floor of the house. It was unfinished when we moved in because we did not need any more bedrooms. When he had framed in a room and put up wallboard, he moved a bed upstairs and began sleeping there. That was clearly ominous to me. One late afternoon, Muriel took me into the dining room, where we had all stopped eating together, and explained that she and my father were getting a divorce. It was a fresh concept to me. Nobody else in Northwood that I knew had one in the family, nor anyone on TV, even. She explained that my father would be moving elsewhere — where exactly was left unspecified — and indeed Henry did not come home that night. Our time as a family was over.

Generally, I had little information about what all this meant, but I sensed it was very bad news. I began breaking down in tears in the middle of class at school. My third-grade teacher, a young woman named Miss Loskill, took me out in the hall and tried to comfort me, or at least get me to calm down, but when I sobbed out the word *divorce* she seemed at a loss to say anything.

The summer of 1957, Roger and I were sent to a sleepaway boys' camp on a saltwater estuary on Cape Ann, Massachusetts, Camp Annisquam. The big thing there was sailing instruction. I spent the first two weeks in the infirmary after driving a three-inch finishing nail into my foot horsing around with my friends in the bunk. It was slow to heal, and after the first week the doctor extracted a two-inch piece of linoleum from the wound that had somehow got jammed in there. I watched a lot of Red Sox games on a small, grainy television on interminable hot afternoons. The camp nurse played the radio in her station: "Wake Up Little Susie," "Love Letters in the Sand," "Diana." I read most of the Landmark series of children's books about famous Americans from the camp library: Lewis and Clark, Wild Bill Hickok, the Wright Brothers. Muriel was in Nevada, getting a divorce. Henry did not come up to see me. I barely heard from either of them. But I healed up and eventually worked my way back into the camp routine, which I loved, especially taking rowboats out at low tide and searching the shallow waters off the sandbars for oddities of nature like hermit crabs.

When I came home from Camp Annisquam, Muriel had a plan. She had a friend, Adele Tierney, down in Roslyn Village, at the bottom of Harbor Hill, who ran an antiques store called the Shooting Box, and I believe my mother had some notion about working there and moving into the village. She'd never worked a job in her life, and hadn't even finished teacher's college, so she must have felt utterly ill-prepared to be on her own. Adele was about the age Hazel would have been, a motherly figure to Muriel. She was, indeed, a very nice older lady, and in retrospect I think she even resembled Hazel physically. She and her husband Bill, a retired gent, were very nice to me. Bill had a Corvette sports car and he took me for spins on the country roads of nearby Old Westbury on fall evenings while Muriel confabbed with Adele.

Though we remained in the same house in the Northwood subdivision that September of 1957, Muriel pulled me out of the Greenvale School and put me in the Roslyn Village elementary school full of strangers. I was very discommoded by this, had no idea what else it portended, and I missed my old schoolmates horribly. I saw my father infrequently that September. Once or twice, a strange woman named Pauline came to the house and picked me up in an MG sports car and conveyed me to a house two blocks away in Northwood where my father was staying — with her. She was an attractive brunette, quite a bit younger than Muriel. Her kids were just toddlers then. One Saturday morning, my father came back to the family house and took me out for pancakes at the Greenvale diner on Route 25A, but we didn't talk much. What I remember was just flipping the metal pages of the little jukebox unit in our booth while we waited for the chow.

Years later, I found out what had happened between my parents back then. I learned this around 1998 at an art opening in New York City for my cousin Kathy Jacobi (Henry's kid sister Lenore's daughter), a successful LA-based painter who was married to a TV actor. Both Henry and Muriel came to the event, the first time they'd been in the same room since 1957. I'm sure it made both of them uncomfortable. At one point, I was off in a corner of the big gallery with Henry, who was then eighty-one (I was fifty), and we'd both had a couple of champagnes. I don't remember exactly what prompted it — I suppose the disconcerting presence of someone he had loathed for a half century — but he disclosed that way back in Roslyn that last year of their marriage, Muriel had been conducting an extracurricular romance with their married friend Larry, the fellow from Great Neck with a sailboat we went out on, and that's what busted up the marriage. So there it was.

Muriel got a pretty poor settlement in the divorce. She complained often about how little he sent her, and a couple of times she hauled him into court. But Henry was in a position to punish her and he did. She would have to work a full-time job. The money from Hazel and Saul was long gone. Curiously, through later years, whenever she spoke of Henry beyond money matters, it was of his good manners, careful grooming, and elegant European clothes. She also offered that he was "boring." She may have known deep down that she *done him wrong* carrying on with another man, and felt some twinges of regret.

In any case, that fall of 1957, her plan A, to work in Adele's antiques store in Roslyn Village, fell through for some reason and in October we suddenly moved out of the Northwood house to a one-bedroom apartment on 93rd Street off Lexington Ave in New York City. Aunt Blanche, my grandmother Hazel's little sister, lived in the building. I had never met her before, for some strange reason, at least not since being a toddler. But the first few months in the city I spent many after-school hours at "Auntie" Blanche's. She was a jolly old gal. She fabricated costume jewelry there in her apartment while sipping Rheingold beer — sometimes she shared it with me in a juice glass — and her hallway was filled from floor to ceiling with cabinets of many tiny drawers and pigeon holes containing shiny things, rhinestones, fake pearls, and sequins. Gold and silver chains hung from hooks. She lived with a dapper fellow named Norman to whom she was not married. He sold men's clothing somewhere in the city, and he took me to a New York Giants football game at Yankee Stadium that fall. I learned how easy it was to get up there on the Lexington Avenue IRT subway line, one of the first orientation lessons I received about life in the city.

The move was a horrible shock to me but I survived and at once began venturing around Manhattan on my own after school, frequently to the Museum of Natural History across the park (admission was free then) to commune with the great blue whale and the shrunken heads. The apartment was cramped and seemed downright squalid to me after the big house on Long Island. Muriel slept on a convertible sofa in the living room. I have no idea what happened to my Lionel train set, or to Kelly the standard poodle, though Tarbaby the black cat came to New York with us. I was enrolled in Public School No. 6 on 82nd and Madison, probably the best public grammar school in the city, and I commenced a very different chapter of childhood.

Muriel found a job at Bloomingdale's department store on 59th Street, in the furniture department. She was charming, attractive, and gregarious. It was a start, at least. Working for a living was a whole new experience for her, and apparently exhausting. She drank rather heavily in the evenings to recover from the rigors of retail, and one memorable night she got falling-down plastered, and I had to fetch Auntie Blanche and Norman to put her in bed. It must have been a lonely time for her, that first year, having to stay home with me evenings. Her whole generation of New York friends from the '40s had moved out to the suburbs. At home on 93rd Street, we existed in separate realms. I watched TV while gluing up model airplanes in my room and she read Lawrence Durrell in the living room or yakked on the phone.

She went out on dates infrequently that first year. She saw a shrink. The summer of 1958, when I was sent to Aunt Lenore's in LA to be with my cousins Kathy and Johnnie, Muriel met a dashing Brazilian fellow named Roberto, and he became a more or less steady boyfriend. Except that Roberto lived in São Paulo — he may have been married, for all I know — and he was in New York perhaps four or five times a year on business. I liked Roberto. He had a dashing style and a wry sense of humor — he liked to call Tarbaby *gato de merda* — but we never went anywhere in the city as a threesome... a *family*. I was given to understand that he came from a prominent family in Brazil, was apparently wealthy, and I must suppose he and Muriel had lively times in the sack. But matrimony was not in the cards. After about a year Roberto stopped coming around.

In 1959, Muriel's fortunes improved a bit. She moved to a new job selling clothes at Henri Bendel on 57th Street, more of an emporium than a department store in scale, but much ritzier than Bloomingdale's. That year she met and began keeping company with Bernard Glaser, Bernie, forty and divorced, who was then the managing editor of a magazine called *Coronet*, which was put out by the company that owned *Esquire*. It was a competitor to *Reader's Digest*, physically the same compact format but aimed at a more educated readership. Bernie had two kids, a girl and a boy, Gail and Garrett, a few years younger than me. Their mother had already remarried, and they lived in a stable household on 72nd Street.

Young Man Blues

Bernie Glaser, 1962

Bernie was a good match for Muriel, intellectually and temperamentally. He was very literary and he almost never got angry about anything. He had a fine bunch of semi-bohemian friends in the *Mad Men* milieu of advertising, magazines, and TV production, a community of lively spirits. Muriel fit right in with her quick wit and her capacity for liquor. He had a little studio apartment near the 59th Street Bridge up the block from Eddie Condon's jazz club, but by the spring of 1960 he was spending most of his nights in the living room of our little place. Before long, they decided to get married, a city hall ceremony. Unlike Roberto, or even my natural father, Bernie was comfortable in the role of family man. With him on the scene, we went out to restaurants, ball games, and Broadway shows. In the spring of 1961, we all moved to a much nicer apartment at 315 East 68th Street, an enormous 1930 building. Apartment 12-E had two bedrooms and two baths, built-in bookcases in the living room, and a working fireplace.

Sometime after that, Muriel persuaded the chief exec of Bendel, Geraldine ("Gerry") Stuz, an early feminist icon, to let her open up a boutique on the ground floor just off the main entrance selling stationery and writing implements: exotic pens, leather legal-pad binders, lap desks, and so on. It worked out really well for her, so well, in fact, that after a couple more years she decided to break away from Bendel and start her own business. She found a backer and silent partner in Larry, the guy from Great Neck she had her marriage-busting romance with years earlier. He had by then become a major real estate tycoon. She rented a storefront on Madison Avenue off 72nd Street, a very posh commercial address, across the street from the historic Rhinelander mansion, a fairy-tale castle from the old robber baron days that, a few years later, was bought by Ralph Lauren for his New York headquarters.

She was very well situated now in the prime of her life. Her business took off. She'd finally landed in something that was fun and rewarding that suited her intelligence and creativity. She designed party invitations and stationery for the carriage-trade wives of the Upper East Side, including celebrities such as Jackie O. Many of them were ladies from her own Manhattan background who had married really well and didn't work — which was not necessarily such a great thing, since many of them, by middle age, were bored and restless.

Young Man Blues

Muriel, 1972

Muriel was not bored. She thrived. She liked chatting up the endless cavalcade of customers from a desk in a corner tricked out with a lot of fun accessories for the writing life: gold bamboo pens, marbled papers, Lucite boxes for this and that, very sixites, very pop. She made a nice chunk of change doing it. Her stationery designs were executed by an arty little job printshop down in Greenwich Village that charged her peanuts and her markup was astronomical. The business, named Ffolio-72 (yes, double "f"), was a success. The catch was that she had to surrender a substantial chunk of her revenue every month to Larry, her silent partner, and he leeched off her like a lamprey on a salmon for the whole thirty-plus years that she was in business there. I never laid eyes on the guy in all that time. He was a phantom.

Our home life at 315 East 68th Street in those years was, at least, very stable. There was never any shrieking or visible strife between Muriel and Bernie. In fact, I can't remember them even arguing about anything. But it's probably clear by now that I led a life very independent of them from age eleven on. They had a lively social life among that gang of Mad men and quasi-bohemians they ran with. There were many raucous evenings of drinking and piano playing at our apartment, and Muriel was an excellent cook, very adept with company. I enjoyed their friends and they treated me like one of their gang.

Muriel had her own social subgroup of young homosexuals she'd become acquainted with in her years at Bendel. These were men in their twenties who worked as window dressers and other "backstage" jobs in the fashion industry. Many a weeknight, she cooked them spaghetti dinners, hosed them down with scotch, and in exchange they were amusing. She referred to them as "my fags," because that was the lingo of her generation. The standout was Joel Schumacher. A few years later, he went to Hollywood and he eventually became an A-list movie director (*The Wiz*, *St. Elmo's Fire*, *The Lost Boys*, a couple of *Batman* movies). But in the years before that he was working his way out of a troubled boyhood of drugs and hustling. Perhaps because he'd already seen so much depraved behavior, his wit was arrestingly sharp. Bernie enjoyed that gang, too, and his presence as the straight husband and father figure seemed to have a moderating influence over their more extreme histrionics. None of them ever came on to me. But, ever after, I got the distinct feeling from Muriel that she would have liked it if I turned out gay, which was not to be. Considering, the fugue of disabling anxiety I'd gone through my last winter at home, and for all my other adolescent ferment, I was not sexually confused. I knew that I liked girls and was not sexually attracted to men, or boys my age. No one ever came on to me in bars.

When I turned sixteen, the year Henry threw me out of his life, and I lost my baby fat and became interested in wearing decent clothes, Muriel began "flashing" me. She found opportunities to present herself topless when we were home together, and more than a few times, often when she'd been drinking, after her gang had said good night and went home, and Bernie had gone to bed, she presented what my generation called a "beaver shot." She would manage to sit in such a way as to open her legs with me sitting few yards away and she would not be wearing any underwear.

At first, I pretended not to notice — thinking, *did I really see that?* — but it disturbed me quite a bit, and by-and-by I realized that, yes, I was really seeing that. I certainly was confused as to why my mother was acting that way around me while it went on, but I didn't say anything to her, or to Bernie, or to anyone. I doubt I even mentioned it to Dr. Sands, who was briefly my head shrinker, because it was so embarrassing. I suppose my sudden transformation from a chubby boy into a lean young man threw some behavioral switch in Muriel's brain. In a chronic error of mind, she routinely called me by the names of other men in the family, either Bernie, or Buddy, her brother. I think it signified a boundary problem about exactly who was who in her life. And, of course, deep in the background was the memory of her daddy,

Saul, gone all those years, who was probably the only person who was ever able to tell her what to do. And he'd done it so much that he broke something in her when he stood in the way of a career in the theater.

One night in the spring of 1966, just before I finished high school and went out to Fire Island to work that summer job at the Catholic real estate association, I finally put a stop to the flashing. It was after a party and Muriel had been drinking. Bernie must have gone to bed. Muriel was wearing a caftan, a long tunic. It might have been a warm night. She hiked up the caftan above her knees as if cooling herself off, but very plainly put her genitalia on view. I had not been drinking — I did not drink around them, at home — but I very plainly told Muriel to quit exposing herself to me, in so many words.

She didn't alter her position physically in the chair or drop the skirts of her caftan. She just denied that she was exposing herself. I sensed that she knew she'd been caught, and now had to pretend strenuously that I was making it up. She said I was crazy, that she had the psychiatrist's bills to prove it, and how dare I accuse her of such a terrible thing. But I didn't back down. I retorted that I wasn't crazy, and that I knew what I was seeing, and I told her in no uncertain terms not to do it anymore. Then, I left the room and that was the end of it. I think she ran that game on me out of a neurotic need to be told to behave herself, making me act like *Daddy*.

A few weeks later I was out of the house for good, never to return except for holidays — many of which I made a point to miss — and stayed far away, wherever I was, in the years after.

My Father

Henry, 1922, the youngest boy

Henry Kunstler was born in 1917 in New York City. His father, Wolf or William Kinsler, Kinzler, or Kunsztler, was born in a little town called Dukla near the present Slovakian border, some 100 miles east of Kraków in what was then the Austro-Hungarian backwater province of Galicia. Dukla is nestled in the foothills of the Carpathian Mountains, which curl south into Romania. With the fall of the Hapsburg empire after the First World War, Galicia ceased to exist and was absorbed into greater Poland. Family lore says they were occupied in the jewelry business or, alternately, ran a small factory that manufactured matches. I like to think that one tree would have supplied them with plenty of wood for a year's production of matches. They were Jews, of course, with the usual political discomforts of old Europe that implies.

Wolf married a Kraków girl named Marie Gutworth. They left Galicia around 1900 and sojourned more than a decade in Antwerp where he learned the diamond trade, Antwerp being the world center for it. In 1914, they departed for New York, via Liverpool, on the RMS *Baltic* of the White Star Line. On arrival at Ellis Island, Wolf changed his name to William and from Kinsler-Kinzler-Kunsztler to the more definitively Germanic *Kunstler*, which means "artist" in German. He started a diamond importing business in the city, acting as a middleman between the wholesalers in Antwerp and the jewelry fabricators in America. William and Marie established themselves on the Upper West Side and added to a large brood of offspring: Helene, Albert, Salome (deceased in childhood), Michael, Charles, Henry, and Lenore. Their mother Marie died of cancer around 1925 and Helene, the oldest child, became the stand-in for mother in the household. The daughter Salome (born 1910) died when she fell off a ladderback chair while changing a lightbulb and a finial on the chair back stabbed her in the kidney.

On October 8, 1927, this headline ran on page 19 in the *New York Times*.

BOY'S PARENTAGE DISPUTED AT TRAIL

Woman Suing for Custody Says He Is Not Son of Kunstler Diamond Importer

Lad, 10 Denies Her Story

Builder Named as Father Asserts He Never Lived with Plaintiff Doctor Tells of Birth

At the time, my grandfather William had a summer house at a town called West End on the Jersey shore. The *Times* reports:

> *Mrs. Mary Diniscia of East Orange, New Jersey, testified yesterday before Supreme Court Justice Valente that the supposed son of William Kunstler, diamond importer, of 590 West End Avenue [New York City], was the illegitimate offspring of a New Jersey builder and that she was the mother.*
>
> *Suing for custody of the boy, Mrs. Diniscia testified that he was her 13-year-old son, John Laudonia, Jr. and that John Laudonia*

of 668 Westwood Avenue, West End, New Jersey, was his father. Mr. Laudonia was poor when she lived with him, she said, but has grown prosperous and has married. He took the boy to live with him, she said, but she saw the lad from time to time. [Note: Henry, my father, was ten at the time, not thirteen.]

Saw Him Last Summer

Mrs. Diniscia said she saw the boy last summer when he was playing on the grounds of a house at West End rented by Mr. Kunstler from Mr. Laudonia. She said she recognized him from a small brown mark under his left ear. The boy had no mark of this kind yesterday and Mrs. Diniscia insisted it had been removed by surgery. She said she would bring four witnesses to say that the boy was her child. She testified the boy had attended a parochial school.

Mr. Kunstler testified that ten and a half years ago, he and his wife Marie Kunstler, who died two years ago [1925], became the parents of the boy now known as Henry Kunstler, and offered a birth certificate to prove it.

The boy testified that he had never seen Laudonia until Mr. Kunstler leased the West End house, and that he had attended only New York City public schools.

Dr. Joseph L. Rubenstein said he was present when the boy was born, and attended him until about five years ago. Under *cross-examination by the former Judge John Palmieri, [lawyer] for Mrs. Diniscia, he admitted that the child showed some resemblance to Mr. Laudonia, although testifying he looked more like Mr. Kunstler.*

Mr. Laudonia appeared to deny the allegations that he was the father of the boy. He said he never lived with Mrs. Diniscia.

Sister Tells of Meeting

Helen [sic Helene] Kunstler, 22 years old, testified that the boy was her brother. At her home later, she told of her first meeting with Mrs. Diniscia.

"It was last August at the entrance to our place at West End," she said. "One day, I started for the Casino in our car [casino meaning something like a beach clubhouse, not a gambling place]. Henry and two others were with me in the car. Just as I drove out of the driveway, I saw a wild-eyed woman with two caddies from the golf course standing right in our way. I jammed on the brakes to keep from running her down.

"She pointed her finger and shouted, 'Stop!' Then she walked over and put her hand on Henry's shoulder and said, 'You are my son. I am your mother.' Then she told me that she was going to get the boy.

"I drove off quickly for a policeman to lock her up for disorderly conduct. He took her and locked her up, but she was later released."

Miss Kunstler said that one night Mrs. Diniscia had crept into the cellar and tried to get into the house. Detectives guarded the home after that, she said.

For a time, Miss Kunstler said, it appeared the woman might drop her complaint. Mr. Kunstler had told the story to a priest, who had discussed it with Mrs. Diniscia, and had wrung from her, Miss Kunstler said, a confession that she was mistaken.

The trial will be resumed on Monday.

From the *New York Times*, October 11, 1927:

Court Decides Boy Is Kunstler's Son

Diamond Importer in Tears as Suit of Woman to Obtain Youngster Is Dismissed

Mrs. Mary Diniscia of East Orange, N.J., failed yesterday in her attempt to prove that the ten-year-old boy known as Henry Kunstler is the son of herself and well-to-do builder John

Laudonia of West End, N.J. Supreme Court Justice Valente dismissed her proceeding against William Kunstler, diamond importer of 590 West End Ave [NYC], who says that Henry is the offspring of himself and his deceased wife, to compel him to give up the boy.

At the adjourned hearing, Mrs. Diniscia, who said that the subject of the legal contest is John Laudonia, Jr., 13 years old, brought into court as a witness Paul Pelusa, 16 years old, of Long Branch, who said he had seen the boy with Mr. Laudonia all summer. Mr. Kunstler, who leased a summer home at West End, N.J., this year, wept during this testimony. To offset Mrs. Diniscia's claims Laudonia had brought to court Nicola Ficca, 12 years old, of 204 East Seventeenth Street, East Paterson, N.J., who was ready to testify that Mrs. Diniscia had insisted two years ago that he was her son by Laudonia. The testimony was not necessary, for Justice Valente interrupted the proceeding to say to Mrs. Diniscia and her counsel, former Judge John Palmieri[:]

"You will agree with me that every opportunity was afforded you to prove your case. However, I believe the evidence is overwhelming against you. I believe you have made an honest mistake. I do not think you deliberately lied. There is not the slightest doubt that William Kunstler is the father of this boy. It is my belief that you worked yourself into an obsession that the boy was yours."

When Mr. Palmieri agreed with the court, and the proceeding was dismissed, Mr. Kunstler threw his arms about the boy and hugged him tearfully. William Jasie, attorney for Mr. Kunstler, told the court that he believed the Pelusa boy had committed perjury, and that he should be committed, but Justice Valente suggested that a proceeding be brought in the magistrate's court if were thought advisable.

And so, the matter concluded. My father never mentioned the bizarre incident to me — I found it searching the family name in the *New York Times* archives — nor did he tell me much of anything else that follows, which mostly comes from my cousin Daniel, the family historian, son of Henry's older brother Michael.

William Kunstler, my grandfather, a widower in the late 1920s, married his accountant, a woman named Bea, who had two children of her own and gave birth to two more with William. When the stock market crashed in 1929, the diamond business in America went to hell and William sought opportunity in a different part of the industry, buying shares in a mine at Kimberley, South Africa. He moved the whole family to Johannesburg, minus Helene who was married and living in Antwerp. Albert, the oldest boy, ran away from Jo'burg to join Helene in Antwerp via Dar es Salaam, the port city of Tanganyika (today Tanzania). Henry, twelve, was sent to a Marist (Catholic) prep school in Jo'burg and his little sister Lenore was educated by nuns. The mining venture didn't work out, since, just then, the De Beers combine was busy monopolizing the global diamond trade.

YOUNG MAN BLUES

So the family returned to New York City around 1934, but Henry, then seventeen, was shuffled off to Antwerp to learn the diamond game at the elbow of his old uncle Adolf, who treated him like an errand boy. During these years, the stepmother, Bea, developed an animus for the children William had with his first wife. William would not allow the boys to go to college, lest they develop professional aspirations beyond the diamond business. I'd heard that Henry had some ideas about becoming an engineer, but that was quashed — like my mother's wish to go into the theater.

Henry, 1935

During the depths of the Great Depression, Henry and his brother Michael worked for a company on the Jersey shore that laundered service uniforms for nurses, waiters, and maids. Sometimes they made deliveries in a horse-drawn wagon. In the late 1930s, the brothers took off for Los Angeles in a beater car, seeking opportunity. According to my cousin Daniel, Henry regarded his older brother as "a lousy driver" and wouldn't let him take the wheel until they got to the wide-open buzzard flats of Nevada, where Michael was unlikely to crash into anything. It also happened to be open rangeland and Michael soon managed to hit a steer that wandered onto the highway. They fixed the car somehow and got to the Golden State, but lasted only a couple of months in LA, mostly goofing off, trying to meet girls.

One day in 1941 Henry had the life-changing accident that broke his neck. He was walking along a sidewalk somewhere in Manhattan with a friend when he tripped into one of those sidewalk elevator shafts used to lower merchandise into the basement below the ground-floor shops. At the time, he had been dating a girl named Pearl Greenblatt from Red Bank, New Jersey. For some reason, Pearl's family took him in when he was released from the hospital — perhaps stepmother Bea didn't want him around — and nursed him through a long recovery. He was not paralyzed by the injury, but his fractured cervical vertebrae had to be fused for stability and it annoyed him ever after. It also happened some months before America entered World War Two, and it kept him out of the army.

Henry married Pearl. One can imagine that the strange circumstance of his convalescence in the Greenblatt house was a big part of that. Perhaps he got her pregnant. Anyway, they had a son in 1943, named for his brother Michael. I remember seeing my older half-brother Michael a couple of times at Fire Island before I was four years old and then never after that until he contacted me when I was thirty-six. By 1948, when I was born, Pearl had remarried a Perth Amboy, NJ, bar owner who became a loving stepfather to Michael. He did not have any contact with Henry through the rest of his childhood. He remembers Pearl grousing as she opened the letters containing his meager twenty-dollar-a-month child support checks.

Michael speculates that his Greenblatt grandparents regarded Henry as a *no-goodnik* and kept him away from his father. One day when he was a sophomore at Rutgers, Michael found himself in the city near Henry's office on 47th Street off Sixth Avenue, called him from the pay phone in the lobby, and went up to present himself. He described Henry as very uncomfortable at the lunch that ensued, and chagrined that Michael had taken his stepfather's last name. My half-brother Michael became a successful lawyer in New Jersey, got married, and had two kids. He tried to get Henry interested in his grandchildren, and to be involved with his young family, but the results, he said, were consistently disappointing.

My Father and Me, 1950

When my parents split up in the summer of 1957, Henry moved in with a young recently divorced woman, Pauline (Weinman) Postel, with two very small children who lived two streets away from our house in the Northwood housing development in Roslyn Heights. I visited him there twice a month for the first five years after the breakup and less often after that. From the time I was about ten, and considered responsible enough to take a train by myself, we established the practice that I would catch a Saturday morning train alone from the old Penn Station out to the Manhasset and he would pick me up, and I would make the return trip Sunday evenings by myself, a lugubrious routine.

He liked to do handyman projects around the house and I was usually asked to "help" him, which mostly involved holding something for him, a wrench, a handful of nails. It was the only way he really knew how to be around me. He could focus on the task at hand. During the spring and fall, he'd have me mow the lawn, and as I grew older I began to resent doing that, since I was only an occasional visitor to the place. Of course, I was never around in the summertime. The really odd thing is, Henry never, ever visited me in the city. Not once, not ever. He never picked me up at the apartment on 68th Street or took me anywhere, never even saw where I lived. What's even stranger is that as a boy it never occurred to me that this was peculiar, that there was anything wrong with it. In retrospect it does, of course. It at least shows how much he loathed Muriel. (And, as my cousin Daniel, who got to know him better much later in life, observed: "Henry really knew how to hold a grudge.")

Outside of those home-handyman sessions, we shared no father-and-son adventures of any kind beyond a trip to the lumberyard in old Roslyn Village. When I wasn't "helping" him build a bookshelf, or mowing the grass, I just beat it at the first opportunity and went to my friends' houses. Henry and I never talked about anything beyond the most superficial chitchat. When he picked me up at the train station he always asked if I'd been "a good boy," and I always said, "of course," and that was that. And so it went through my childhood until that March afternoon in 1965 when he flew into a rage and threw me out of the Roslyn house.

My father always said that life was *a struggle*, and I don't doubt that was so for him. He carried many burdens. Though he was the youngest son in a large family, he often had to step in and help his older siblings. He financially supported his crazy, much-divorced big sister Helene for years into a very old age, and sometimes had to bail out his brother Michael, who eventually settled in Antwerp, didn't thrive in the diamond business, and had three sons to support. Plus, of course, he paid child support to Pearl and Muriel for years.

I don't remember ever meeting William, my grandfather. Nor Bea, who had pretty successfully alienated William from his first brood of children. My father would visit the old fellow now and then in a nursing home in New Jersey into the early 1960s. I was not informed when he passed on. And then a vicious court case ensued over his estate with the first group of children against the second, which the latter won. Henry was left nothing by his father. When Henry passed away he did the same thing to me.

My Stepparents More Briefly

Bernard Glaser, Bernie, was born in 1919 and raised in Winthrop, Massachusetts, a beach-town suburb of Boston out next to the marshes where Logan Airport would later be built. He graduated from Tufts University, distinguishing himself in theatricals while he was there. After Pearl Harbor, he went into the army. He was picked for officer candidate school and became a lieutenant. The army shuffled him from base to base around the USA, instructing recruits. While out in California, he impulsively married a girl named Juanita. He was sent to Europe after D-Day to reinforce General George Patton's Third Army in the developing action in the Ardennes Forest, the Battle of the Bulge. In the vicinity of Bastogne, he was wounded in the thigh with shrapnel from an artillery shell and came out of the battle with a silver star for heroism and a purple heart. The marriage to Juanita was over before the war ended.

Like for many men of his generation, the war was probably the highlight of Bernie's life for sheer, vivid action. When it was over, he gravitated to New York City and got into the magazine game, because he was literary and liked to hang out with writers — though he lacked creative drive himself. I came to understand that editors were a special personality type, and played an important role in the world of letters. There were not a few great editors in that small world.

After a brief recall to the army during Korea (served in Washington), he married a woman named Merrill, had two children named Gail and Garrett, and settled for a while in suburban Tarrytown. The marriage broke up, and when he met my mother he was living in a studio bachelor pad near the Queensboro Bridge.

He was managing editor of *Coronet* magazine at the time, but around 1962 he became an account executive with William Safire's public relations firm — where Safire hid out and made some money between Richard Nixon's loss to JFK in 1960 and his election victory in 1968, after which Safire became a White House speechwriter. When I left for college in 1966, Bernie had moved to a job doing publicity for the New York League of Theater Owners — Broadway's trade organization. He got a lot of tickets to shows, but I think by then he was disillusioned and disappointed with himself, working as a PR flack approaching age fifty. The truth was, through the *Mad Men* era, he was drinking too much, quietly, without any alcoholic emotional melodrama. But it was enough to derail whatever career aspirations he came home with from the war.

He was good to me, in any case. He worked steadily and was good to my mother, and certainly stabilized her. They never fought. He didn't raise his voice or antagonize me, as stepfathers are known to do. We did some things together as a family: those Broadway shows, restaurants, Yankees games. On weekends, when he didn't go somewhere with his own kids, we sometimes went to museums and movies together. He read my adolescent poetry and annotated it intelligently. He urged me to read the popular authors of the day: Updike, Heller, Mailer, Gore Vidal, early Pynchon. He didn't offer a whole lot of life guidance, teach me how to do things, or indulge my teenage emotional fugues. But he probably set me on a career path into literature. I was lucky that he came into my life.

I know much less about Pauline Weinman, Henry's third wife, since I was only an occasional visitor in their household. She was from Brooklyn. Her father was a dentist. She was married briefly to a man named Martin Postel in the early 1950s when they landed in the Northwood development in Roslyn, Long Island. Her children, Jonathan and Madge, were five and three when she ditched Martin — who moved to Florida and never visited his children afterward. Pauline was eleven years younger than my father when Henry, then forty, came on the scene. I never heard how they met, but it was evidently around the same time that Muriel was carrying on with Larry from Great Neck.

Pauline was tall, slim, dark-haired, and rather glamorous. She'd gone to Beaver College (now Arcadia University) in Pennsylvania. She didn't work or have a vocation but she took art classes for years and produced some creditable sculptures and paintings. Henry and Pauline always had live-in housekeepers. Their particular split-level was designed with a maid's room and bath off the garage. One year, they employed a "girl" who was arrested on a night off in a stolen car in Mineola and discovered to be a man when the police booked him.

As I said earlier in this chronicle, Henry had an animus for little Jonathan and it was painful to watch him persecute the kid. I know that it was hard on Pauline, but she hung in there with Henry until Jonathan was out of the house and off to art school in Kansas City. It seemed to me that, apart from the children, Henry and Pauline had a nice life together, appreciated each other, and were mutually tuned in.

They took trips regularly to Europe and South America, often went to dinner and the theater in the city on Friday nights, when Pauline would drive the twenty miles into the city from Roslyn and they'd drive home together. They had a very active social life in Roslyn too — they must have been a popular couple. In fact, the weekends that I was on hand, they were absolutely never home on a Saturday night.

Pauline was friendly enough with me, though more than once she twanged on me about checking in and out of her house like it was a motel, because I took every opportunity to escape to my friends' houses. We remained friends long after she split up with Henry, but I get ahead of myself now.

Part Three

Out of the House

On the last day of August 1966, in the cool of the evening, I stepped off the Greyhound bus on Main Street in the little town of Brockport, New York (population then about 7,000), sixteen miles west of Rochester, way, way, way upstate — so far away from the city it felt like Indiana. The driver fetched my luggage from the hatch on the side of the bus: a heavy leather-trimmed canvas valise, a turquoise Smith-Corona typewriter in a hard-shell case, and a beat-up jazz guitar, dark brown with f-holes. Up the street, the marquee of the Strand Theater, an unusual triangular wedge shape, said "Welcome Class of 1970" over the title of the current attraction, *This Property Is Condemned*. I was a little woozy after the nine-hour bus trip on the old state highways, including rest stops at Binghamton and Syracuse, and had to wonder why the perfectly okay-looking art deco theater was condemned — and why they would announce it so proudly. Nineteen seventy was still four years away and it seemed wildly futuristic — a coming era of flying cars and robots.

This was my new college town. The State University of New York College at Brockport was its formal name, a mouthful. SUNY Brockport, Brockport State in plain talk. Only a year or so earlier it had been upgraded from a teacher's college, with an emphasis on phys ed, to a regular liberal arts school. Governor Nelson Rockefeller was just beginning an epic campaign to pump massive amounts of money into the SUNY system. He wanted to compete with the California system. New York was way behind. There were several big new buildings going up on campus that autumn of 1966, and many more would come shortly. They were hiring faculty like mad too. It must have been a great time for freshly hatched PhDs.

The Brockport student body would go from about 2,500 to nearly 10,000 in four years. SUNY charged roughly $500 a year. By some fluke I'd scored well enough on a scholarship exam to get $250 of that lopped off, and my mother didn't fight about paying the difference. She was doing well in business by then, with Bernie backing her up, and must have been glad to have me out of her hair and under state supervision for a measly two fifty per annum. Psychologically, I'd left home months earlier when I got that job on Fire Island and lived by myself in the garret of the old Coast Guard station, so I was used to being on my own. Now I was safe, in college, a small miracle. The war was on in earnest.

This remote corner of upstate New York between Rochester and Buffalo quickly revealed itself to me as a weird alien culture, essentially midwestern. The locals spoke in the harsh flat-A dialect that you find all around the Great Lakes. Lake Ontario was just ten miles due north of town. The landscape along the apron of the lake was dead flat, indeed like Indiana. Once you left Rochester behind it was all horizon, sky, and endless farm fields: squashes, beans, some corn, some orchards. (There was an applesauce cannery just north of town.) The regional cuisine whether in the college dining halls or in the town's few restaurants was all strictly cafeteria quality. The "best" off-campus restaurant was the dopey Robin Hood Room in the town's first, and then only, strip mall. When I ordered a glass of red wine there one of my early nights in town it was served on the rocks.

Brockport owed its existence to the Erie Canal (completed 1825). The state still maintained the waterway immaculately for scant barge traffic. The old towpath along it would turn out to be a lovely place for long walks in the fall. Compared to the frightful scale of Manhattan, the town was cozy and comprehensible to me, like a comfortable old sweatshirt. There were quite a few Greek Revival houses, popular in the decades of its settlement, and handsome fieldstone warehouses from the canal days. Main Street had its complement of little shops and several student dive bars. The drinking age was still eighteen in New York, and Brockport was known throughout western New York as a college party town.

The campus, on the other hand, was pretty charmless except for the "old main" building, Hartwell Hall, with its tower and gilded dome. The dorms and other buildings from the 1950s were three-story boxes right out of a Soviet pattern book. But my own lodgings were in a brand-new dorm, Harmon Hall, just opened that month. It was also a basic box, but the furniture in the lounges was all new, and there were color TVs, and the bathrooms were oddly luxurious, with marble shower stalls.

Young Man Blues

The roommate assigned to me was a gloomy kid named Frank from Cheektowaga, one of the steel-factory towns that ringed Buffalo. He apparently didn't like me much, because he arranged to swap quarters a few days later and moved out. His replacement was a jolly sophomore named Bruce, nicknamed "Pussyface" for his romantic exploits, casually just "Puss." He hoped to become a marine biologist. We got along fine, though we didn't become boon companions. He found my New York mannerisms exotic, and often said so.

The first week or so, we freshmen had to endure hazing so as to cement our allegiance to the school — one of the few rites in a state college almost devoid of any tradition. (Fraternities were banned there.) We wore humiliating green-and-gold beanies and marched through the town streets at twilight singing football fight songs. I rather liked the midwestern *normality* of all that. It was such a relief after all the fey boho sophistication of my high school. And it was reassuring to feel part of *something*, instead of completely alienated from everything around me.

At registration that first week I was astounded to find out you had to go to only three classes Monday, Wednesday, and Friday and just two on Tuesdays and Wednesdays. After the arduous load of high school it seemed like a joke. What were you supposed to do the rest of the time? The word *study* never would have entered my mind because I went all through high school without studying or doing homework.

Besides Puss, I made a couple of freshman friends that September. Thad was from Long Island and felt the same culture shock that I did. He had a record player and let me listen to Bob Dylan's magnificent *Blonde on Blonde* album over and over in his room until he finally got sick of it. (He would transfer away sophomore year.) The other new friend was Russ from nearby Rochester. Hippiedom was still in the incubator that fall — at least in western New York — but Russ was a sort of beatnik-slash-hipster. Rochester had quite a music scene and some fine jazz clubs because the Eastman School of Music was there, and Russ was on that scene in his teenage years. He also had a record player, but we listened exclusively to comedy albums of which he had a great collection: Lenny Bruce (who had died just that August of 1966 at forty), Moms Mabley, and our favorite, Jonathan Winters. We worked on some comedy improv riffs of our own, too, mostly Nazi routines. We had a certain comic chemistry, but it never went anywhere because, alas, Russ dropped out after the fall semester and, sadly, I never saw him again.

I chatted up some girls in the bars and made some female friends, but *scoring* with coeds was impossible unless you had a car. (Puss had a car; I didn't even have a license.) In those long-ago days the women who lived on campus had curfews. They had to sign back in to their dorms at ten o'clock on weeknights and midnight on weekends. A "house mother" lurked on the premises to enforce the rules. Men had no curfews and were only lightly supervised by RAs (Resident Assistants), seniors who lived in the dorm for free, on hand mainly to keep order and break up fights. We were not allowed to have the opposite sex in our rooms under any circumstances. Anyway, I was still sexually inexperienced except for that one awkward night on Fire Island in August.

I went to my classes dutifully that fall, but I didn't study, just goofed around, walked the canal towpath on bright October days, caught the weekly movie at the Strand, explored the bars. I was seventeen until October 19 — the day I had to register for the draft at Brockport's town hall — but I still had a phony ID and had no trouble getting served. I didn't have a whole lot of money for drinking, but draft beers were only a quarter and you could get a buzz on for a buck. That fall, I got into a few fistfights with some of the older students, athletes who were holdovers from the college's phys ed teacher days. I went around in a seersucker jacket, which apparently offended them as a snooty symbol of unwelcome change. Also, I was a wise guy and when they started up with me I sassed them back, no matter how large they were. I was never hurt badly. Eventually I would make friends with some of them.

At Thanksgiving break, I opted not to go home. The journey was just too long and punishing for a four-day visit. The dorms and one dining hall were kept open for people in my situation. Instead, I bought a bottle of cheap gin and some wine and just hunkered down in my room, pretending to write short stories à la F. Scott Fitzgerald. It was dreary, of course, and I suppose I felt a little sorry for myself, but that self-pity worked nicely with the tragic young writer persona I was still cultivating. The stories didn't add up to much because I knew next to nothing about how things really worked in the world, but I gave the Smith-Corona a workout.

A few weeks later I did go home for the two-week Christmas break. I caught a ride with a sophomore named Dean from Staten Island. Riding shotgun down the NY State Thruway (a seven-hour trip), my old anxiety revved up the closer we got to the city. I began to develop a phobia that stuck with me for decades: seeing the moon through the car window, I got the idea that it wasn't stable in its orbit, but might somehow escape and crash into the earth. I couldn't bear the sight of it, looming dangerously up there. I suppose it represented my fear that the universe was not a safe place, that something fantastically catastrophic could happen at any moment. It disturbed me to discover that I could still summon the seemingly psychotic ideation that had overcome me a year ago the previous Christmastime in the city. I'd thought I was over it. But something had imprinted on my brain.

I was in a state of marginal panic those vacation weeks in Manhattan. The scale and bustle of the city overwhelmed my senses after being in a small town for four months. What kept me together in the city was knowing I'd soon be back upstate, far far away, in a place where I was beginning to feel comfortable. I paid a dutiful visit to my father in his office on 47th Street but spared myself any overnights at his place out on Long Island, and he was okay with that. We were strangers to each other. I couldn't find a way to reach him, and he didn't make much effort to reach me. Bernie and Muriel were in a very stable period of their lives. Her business was thriving. Bernie was busy doing PR for the New York League of Theater Owners (He got me a ticket to the brand-new musical *Caberet*.) I went along to a couple of parties thrown by their TV and advertising chums and took advantage of the free booze. I spent most of my Christmas money out in bars. The city didn't scare me so much with a load on, but the hangovers only amplified my anxieties. Days, I took in every movie that would never come to Brockport's Strand Theater (*You're a Big Boy Now, Blowup, King of Hearts, Is Paris Burning?*).

Young Man Blues

Returning to campus in the new year, 1967, I learned that I'd flunked the first semester of Spanish (a language requirement for the Bachelor of Arts degree). I eventually opted for a Bachelor of Science (no language requirement). I never had to take another math class either, thank God. And I got a D in Intro to Philosophy, which I found abstruse and confounding. The dean of students sent me a letter warning me "to not fall further behind," but there were no other consequences. I was otherwise pretty aimless, just floating, until something happened in February of the spring semester.

A Life in the Theater

On a wintry day, I tagged along with a girl I'd met named Sally into an audition for a college play. It hadn't occurred to me to try out, but the director, a prof in the Speech and Rhetoric Department named Lou Hetler, asked me to come onstage and read for a part. Since I was there, I did. The play was *The Crucible* by Arthur Miller, written as a parable for the communist witch hunt of the early 1950s led by Senator Joseph McCarthy. The play is set during the witchcraft uproar among the Puritans at Salem, Massachusetts, in 1692–93. I was cast as Reverend John Hale, the young clergyman who emboldens the hysterics of a few deranged teenage girls, whose antics led to the prosecution and hanging of many innocent colonists. It was a histrionic role and I got good reviews in the school paper when the play opened weeks later. Suddenly, I was learning a lot about something that actually interested me.

In April, I was invited to act in another play, directed by a campus administrator named Bob Denning, a young family man who had just been hired that year to run the office of campus planning — overseeing the big expansion underway. He'd done a lot of community theater in his previous job downstate and he'd played the role of Governor Danforth in our production of *The Crucible*, where we became friends. His play was *The Spoon River Anthology*, an eccentric and lovely bit of Americana about the denizens of a small-town cemetery, based on the poem cycle by Edgar Lee Masters. During that spring I often stopped by Bob's office in Hartwell Hall and we'd do some comedy improv. He was a fan of Mel Brooks and Carl Reiner's *2000 Year Old Man* routine. Bob would play a pivotal role in my finally growing up a few years later.

During the run of *The Crucible* I was introduced backstage to a visitor who would also influence me deeply. David Hamilton, twenty-eight, had just come through the Syracuse theater program with an MA. He was at Brockport that night for a job interview. I had a long chat with him in a stairwell before the curtain went up. We hit it off. He had a lively sense of humor but was obviously a serious person. The people in charge of the college had decided to start a stand-alone Department of Theater Arts, pulling it out of the stodgy old Department of Speech and Rhetoric. They would hire a dozen new faculty over the next two years and open a new building with a main stage, a black box theater, state-of-the-art lighting, scenery shops, costume shops, all fully equipped and staffed, offices for everyone, and very luxurious dressing rooms with those signature marble showers of the Rockefeller years. Dr. Hetler, now department chair, was recruiting students to become majors. I signed up. Suddenly I had a scaffold to hang my existence on: theater major.

The new department got going fast. It was a very flush time for the nation, even with the war in Vietnam intensifying. It happened that Brockport had a little auxiliary campus ten miles west of town in the middle of nowhere, a recreation center with a boating pond, stables and riding trails through the woods, bunkhouses for men and women, and a big rustic lodge for dances and conferences. There was also a run-down outdoor amphitheater beside the pond. Many of us new recruits were enlisted for a new summer theater program out there. David Hamilton joined the faculty to teach directing for the stage and to direct plays. He was tall and gangly, chain-smoked cigarettes (we all did), could play barrelhouse piano, liked to drink martinis, and went about directing plays with impressive authority. He'd gotten in trouble for something in the navy and liked to tell the story of being sent home from the Mediterranean on a punishment ship. He was married and his wife had a kid on the way. His pal from grad school at Syracuse Rick Miller, short and compact with a wicked wit, was hired to teach scene design and supervise the building of sets. His tech crew renovated the amphitheater while we started rehearsals.

As we settled into a routine that summer of 1967, Dave asked me to stage-manage the first play of the season that he would direct: Arthur Kopit's *Oh Dad, Poor Dad, Mamma's Hung You in the Closet and I'm Feelin' So Sad*, a dark comedy about a boy with a monstrous, narcissistic mother. Dave's mise-en-scène was hallucinatory. The mother character, Madame Rosepettle, was a dead ringer for Muriel in her psychological fine-tuning. It seemed absolutely right to me. I began to understand some of the dynamics in my relationship with her as depicted in nightmarish comedy, especially her imperious self-presentation and its use as an implement of torture.

Dave knew nothing about my internal workings, but he seemed to appreciate my competence in getting things done. During the three-week rehearsal period, several of us involved in the show finished every working day with a cocktail hour at a bar a few miles down the road in the nearby village of Holley, NY. It was great to be a part of something fun and purposeful, in a community of my own.

I learned a tremendous amount about directing from Dave as his stage manager. He had firm ideas about keeping the action onstage in motion. Dave hated static dialogue, actors just standing in place pitching lines back and forth. He choreographed his actors to cross — move from point A to point B — on almost all of their lines, even if only a step or two. It was visually dynamic, and he used that swirling motion to emphasize the velocity of the story. When the actors annoyed him, he'd yell up at the stage, "Quit the acting and get on with the play." I sat beside him those weeks of rehearsal, watching him work out every line-by-line blocking decision. Sometimes he asked for my opinion of a line reading or bit of business. It was gratifying to be taken seriously.

One of my duties was to drill the actors in rehearsing their scenes in the mornings, when Dave had faculty meetings and office work. He'd showed me how to construct a loose-leaf binder recording all the blocking — the movement on stage — on Rexographed pages with a template of the set. Every cross and bit of business was recorded. Once the blocking was fixed, Dave expected the actual performance to come off exactly as directed every time, with no changes, improvisations, or sudden inspirations. I liked telling the actors what to do, and they took me seriously too. It was really the first time in my life that I'd worked hard at anything. During the week of performance, I had to run the lighting and music cues from a booth behind the audience. This was before computers. I had a crew of two other kids throwing the dimmer levers and working the reel-to-reel tape deck. It was exacting work.

I don't know how they induced audiences to come all the way out to the auxiliary campus in the rural township of Fancher, NY. But we had full houses for all our plays. (Gasoline was around thirty cents a gallon then and motoring was still the national pastime.)

Another bunch of actors went into rehearsal for the second show of the season, directed by a young professional from the city named Roger Ochs who might have been auditioning for a job on the faculty (he didn't get one). This was *Little Mary Sunshine*, a 1959-vintage spoof on turn-of-the-century Victor Herbert–type operettas, a crowd-pleaser. I had little to do with it after the run of *Oh Dad, Poor Dad* except hanging lights with the tech crew. The third play of the season, also directed by Dave Hamilton, was a very ambitious choice: Peter Weiss's *The Persecution and Assassination of Jean-Paul Marat as Performed by the Inmates of the Asylum of Charenton Under the Direction of the Marquis de Sade*, usually referred to as *Marat / Sade*. The Royal Shakespeare Company production, directed by Peter Brook, was a sensation on Broadway the year before. The action of the play is a re-creation of the French Revolution performed by lunatics. Dave cast me as the inmate playing Jean-Paul Marat, an even more histrionic role than the Reverend Hale in *The Crucible*, a real scenery chewer.

Marat / Sade is a large cast play, very demanding, with musical numbers and a little chamber orchestra, and a great deal of colorful swirling motion, as befits *a revolution*. My character, the firebrand Marat, spent almost the entirety of the play seated in an antique bathtub, naked just off center stage. (The real Marat suffered from a skin disease and this was the only way he could keep comfortable, as depicted in Jacques-Louis David's famous painting of the martyred Marat dead in his tub.) The three weeks of rehearsal took place in daytime, but when it came to the tech rehearsals to set the lighting levels and integrate the little orchestra into the play things changed. The outdoor amphitheater was, as I said, bermed into the sloping bank beside a big pond. As twilight gathered, I was seated onstage in the bathtub under the beam of an intense 750-watt Leko light, required to sit motionless for about the first twenty minutes of the play. As soon as that light hit me, so did every flying insect in Orleans County, including some really large things, and that's how it went through a whole week of performances. It almost ruined the run of the play for me, but I soldiered through. Everyone in the cast was sympathetic.

Off Campus

The first two years of college were probably the happiest and most stable of my life since early childhood. My problem with crippling anxiety reemerged only when a holiday compelled me to go back to the city, or when I had an especially vicious hangover, which would plunge me into a state of restless agitation. I did not drink routinely, but I got hammered some Saturday nights. To me, it was a safe, reliable, and familiar high, which did not play dirty tricks on your brain the way marijuana could.

By the fall of 1967 a much larger entering freshman class arrived, including more downstate students from the NYC metro area, and they brought the new pot-smoking hippie culture with them. The Age of Aquarius was on, even at provincial little Brockport. The Beatles had released their "trippy" *Sgt. Pepper* album the summer of '67. Every guy on campus was growing his hair long, including me. I was especially careful to avoid LSD. Anyway, during those years I was constantly in rehearsal every night, and that tended to keep me out of trouble.

That sophomore September I moved out of the dorms into a squalid rental in town with two other theater majors, where all three of us had to share a single bedroom, but that lasted only a few weeks. One of my friends, Eric, who'd played guitar in *The Spoon River Anthology* the previous spring, had a place four miles outside town in a tiny hamlet called Adams Basin, long ago a stop on the Erie Canal, with an inn that was now a stately ruin behind the towpath. Eric's place was an old barn that had lately been an antiques store. The landlord was the Adams Basin postmaster who ran the post office out of his little general store next door that was the only commercial enterprise in the hamlet. Apparently, he couldn't be bothered to run the antiques store anymore.

The barn was spacious, pretty grand for student housing. The downstairs had three separate "bedroom" areas — there were stud walls, but with a twelve-inch gap between the Sheetrock and the ceiling, and curtains instead of doors. There was a bathroom with a cheap metal shower stall, a kitchenette with a stove and fridge, and an excellent forced-air oil furnace that roared reassuringly on winter nights. A good-sized living room occupied the center between the bedrooms. The big loft upstairs was just a storage space for pieces of the landlord's beloved 1930s-vintage hot rods.

The barn was all tricked out with antique furniture. The bedroom I took over had a big brass double bed, a fine old mahogany dresser, and no windows, a perfect cave. I fell in love with the place. There was a rolltop desk that nobody was using in the hall off the living room and I installed my Smith-Corona in it. Eric had a decent stereo in the living room. At the time, he was big on Country Joe and the Fish, the Jefferson Airplane, and the Vanilla Fudge. The third roommate at the barn was a humorously thoughtful fellow from the Finger Lakes who had spent a year at a college in California and then taken another year off: Billy Grant. He was three years older than me. We would become great friends. Less than a month later, Eric impulsively dropped out of school and took off for parts unknown. Billy replaced him with Duane, who he knew from their hometown, Auburn, New York, in the Finger

Lakes region. Duane went back there every weekend to play drums in a rock and roll band.

I loved living out in Adams Basin. Time stood still there. My share of the rent was $27 a month. The landlord's post office / general store on the corner sold beer, cigarettes, hamburger for thirty cents a pound, and anything else you needed. I extracted enough money from Henry and Muriel to cover my living expenses. I would come to regret it. I would have been a lot better off working somewhere for a few hours a week, but I was too immature to know how important that was, and later on I paid the price.

I caught rides back and forth from campus with Billy and Duane, and sometimes hitchhiked. Duane drove a beat-up old Rambler made by the now long defunct American Motors Company. Billy had a 1959 Ford Thunderbird, a great big boat of a car, with a souped-up 345 horsepower V-8 engine, and a four-on-the-floor Hurst transmission. It was a monster. Little things on it were constantly failing — the solenoid, a valve lifter, an oil pan screw, a directional light — but nothing fatal. Billy managed to keep it running and he taught me how to drive. I had zero experience with cars before that.

One Friday in October, after a few weeks of sporadic lessons, Billy asked me to come along to the airport in Rochester so he could fly to Ann Arbor, Michigan, and visit his old high school girlfriend. He didn't want to pay for three days of airport parking, so I was supposed to drive the T-bird fifteen miles back to the barn on my own, and then return to pick him up Sunday night. It was a nerve-wracking journey back to Adams Basin. I'd gotten pretty used to the four-on-the-floor gear shift but I had zero experience driving on big expressways, and you had to take I-390 just to get away from the airport to the back roads. I hadn't applied for a learner's permit either, and the big souped-up T-bird seemed the kind of car that might attract the attention of the law. But I managed to get home without any trouble. Billy hadn't said anything about me using the car while he was gone, so I agonized over that for a while, and after a beer or two to calm me down I decided to drive into town.

It was a lovely fall night. Brockport was bustling with people cashing their paychecks, folks shopping, and college kids hitting the bars. I was cruising happily up Main Street trying to figure out where to park when I saw a cop up ahead directing traffic at the intersection where the Lincoln Rochester Bank was. He motioned at me to stop. I almost had heart attack, knowing I had no license. The T-bird's big engine had a conspicuous growl when it idled. You could hear the valves tapping too. The cop made a crack about whether I could handle such a monster. I figured my life was over. But he only told me to turn my headlights on because twilight was falling. It took me more than a few seconds to even find the headlight switch on the dashboard. Cars were honking behind me and he waved me on.

The encounter freaked me out so much that I didn't stop in town after all, but kept driving north after Main Street turned into Route 19, halfway to Lake Ontario, chain-smoking cigarettes, trying to settle my nerves. Eventually I navigated the lesser country roads back to Adams Basin. I practiced driving some more the rest of the weekend. The roads of pancake-flat Monroe County all ran perpendicular along the old one-mile section lines, so you couldn't get lost easily, and there was little traffic. Sunday night, I managed to find my way to the airport to pick Billy up. The next week, he took me over to the motor vehicle bureau in the Rochester suburbs to get the learner's permit, and before Christmas I had a driver's license. Billy was the big brother I never had.

GIRLS

I had an awkward romance with one of my fellow cast members in *The Crucible* the previous spring. It was my first truly romantic sexual adventure, but for the fumbling twenty-minute episode on Fire Island with a girl I didn't even know. Leslie and I both lived in the dorms but got to sleep together at an off-campus house after the cast party there. Leslie was a year older than me, a sophomore, with fine-featured, feline beauty. She was a good actress, and athletic, and had a jokey personality. She would have been a great girlfriend but I still had no idea how to be a proper boyfriend, and apparently didn't want to be one.

We had another opportunity to sleep together at the motel we stayed in at a college theater festival where we shlepped *The Crucible*. But that was all. We didn't date and I wouldn't have known what to do with her outside a bedroom. With so few friends of either sex through high school, I'd hardly passed any time around girls my own age. That summer of 1967, Leslie had also signed up for the summer theater program and she played the lead roles of Rosalie in *Oh Dad, Poor Dad* and the assassin Charlotte Corday in *Marat / Sade*. We had a few trysts in the bunkhouse when nobody was around, but they obviously made her unhappy. By then, she understood that I was not boyfriend material: immature, furtive, not bondable.

The birth control pill was suddenly on the scene and it was altering behavior rapidly. The side effects were barely known then and there were few disincentives for girls to *not* take it — aside from, maybe, religious scruples or the cost of the prescription. So a lot of coeds were on the Pill, freely experimenting in ways that would have been unthinkable a few years earlier. Some were quite aggressive, making it clear that they were sexually available without expecting anything resembling courtship. In my sophomore year, I had a few casual romantic encounters with girls like that but no one stuck and I did not stick to anyone. Billy and I threw parties at the barn and it was not hard to get a girl who lived off campus to stay overnight.

So, all of sudden, in colleges all over the country, young women were eager to experiment with sex. The old traditional venereal diseases were supposedly still around, but they could all be defeated with modern antibiotics. Canceling the fear of disease, and of pregnancy, lowered the barrier for entry into sex. You didn't have to be careful anymore. That, and the hippie culture around it, put sexuality front and center in daily college life. Woman had quit wearing bras. Sitting in class, you could gaze across the room at a girl's nipples within her sheer peasant blouse, and the beautiful arc of her breasts as sunlight shone through the window, or see them in motion, joggling around inside their clothing as you walked in and out of class. Surely, they knew they were putting their charms on display. Every day on campus was a three-ring sexual circus in the brain.

Things Start to Go Wrong

For all that, most of my energy that year went into acting and stage managing plays. Dave Hamilton decided to direct Samuel Beckett's *Waiting for Godot* as the big production that fall of '67. Beckett was an Irishman who, in youth, had served as James Joyce's secretary. He lived in France for most of his life. *Godot* was labeled as "theater of the absurd" because the action leads nowhere, but it's also a rich philosophical comedy with plangent overtones of loss and decay. Beckett's lyrical language itself was the star of the show in which two bums on a country road in a desolate corner of France are instructed to wait for an appointment with the mysterious Monsieur Godot, who sends a messenger boy once in each of two acts to inform the bums that Godot won't come today but will surely come tomorrow. While waiting, the bums act out a series of routines that amount to old vaudeville gags, the type Beckett might have seen in the Irish music halls of his youth. In each act the two bums, Vladimir and Estragon ("Didi" and "Gogo"), are visited by a bombastic, holding-forth buffoon named Pozzo and his skeletal "slave" attendant, Lucky, who carries Pozzo's bags and whom Pozzo routinely mistreats.

I was cast as Lucky. I had only one line in the play, near the end of Act One, but it was three pages long, running a good five minutes of stage time, and it consisted of carefully composed poetic gibberish. The speech was very hard to memorize, and I didn't get the whole thing completely down until the week before tech rehearsals, which annoyed Dave Hamilton and freaked him out. Leslie had the small role of the boy who enters at the end of each act and informs the bums that Godot isn't coming. We had moved on from each other as lovers but got to be friends. After the play's regular two-week run on campus, we took it to the New York collegiate theater festival and won the top prize, which was a cash grant for touring the play to other colleges all around the state.

At a party the Saturday night of the festival, after we'd performed *Godot*, I was in a hotel suite and someone passed me a joint, which I actually took a hit off, probably the first time I'd done so since Christmas 1965. I'm sure I'd been drinking at the party, too, and it didn't spark off any distressing feelings. Marijuana back then was weak. You had to smoke quite a bit to even get off. I probably did it so as not to appear uncool. Anyway, Dr. Hetler happened to see me do it and it put me in the doghouse. He reamed me out Sunday morning as our entourage was getting ready to drive home. In the meantime, though, I had to go on tour with the play, and they couldn't easily kick me out of the cast and replace me. The tour kept me very busy through the winter. Every week, we were off to some distant corner of New York State in a station wagon following the truck that hauled our set and a couple of techies.

One of the schools we played was SUNY Stony Brook out on Long Island. I informed my father that we would do a show there — Stony Brook was an easy drive east of Roslyn — and he actually showed up with Pauline. Meeting up backstage after the show, he didn't have much to say about it, and I suppose he found the play irritatingly pointless, but we in the cast understood that the play was tough on audiences —

wherever we went, we usually saw walkouts before the curtain fell on Act One. It certainly wasn't the kind of Broadway fare Henry was used to. And Lucky's tirade was the least comprehensible thing in the show. But my father gave me a pat on the back, and Dave told him that I was "a trouper." I felt that I had demonstrated I was good for something. That was the only time Henry ever saw me onstage. Otherwise, he didn't make it up to Brockport during the years I was there.

Early in the spring semester of 1968, Dave asked me to stage-manage a surreal, dark comedy, *Epiphany*, by Lewis John Carlino (later, a big Hollywood screenwriter), about a henpecked husband who turns into a chicken. The guy who played the husband was a transfer student who had served a four-year hitch in the navy and was well into his twenties. His name was Timothy Leary — and, of course, he never heard the end of cracks about that, considering how much publicity the other Timothy Leary, the LSD guru, was getting in those years. But Tim was a fine actor and a splendid fellow, and when Duane dropped out of school in late winter Tim took his place in the barn out in Adams Basin. Tim was gangly, with a large, strangely off-center chin, like Popeye the Sailor, but he had a booming stentorian voice and great range as an actor. He drove an ancient bulbous Volvo and I caught a lot of rides into the campus and back home with him, so we got to be good friends. I learned a lot about acting just being around him. It was a very happy time for me.

After *Epiphany*, early in 1968, Dave Hamilton made a misstep. For the winter main stage production he chose a restoration comedy, *The Country Wife* by William Wycherley (1675). Being mainly about adultery, the play expresses the libertine exuberance of a society that had emerged from the grim Puritan interregnum of Cromwell. Dave decided to do it in the manner of *Hair*, the sensational rock-and-roll hippie musical playing on Broadway. Dave was many things, but he was not a hippie or a rock and roller. The band he patched together sucked, the songs we added to the play were unmemorable, the costumes were embarrassing, and Dave visibly struggled with the cast's discomfort. My character was Mr. Dorilant, sidekick of the lead character, Mr. Horner, with not much to do onstage. We soldiered through it out of respect for Dave.

Our main stage production in spring 1968 was Bertolt Brecht's *The Threepenny Opera*, which the department chairman, Dr. Hetler, directed. I got a minor role as the pickpocket Filch, who doubles at the end of Act Three as the Mounted Messenger, a deus ex machina character, who gallops down the aisle and onto the stage wearing a papier-mâché horse costume around his waist and magically solves all the characters' problems. Dr. Hetler recruited several ringers, older adults from the Rochester community theater scene, to play the major roles of Macheath, Jenny, and the police chief Tiger Brown. The rest of us were supernumeraries. We were all disgruntled about the ringers and I instigated a rebellion.

The night of the tedious tech rehearsals many of us got plastered. I got the blame for collecting the money, buying the liquor, and stashing it backstage. That stunt would put me completely in the doghouse of the theater department. Meanwhile, events were running furiously ahead of everyone. The next night, our dress rehearsal, Martin Luther King Jr. was shot in Memphis. The campus went into collective mourning with everybody else in America. Riots broke out in dozens of cities, including nearby Rochester, which had a big black ghetto. Hardly anyone came to the performances of our play. When the run was over, Dr. Hetler and Dave Hamilton called me into a meeting and said I would be banned from performing onstage for the next year for organizing the cast drinking spree.

A few days after that, I got elected president of the student government by an utter fluke. Between the end of *Country Wife* and rehearsals for *Threepenny Opera*, when I actually had some free time, I'd been out in the bars one Saturday night and a campus go-getter approached me about becoming his campaign manager in the student election. I'd gotten a reputation on campus for being a clever fellow, and he apparently thought I might add some dazzle to his image. There was a distinct dividing line between the old-school upperclassmen, who represented the lingering 1950s "straight" culture, and the freshmen and sophomores who were all turning into hippies. I told him I'd think about it. Amazingly, the next night, Saturday, the guy's opponent, an equally straight junior of the old phys ed major type, cornered me in a different bar, the Roxbury Inn, and asked me to manage *his* campaign. I decided to run against both of them as a goof.

I had no interest in actually managing the student government, the BSG, which was essentially a service org for funding student activities, dances, concerts, lectures, trips, et cetera. I was barely capable of managing my own affairs. The election was just a joke and an ego trip, and my campaign was just another *performance*. I wasn't politically involved in anything, including the gathering antiwar struggle. I'd been preoccupied with working on plays. We didn't even have a television in the barn to watch the evening news, though I read the *New York Times* most days out of habit — unlike so many of my fellow theater majors who were quite oblivious to current events.

I was as skeptical of the antiwar movement as of the Vietnam War itself.(And, of course, I had a student deferment from the draft, quite an exorbitant privilege, though I did not recognize it at the time.)While I certainly enjoyed the new, wide-open sexuality of the day — with my own hormones raging — I found a lot about hippie culture to be creepy or annoying: the pseudo-orientalism, the "hey man" lingo, the psychedelic drugs that frightened me, and the boringly earnest student radicalism, with its shibboleths and Marxist bromides.

As the election campaign revved up, I had only one issue to run on: getting rid of women's dorm curfews. By then, spring of 1968, the policies seemed absurd, but they were still being followed out of sheer inertia, as far as I could tell. A small minority of prudish older coeds opposed any change, but mostly everybody else wanted the curfews gone. They were just unfair. I went around campus giving rousing speeches inveighing against the curfews. And in the election I got twice as many votes as the two juniors I ran against combined. I was suddenly a Big Man on Campus, the makings of a fiasco.

Bad Ego Trip

Since I was suspended from acting in plays, there was no point in signing up for the summer theater program. When the semester ended in May, I went straight down to Fire Island to look for a summer job. I got hired to wash dishes at the Sea Turtle, the most popular joint in town. The job came with a spot in the staff bunk room upstairs so I wouldn't have to stay with Bernie and Muriel. But then, the first week of June, the night of the California primary, Bobby Kennedy was shot in Los Angeles. It made me despondent since he'd won the primary that night and was clearly on track to win the 1968 presidential election. To me, and perhaps many others, it was personal. You felt that RFK winning in 1968 would at least partly patch up the crack in the cosmic egg that opened up when his brother JFK was assassinated in 1963 — and now that Bobby was gunned down, too, it seemed like the soul of the nation had flickered out.

Bobby died the next day. Fire Island suddenly looked to me like a panorama of degeneracy, another Hieronymus Bosch nightmare. I quit the Sea Turtle and got on the Greyhound bus back upstate. Billy and Tim were at the barn in Adams Basin, and my room was there waiting for me. I got a job bartending at a dinky, small town country club a half mile up the road from the barn. My little world looked safe and coherent again. But I was turning political now, in my own way. I was president-elect of the Brockport student government, though I made absolutely no effort to study my duties and responsibilities for the upcoming academic year. With Bobby out of the picture, I followed the jockeying for Democratic Party leadership in the news. Many on campus rallied behind Senator Eugene McCarthy of Minnesota, another antiwar candidate, while the *straight people* supported the clownish vice president Hubert Horatio Humphrey, also of Minnesota.

While I ignored my upcoming BSG responsibilities, what I did do was use my glorious election victory to persuade my father to help get me a car, since I was sick of cadging rides with my roommates and hitchhiking to campus and back. I had a few hundred dollars saved from my summer jobs and hoped he might kick in to get me a halfway decent beater that wouldn't break down two miles from the lot. To my amazement, Henry agreed. I took the bus back downstate, went to Henry's office, and we caught the commuter train out to Roslyn.

At the time, Henry's train station car was an Opel Kadett wagon, a cheap German import that was being sold out of Buick dealerships. So, on a Saturday morning, to my surprise, he took me down to the dealer in Manhasset and he bought a brand-new Opel sedan. Just like that. Altogether, I think the price was $1,500, which was a lot of money in 1968. I can't account for his extravagant gesture. It was quite out of character. Maybe Pauline twisted his arm. Maybe it was his way of making up for the years of neglect, trite as that sounds. He didn't make a show of recognizing my "achievements" in college, and we were otherwise as mutually inaccessable as ever. But I was certainly grateful, and amazed he did that, and that he was possibly proud of me. But it was a terrible mistake. I should have just bought a beater on my own, with my own money, and learned how to fix a few things when they broke. Cars were simple in 1968, before they got computers onboard. Why didn't I? Immaturity . . . a wish to be taken care of . . . laziness.

Anyway, I didn't stick around his house long. Getting off of Long Island even in light Sunday morning traffic was another nightmare — I'd never driven in city traffic before — and then through the maze of freeways across the Bronx. But eventually I hit the New York Thruway across the Tappan Zee Bridge and I was able to calm down for the remaining 300 miles upstate. Billy and Tim were astounded that I came back with a brand-new car.

A Political Year

Around two weeks later, I got fired from the country club for backtalking a golf player at the bar. After a week of doing nothing in late August, I was inspired to go out to Chicago to the Democratic National Convention. Something big was going to happen there, the hippie grapevine said. A campus acquaintance named Bill Murphy, who was more political than me, wanted someone to go with him and share the driving. We took off the morning of August 25 in his Rambler and got to Chicago about eight o'clock at night. On the radio, you could hear bulletins about demonstrations on the North Side. We had maps, of course, and we navigated up to Lincoln Park, where the action was. Somehow, we found a place to park. A riot was going on, sirens blaring, police lights slicing through the night, tear gas billowing, fireworks going off, mobs in motion.

Through the next several days, we followed the riotous blob of hippies and yippies (followers of youth *influencers* Jerry Rubin and Abbie Hoffman) around Chicago, from the North Side to Grant Park off the Loop, where National Guard troops crouched on the roof of the Art Institute with their rifles poised, and onto the streets, notably Michigan Avenue where the grand hotels of the candidates stood — the convention itself took place far away, in the arena down at the old Chicago stockyards. Murphy and I were not eager to get our heads cracked by the aggressive Chicago police, so we mainly stayed on the edge of the action, except on Michigan Avenue, where it was impossible to evade the clouds of tear gas in the skyscraper canyons.

We slept in the Rambler (it's winning feature: reclining seats!) in various parking lots around the city. It was exciting to watch history made, of course, but I was ambivalent as ever about what I saw of radical street politics, in the same way that I was dubious about hippiedom generally. As the movement grew, it seemed to attract more and more lowlifes who simply liked to get stoned and act out. Anyway, in the end, none of the mob's favorites, neither Senator Eugene McCarthy ("Clean Gene") nor Senator George McGovern, won the nomination, which went to the old cornball party hack Vice President Humphrey. The highlight of the whole week in Chicago, for me, was seeing a sign that depicted Mr. Humphrey with a Hitler mustache over the statement "Mein Humph," in gothic lettering.

I sent postcards to my mother and father, bragging on taking part in history. As soon as I got back to college, Henry called and reamed me out for driving the brand-new car he just bought for me all the way to Chicago. I couldn't convince him that I hadn't done it. There was no arguing with him about it. I should have taken a snapshot of the Opel's odometer, which, after maybe two weeks — five days of which I was away — was well under the roughly 1,200 miles that would have represented the round-trip out there. But to that point in my life I'd never owned a camera, and neither Billy nor Tim had one, so it just didn't occur to me. Henry ended the conversation in his usual way, by saying that I was "skating on thin ice." I was back in his doghouse.

I was also in the doghouse over at the theater department with Dr. Hetler and Dave Hamilton because of my aforesaid antics. But

I discovered something interesting about my job as president of the student government: I had some discretionary control over the amount of student activity money that made its way into the theater department for play production through the student org called the Harlequins, which was a vestigial remnant of the days before the theater department was created. I dropped by Lou Hetler's office in September to let him know that I discovered this little mechanism. He quietly replied that he was *confident I would do the right thing.*

I also discovered that being president of the BSG came with a salary of $500 for the year, which was a huge surprise. Accordingly, I acted irresponsibly, managed to draw the entire sum in one check, went to the musical instrument store in the town's strip mall, and bought myself a Gibson twelve-string guitar (the B-45-12). The retail price was around $350. I never learned how to play it very well.

That fall of 1968, I introduced a resolution to the student legislature to renounce women's dorm curfews. It passed easily, though not unanimously. We sent it to President Albert Brown's office and within a week the college council, composed of various deans and department chairs, abolished the old curfews. They had enough trouble with all the antiwar agitation and just gave in — and anyway, it was a trend on campuses all over the country, so they just went with the flow. After that victory, I began to lose interest in student government and did minimally what I was obligated to do: preside over boring meetings. The job also came with a cushy office in the brand-new student union building. Much of my time was spent interceding in fights between with burgeoning gang of campus radicals led by a sophomore who went by the name of "Spaceman" and the older guard of conservative of seniors, still mostly education majors, who held all the other elected BSG posts.

The Vietnam War saw several watershed events that year: the Tet Offensive, the My Lai massacre, the saturation bombing of North Vietnam, and a week of the highest number of US soldier deaths (543) in the whole war. In November, Richard Nixon won the presidential election over Humphrey, with former Alabama governor George C. Wallace queering the race on a third-party ticket that took five states in the Deep South. The country was in a sour mood and the campuses were simmering. At Brockport, there were incessant marches, "teach-ins," and uproars.

But that fall I got distracted by a romance with a young faculty hire in the theater department. "L" was about twenty-five, petite, pretty, curvy, and apparently lonely those early months of her new job in a remote corner of the state. She also came out of the Syracuse theater grad school, was a friend of Dave Hamilton, and was brought in to teach the business side of theater, mainly box office management. She had a new Ford Mustang and a garden apartment on the north side of the Erie Canal. It would be fair to say that she was in charge of our liaison. I didn't exactly *ask her out on a date*. We hooked up after a September meet-and-greet for theater majors and faculty. Wine was served (the drinking age was still eighteen). There were no strictures about faculty-student romances in those days, but "L" didn't want to be on display with me anywhere in public, so our "dates" all took place in her apartment. She was wonderfully avid, but we had almost nothing to say to each other. This went on for about a month, until I started actually dating a freshman we'll call "Stella," a dark-haired, fox-faced cutie who was a dead ringer for the actress who played Juliet in Franco Zeffirelli's *Romeo and Juliet*. "L" caught on that I was spending time with "Stella," and we had a spat in the hallway of the department offices. The romance with "Stella" didn't work out either. It became obvious that she was troubled about sex, not really ready for it on any kind of regular basis. So she just made herself unavailable, and I let it be. I stayed stuck on her for years, though.

That fall, Dave Hamilton directed the play *Shelley, or the Idealist*, by Ann Jellicoe, about the English poet and his entourage of lovers. It annoyed me to watch the performance. I'm sure I would've done the title role nicely, but I was still banned from the stage. Through that winter I felt like I was just marking time, stuck in the BSG job, sitting through rancorous meetings between the radicals and the old guard, faking my way through classes I was uninterested in (medieval English lit). I'd lost the sense of purpose that I'd found blundering into that audition for *The Crucible* two years earlier. And then I badly misstepped.

One Saturday night in March I went around to a bunch of parties off campus, got wasted, and had three crashes in my new car. I had a girl in the car with me, a fellow theater major I picked up at one of the parties, and was taking back to the barn in Adams Basin. She'd been drinking too, of course. In the first crash, a mile out of town, I misjudged a turn at a T-junction and drove up an embankment. No damage done. I continued on. Minutes later I scraped a guardrail leading to a bridge over the Erie Canal. That damaged the right front quarter panel. We made it to the barn and I got the girl into bed with me. She was sick afterward from all the booze, spent a half hour in the bathroom heaving, and then asked me to drive her home, which I did. I made it back to town without incident and dropped her off at her dorm, but heading out of town again I hit a parked car on State Street and bashed in the front end on the passenger side. A piece of metal was wedged up against the front wheel and the car was undrivable. The police materialized magically minutes later and took me to the station house a few blocks away. I called the only person I knew who lived in town who might help me out: "L."

She mercifully came down to the police station. For some reason, the police did not charge me with drunken driving. The breathalyzer device was just coming on the scene and not all police forces had them. "L" helped me arrange to have the car towed to the Buick dealer at the edge of town. We went back to her apartment where I had the kind of sex that only desperation can incite, and the next day she drove me back to the barn.

I had to call Henry Sunday morning and tell him. When he stopped fulminating, I was able to give him the practical information about the Buick dealer and we left it at that for the time being. I was only dimly aware of what was going on in his life. We barely talked over the phone — long-distance calls were expensive in those days. If he sent me an occasional letter, with a check, he never spoke of his own doings or feelings, just admonitions about behaving myself.

I suspect he felt heavily burdened, and unfairly so. His stepson, Pauline's kid Jonathan, was going on sixteen, preparing for college (which Henry would resent paying for). They never got along and, as far as I could tell, Henry did nothing to cultivate a rapport with him. Henry doted on Jon's little sister, Madge, about thirteen then. Henry was also obliged to support his oft-divorced older sister "Helene" late in life, out in Los Angeles, and he often "helped out" his closest older brother, Michael, in Antwerp who was often in financial straits. On the surface, my father led an extremely orderly suburban life. But Pauline would end up dumping him for another guy a few years later, so there must have been a lot of tension in the household. My hijinks probably didn't help my father's styate of mind.

I was horribly hungover the day after the crash, wracked with anxiety and remorse. Everything soon got a whole lot worse. Tuesday, Henry called and informed me that because of my car crash the insurance on all the cars in his household had been canceled — my Opel, the Buick Riviera that Pauline mostly drove, plus his Opel train-station car — causing him a huge and expensive pain in the ass. I barely understood how car insurance worked, and Henry was volcanically angry, so I didn't learn the details. He concluded by saying that when the car was done being repaired, I would have to drive it back to Long Island and then we'd see about me ever getting it back. He also said he was a fool for thinking I could handle the responsibility.

I had to incorporate another big dose of being an unworthy son, a dope, and a fuckup. I didn't have a plan for making amends, or earning any money to pay my father back for what my screwup had cost him. I didn't see how. I was not an autonomous person able to handle what life threw at him. I was still functioning as a child, passively depending on others. My roommates, friends, teachers probably didn't see me that way, since I was superficially clever and witty, and was supposedly a big man on campus. But my self-respect was in shreds, due entirely to my own reckless behavior. On top of all that I'd lost my practical means for even getting around.

Muriel and Bernie knew only that I had crashed the car Henry bought for me but was not hurt. There was no awareness or discussion beyond the superficial details. Muriel was appropriately dismayed at my fecklessness, but not otherwise interested in how it affected me. At that time, Bernie was beginning a slide into alcoholism that would eventually torpedo his career, and he had children of his own ready to go to college, so he had little to say — and he was still the guy who had been to war when he was my age, and my little problems must have seemed trivial. I really could not find anyone to help or advise me, and I badly needed help growing up. Billy Grant, the person I was closest to then, was a sympathetic friend, and Tim Leary, too, but neither saw how I was starting to sink psychologically. Dave Hamilton was having marriage problems and didn't need a side job helping to straighten me out, and the truth was he probably didn't care. The days of me being his little sidekick were long over.

I became so inattentive as BSG president — not even bothering to attend meetings — that early in the spring semester of 1969 the other elected BSG officers decided to impeach me. I was duly notified and I treated the whole thing as a joke. It was a peculiarity of the BSG constitution that the elected president served also as speaker of the student legislature. So my career in student politics ended in a fluke as it began: I presided over my own impeachment.

The proceeding was held in a fancy new lecture hall in the brand-new Communications Building. I had learned enough about *Robert's Rules of Order* to confound my antagonists (which included pretty much everyone, the new student radical faction as well as the old-time conservative education majors). I turned it into a circus, something that did not yet have the name *performance art*. Everyone was suitably dissatisfied. The next day, I sent a letter of resignation to the guy who was vice president. On Friday, the student newspaper, *The Eagle*, ran a big headline over a picture of me in the lecture hall, dragging on a cigarette: "Kunstler Resigns!" Nobody commiserated with me. Billy and Tim played it as a goof, which was our generation's cynical way of pretending that nothing mattered. I'm certain it was generally understood that I was a terrible student government president, a failure even as a prankster. I was too detached from my feelings of humiliation to act as if I cared.

Shortly after that, my one-year banishment from performing on stage was lifted. The theater department had just moved into the brand-new Fine Arts Building, with its fabulous main stage theater, and Dr. Hetler had decided to honor the event by putting on Chekhov's bittersweet comedy *The Cherry Orchard*. He cast me as Trofimov, the student revolutionary, a signal irony. It was a wonderful production. Rick Miller designed elaborate box sets for the various rooms of the family mansion that hung from the counterweight system. My roommate Tim Leary played Gayev, the head of the family who loses their ancestral estate out of aristocratic fecklessness. I was at least able to get rides home from rehearsal with him, now that I was carless. I think we properly honored the opening of the new theater with the show. The end of the run brought us into finals and the semester's end, May 1969. I plotted a course of action for summer that would land me in a mental hospital months later.

Provincetown

I didn't know what I was doing in the spring of 1969. It was not so much that I wasn't in control of my life; more like I didn't even know one *could be* in control. I made choices and took actions of a mostly schematic kind, living the outline of a life with no clear sense of its content or its direction.

I didn't want to spend the summer around Brockport. I still had a lot of affection for the town itself, and especially for the barn and my roommates in Adams Basin, but I felt impelled to get away for a while to someplace where I wasn't a known personality with a checkered reputation, someplace on the ocean where I could make some money and hang out on the beach. I definitely didn't want to go back to Fire Island, and not just because Muriel and Bernie would be there, but because I couldn't shake my association of the place with those horrible days the year before when Bobby Kennedy got shot, hung on a thread overnight, and then died the next morning. I'd never been to any other beach towns in my corner of the country, but I wasn't afraid of going to an unknown place.

I studied the map of the New England coast and focused in on Cape Cod, which I knew a little about from reading Thoreau in my nineteenth-century American lit class. One thing you could tell: the farther out you went it, the less it was cluttered up with towns, highways, and people. So I decided to hitchhike out to Provincetown at the farthest tip of the Cape. Exams were over by the second week in May. Then, early one bright weekday morning, Billy gave me a ride down to New York State Thruway on-ramp no. 47 at Le Roy, about twenty miles south of Brockport. I was lugging a suitcase and my Smith-Corona typewriter — still bethinking myself a reincarnation of F. Scott Fitzgerald who, any day, would turn out a classic short story — and I'd made a crude cardboard sign that said *Cape Cod*. I was too excited about setting out on an epic life adventure to rachet myself into an anxiety attack.

Hitchhiking was not so difficult in those days before America became infested with serial killers and other desperate maniacs, and hippies were notably altruistic toward each other. I made it all the way to the outskirts of Boston around Framingham the first day with no more than three rides. I didn't want to be out on the road at night, so I lugged my stuff to a motel nearest the off-ramp and checked in. The next day, I set out early and made it all the way out to Provincetown. I was correct that the human presence became generally sparser when you cleared the elbow of the Cape at Orleans. But I became a bit dismayed when I finally got dropped off on Commercial Street, the main drag of Provincetown, by my last ride, a bread truck driven by a hopped-up college kid blasting the radio who offered me hits on his doobie, which I declined. Provincetown was not the mellow old whaling village I'd imagined. It was at least as dense and bustling Greenwich Village.

It was still pretty early in the season, not yet June, and perhaps the second or third restaurant I popped into had a job opening for a dishwasher. I signed on to start work that very night. The place was called the Penny Farthing, on Bradford Street. It had nothing to do with mutton chops or anything British. It was owned by a forty-ish Cuban named Benito Narciso. The menu was a mashup of international this-and-that, such as Benito's "pork Javanese" (skewered with pineapple and peppers) and that crowd favorite veal parmigiana, and various seafood specialties such as Lobster Fra Diavolo and scampi, and, of course, steaks. After hiring me, Benito sent me a couple of blocks back over to Commercial Street where a friend of his, a German immigrant in his thirties named Frank, ran the White Horse Inn. Frank had a spacious apartment on the ground floor filled with architectural bric-a-brac and his own excellent photographs, and he rented me a tiny room upstairs in the back for $25 a week. That was quite a large sum of money then, $100 a month for a space barely big enough for a single bed. But based on what I'd been making briefly at the Sea Turtle on Fire Island the year before, about $75 a week, I figured I'd have plenty left over for meals and beer. (Rent for the barn in Adams Basin for all three of us was $80 a month total.)

What I didn't figure on in making these arrangements was saving any money to repay my father the insurance company's deductible charge I owed him for the car crash and to buy my own insurance in order to get my car back. I just could not bring myself to think about any of that. At twenty, the judgment region of my brain remained undeveloped. I couldn't face the shame and humiliation associated with the car, so I just stuffed it all in some dark basement corner of my mind. Ironically, if I'd faced the discomfort, and saved enough money over the summer to meet those obligations, I might have overcome all that juvenile, defeatist emotion. I would have taken the required action of an autonomous adult, demonstrated some basic competence in problem solving to myself, and developed some confidence. I did not know then that these neurotic gales of gothic emotion can be overcome by working out the practical problems of existence. My main practical problem was keeping myself dependent on two parents I didn't get along with.

The Kitchen

From the first night working at the Penny Farthing I fit in nicely. There were three of us in a room about fifteen by twenty. Rick Librizzi, the line cook, was in charge. (Benito managed the "front of the house," the dining room.) Rick grew up in a small industrial town in the Berkshires, but had bugged out to Greenwich Village in his teens. He was now in his late twenties, tall and lanky with a manner of speech that at first seemed goony, almost retarded, like a punch-drunk prizefighter. He soon revealed himself to be a something else entirely. He was a serious artist, in a town that, as yet, I barely understood to be a mecca for painters, writers, poets, and theater types. That's how ignorant I was. I wasn't even aware of the connection between Eugene O'Neill and Provincetown — O'Neill was out of style in the late sixties. We were all caught up in Beckett, Ionesco, Genet, Pinter… the Absurdists.

Later in life, Rick became a downtown New York art dealer, in Warhol's orbit, and especially active in the years of the graffiti kids Keith Haring, Jean-Michel Basquiat, and others. For many years he was an agent for the wealthy collector Walter Chrysler Jr., son of the founder of the car company, who, by 1969, had set up a museum in an old church a block down Commercial Street from the White Horse Inn. I didn't know about any of that. In the summer of '69

Rick already had a wife and a baby girl, with another child on the way.

The second guy in the kitchen, Rick's assistant, name forgotten, only lasted about a week. I proved to be adept at dishwashing and pot washing, and keeping my end of the kitchen orderly. Benito was impressed enough to promote me when the other guy bounced. I knew a thing or two about cooking, having fixed my own dinner for years as a teenager and assisted the chef at the Fire Island Summer Club the summer of '66 and I cooked a lot at the barn for my roommates. My new position at the Penny Farthing was combination prep cook and sous-chef. I came in at four o'clock, chopped all the parsley and the garlic, scrubbed the "beards" off the mussels, cleaned fish that were delivered whole, prepped up about twenty baguettes with garlic butter to make garlic toast, filled a bus pan with portioned-out nests of half-cooked spaghetti, fixed salad dressings, and got the "line" (the region in front of the stoves) ready for action, which generally started about five-thirty. Of course, we had a radio blasting the whole evening. The big hits of that summer: "In the Year 2525," "Sweet Caroline," "The Age of Aquarius," "Spinning Wheel," "Bad Moon Rising," "Sugar, Sugar," "Honkey Tonk Women," "In the Ghetto" (Elvis), "A Boy Named Sue" (Johnny Cash), "Poke Salad Annie" . . . I got to hate most of them.

Rick and I were a good team. I could anticipate what he needed and pick up the ball in a rush and we were both working the line together in a blur of coordinated motion. Meanwhile, the bratty waiters would be clustered on the backside of the line screaming for their orders. Cooking in a restaurant is exacting to an extreme.

Young Man Blues

Eleven seconds too long under the "salamander" — a sort of superbroiler — will incinerate the mozzarella off a veal parm and ruin a halved lobster. In those close quarters and frantic moments, Rick and I naturally fell into clowning around, improvising comedy routines, and he revealed himself to be very knowledgeable about art and literature in the process. He especially enjoyed one of my gags: reciting all the parts from the quarterdeck scene of John Huston's 1956 movie of *Moby Dick*, which I'd memorized as a teen from watching it repeatedly on WOR-TV's *Million Dollar Movie*. Rick regaled me with wild tales of the life of the renaissance artists, including his favorite: the swashbuckling and slightly crazy Benvenuto Cellini. A bonus working for Benito was that he generously let me cook a decent dinner for myself on the house before work each night, anything except a steak or a lobster. And, of course, when you're working hard on the line on a long weekend night, a lot of wayward leftovers find their way into your mouth.

I learned a few things about the dark side of the restaurant biz at the Penny Farthing too. Benito's pièce de résistance on the menu was paella, which we made only as a weekend special. Paella is a complex Mediterranean pilaf dish. In the late afternoon I'd prep up the saffron-scented rice base with shrimp and chorizo sausage in a giant ten-gallon covered pot. To serve, we'd mound the rice on these hokey little tin individual paella pans, stick half a broiled chicken on one side and half a boiled lobster on the other. Between those, we'd deploy half a dozen each steamed mussels and clams and garnish the whole deal with pimento slivers, fresh green peas, and parsley — a very grand presentation!

Only on the Saturday night of the Memorial Day holiday weekend, the place was jamming so hard that we ran out of the rice base before nine o'clock. Customers were still coming in and ordering paella. We informed the waiters that it was "eighty-six" on the paella, but Benito wouldn't hear of it. He came into the kitchen and instructed us to scoop the rice off the half-eaten pans returning from the dining room — it was so much food that customers could hardly get past the chicken and lobster — and re-form a new mound on a new pan with the old rice, hit it with more chicken and lobster, etc., and send it back out again. A few of those paellas must have made three circuits in and out of the kitchen and dining room that night. Same thing on the Fourth of July weekend.

Another Friday, for some reason the seafood purveyor forgot our mussels order. In a panic, Benito ordered a couple of waiters to go down to Provincetown Bay and pull a couple of buckets of mussels from a pie down there. Those mussels were pretty sketchy. About every fifth one was dead and stinky when they came out of the steamer. We also occasionally got bargain lobsters from a particular type of P'town desperado called a lobster rustler. These were guys without licenses who raided the lobster pots of the licensed fishermen, considered a capital crime in that milieu — you'd turn up with your throat cut, and no one would rat out the killer. Drugs might have been behind it. I learned over the weeks that there was quite a heroin scene in town that summer. It was one of the signs that the Age of Aquarius was going sour.

One thing I discovered early on, to my dismay, was that the drinking age in Massachusetts was twenty-one. I'd be twenty until

October, and I looked even younger. I didn't carry my old fake ID anymore, since I didn't need it back at college in New York State. So I had to buy India ink and a crow quill, some cheap watercolors, and plastic laminate to forge myself a Wyoming driver's license. The first place I used it, the bartender gave me the hairy eyeball and called me "cowboy."

The second week I was there, I met a college girl named Janice who worked for the pastel portrait artists that set up along the sidewalk at the heart of town, just off the main town piers. Janice was energetic and magnetic, with frizzy dark hair and big dark eyes. Her job was to hustle clients to sit for portraits from the tourists plying the street. She tried to hustle me, but we just ended up yakking and hit it off. I met her downtown again later that night, after work at the restaurant. She took me to the Atlantic House, a raucous disco, and then to a party thrown by her artist pals in an old sail loft. It was the first time I actually ever saw men making out with other men, though obviously I knew it was *a thing*. There were a lot of them at it and the scene disturbed me. When I'd scoped out P'town on the map, I had no more idea that it was a gay mecca than I knew it was an artists' mecca. The decadence of the times was getting to me, and Provincetown especially. I was sorry I'd landed there, but felt stuck since I had a summer job. The word "decadent" reverberated in my head as I went around town and took in the scene.

Janice became a friend while I remained in town, but I avoided sleeping with her because she looked unnervingly like Muriel, my mother — at least what Muriel might've looked like at twenty. Anyway, it was enough to disconcert me. In fact, I'd spent very little time around my mother during in those years, avoiding many holiday trips home. At that point in my life Muriel inhabited my imagination as a kind of monster in the attic. I felt bad about spurning Janice, because there was really nothing wrong with her, and I suppose she must have concluded there was something wrong with me — which was true, though of the various confusions in my young life, sexual identity was not one of them. I was too embarrassed to tell her it spooked me that she looked like my mother. We just remained friends, with an awkward edge. She seemed to be sympathetically studying me, trying to figure me out. Years later, she ended up being a psychiatrist.

Anyway, around the same time in June, I ran into a couple from Brockport State I'd known on a tangent of my social circle: Bob and Judy. They'd graduated that year. Days later, they broke up for some reason and Bob split P'town leaving Judy behind. So I started a romance with her, if you could call it that, meeting up at her place after we shut down the Penny Farthing kitchen. She had a room in a rented house with five other people I didn't know, and never got to know. She was athletic and sexually avid, an education major. We had almost nothing else in common besides going to the same college, and all we did until she left a few weeks later was sleep together. We just had nothing to say to each other. Janice was different. I could talk to her about the world, politics, movies. Judy left town before the Fourth of July.

Otherwise, I was strangely lonesome those months at land's end on Cape Cod. I didn't make any other friends. Rick and I had enough of each other's company each night in the kitchen. We didn't pal around outside of work, and he had both his art and a family to keep him occupied. I got out to the beaches only twice that whole summer. You needed a car or a bicycle to get to the ocean from town, and I had neither and it was a miserable trek down a busy highway on foot. I could swim in the bay, right across Commercial Street from the White Horse, where there was a dingy little beach, not the kind of place you would want to hunker down and read among the kelp and broken Styrofoam cups. Much later in life, when I'd taken up painting seriously again, I would carry an all-media sketchbook and a little watercolor kit everywhere, and engage my attention whenever I had a few minutes. If I'd developed that practice sooner, it might have helped keep me sane that summer, but apparently back then I'd rejected everything about my former life in New York City, including my high school art training.

My days were routine. I'd spend four bucks on a big long, lingering breakfast at a diner on Commercial Street and read the *New York Times* from end to end. I was a maniacal newshound and the summer of 1969 was an extravaganza of sensational news. In June, Judy Garland died of a sleeping pill overdose and days later the Stonewall Inn riots happened in Greenwich Village — both events were big deals for P'town, with its huge gay contingent; in early July, Brian Jones of the Rolling Stones drowned in his swimming pool in England; the next day the "Zodiac" serial killer struck again in California; July 16, the Apollo 11 spacecraft blasted off on its moon-landing journey; on July 18 — with the nation in thrall to the astronauts — Senator Ted Kennedy ended a night of drinking on Martha's Vineyard by driving off a little bridge over the

Chappaquiddick inlet with his Senate aide Mary Jo Kopechne, who got stuck underwater in the car and drowned (and then Kennedy foolishly skulked back to his hotel in Edgartown and waited ten hours to report it, setting in motion a spectacular scandal); on July 20, with all that going on, the astronauts landed on the moon in the afternoon, took a nap, and, around eleven o'clock that night, Neil Armstrong floated down the steps of the lunar landing module to become the first human being to set foot on another heavenly body.

In the background of all these events, the war in Vietnam revved into its *Apocalypse Now* phase of pointless insanity. Until mid-July, I spent the hours between those long newsy breakfasts and going into the Penny Farthing to work typing letters to my friends back in Brockport, and reading out on the front lawn of the White Horse Inn. I occupied myself with the essays on theater of Robert Brustein, who was dean of the Yale School of Drama (a place I imagined myself going to eventually). I also became enamored of Robert Lowell's American play trilogy *The Old Glory*, thinking I'd do one of the plays for my senior project. And I read Norman Mailer's *The Armies of the Night*, his sensational "nonfiction novel" about the big antiwar protests in Washington a year and a half earlier. In an instance of synchronicity, Mailer, who famously had a summer house in P'town, actually walked past the White Horse Inn on Commercial Street one day when I was reading his book out on the grass in front. I jumped up and hailed him and chatted him up on the sidewalk. He was very pleased to see his book in my hand and we yakked for twenty minutes.

Young Man Blues

In mid-July, though, growing desperate for money, I took on two additional jobs. Benito had acquired a broken-down motel out where Commercial Street melded into the sparser duneland of Truro and he'd started renovating it. He got his waiters up to scraping and painting the rooms. He put me to work for a few hours every morning cleaning the stoves, ovens, and refrigerators in each housekeeping unit. It was disgusting work. I got an additional gig working noon to three p.m. behind the counter at a hippie jewelry shop downtown that was owned by a friend of Janice's. I was working around the clock. No more lingering breakfasts, and no reading on the grass. At midday, it was a long walk from the motel on the edge of town to the McMillan Wharf. At three, it was another trek from the jewelry store in the center of town back to the White Horse where I changed into my kitchen togs, with just a few minutes to scurry over to the Penny Farthing on Bradford Street to scale striped bass, scrub mussels, and perform countless other prep duties before the rush. I was usually out of there by midnight. I'd scurry back to the White Horse, shower all the grease off, and go out and hit the bar that first served me with my phony ID. For some reason — lingering Puritanism? — closing time for bars in Massachusetts in 1969 was one a.m., so instead of beers I'd order vodka on the rocks and pound down two or three of them rapidly before last call to calm my system down enough to get to sleep.

By late July I'd managed to save maybe a hundred dollars. It wasn't enough, and I knew I couldn't keep up the pace of working around the clock. I started sinking into the familiar state of continuous phobic anxiety that I'd gone through back in the winter of my senior year of high school, on the edge of panic all my waking hours. Provincetown was taking on that spooky, *Cabinet of Dr. Caligari* look — the buildings seeming to tilt at odd, psychotic angles, casting sinister shadows, the people on the streets looked hollow-eyed and gaunt. I was aware that I was cracking up again, and this time it hadn't been triggered by any pot smoking. That dreadful awareness only amplified and ramified my out-of-control anxiety. I was sure I was going insane. I'd read enough about abnormal psych to know I was at the age that young men with a certain genetic inclination turned schizophrenic. I thought: why not me?

I've written in an earlier book (*Too Much Magic*, 2012) how disturbing the moon landing was to me. We had a tiny black-and-white portable TV running on top of the big reach-in fridge in the Penny Farthing's kitchen the night of the Apollo 11 lunar module's first moon walk. I've written that I developed a weird neurotic terror of the moon some years earlier — I couldn't stand looking at it in the night sky. I was so untrustful of the universe that I feared the moon would become unmoored from its orbit and crash into the earth. So I could barely stand watching the extravaganza on TV. The mere thought of the astronauts being up there in space, so untethered from the earth, terrified me, caught up as I was by my own psychological untethering. Everybody else in the kitchen was glued to the tiny TV screen, including Benito and the waiters who had finished their tables. I just went about my regular business shutting down the line and putting away all the garni while Neil Armstrong floated down from the lunar module and spoke that staticky, banal line about *one small step for a man*, blah blah. I split as soon as I was done with my chores. After that night, anxiety seeped into every cranny of my existence in Provincetown. It became agonizing to just walk down crowded Commercial Street. I quit the jewelry store job. I told Benito I was too worn out to work on his motel project in the mornings — which pissed him off. And I began to feel unendurable panic in the one place that had been a sort of refuge: the Penny Farthing's kitchen.

Rick Librizzi seemed to sense that I was in rough shape, but I was becoming a problem for him by showing up late for work and neglecting some of the many essential prep chores. Benito was on Rick's ass about it, I learned, and threatened to fire me. In desperation, I turned to the only other adult around in my world, my landlord, Frank, for help. I'd chatted him up almost daily since arriving in May, in my comings and goings from the White Horse. He left the door open to his stylish ground-floor boho apartment so walk-ins looking for a place to stay in P'town could find him easily. I often strayed in after breakfast and we'd developed a friendly joking relationship. He seemed surprised to learn that I was not the happy-go-lucky kid he thought I was. I knew that he saw a shrink somewhere on the Cape because he was always joking about his many neuroses. So I just came clean and told him I was having mental problems, terrible anxiety dogging me, and he gave me his shrink's phone number.

I made an appointment pronto, and one August morning I hitchhiked down the Cape to Orleans on Route 6, about twenty-five miles. The shrink's house — name forgotten — was tucked away in a quasi-wilderness of winding, sandy roads and scrub pines, which I had to explore on foot after being dropped off on the highway by my last ride. I'd set out extra-early to leave time to find his place and had to kill the better part of an hour before my appointment after I'd located it. I found a small rural cemetery near his house and waited there, perusing the ancient tombstones with the names of old New England mariners and their wives and children. Finally, I presented myself at the shrink's door.

I remember nothing about him other than he was a serene man of late middle age, very professional and accommodating. He took me into his study, a spacious room full of books with oriental rugs and plush furniture and a huge picture window with a view of the salt pond behind his house — a scene of Zen-like natural order. It was the first time I'd felt calm in weeks. I sank into one of his soft chairs and blabbed for the requisite fifty minutes, mostly, I'm sure, about my array of disturbing phobias and symptoms, staring at the salt pond all the while with its soft grasses bending gently in the ocean breeze. I didn't say much, I'm sure, about my practical predicaments — my relations with Henry and Muriel and my failing attempt to raise money to get my car back. But I left his office temporarily calmed and hitchhiked back in time for work.

Within another twenty-four hours, through some alchemy of the unconscious, perhaps provoked by something the shrink said, I decided to bug out of Provincetown and return to Brockport. Once I had decided, I couldn't face Benito, but I did call Rick on the phone and explained that I was going crazy in P'town and had to leave for the sake of my mental health. Rick was yet another older brother figure that I let down. My room at the White Horse was all paid up for the week. He gave me back some of the money pro rata and sincerely wished me well getting my head straight. I caught a morning bus to Boston, changed to one to Albany, and then Rochester, and sometime after night had fallen Billy Grant met me at the Rochester Greyhound terminal and drove me back to the barn in Adams Basin.

Last Stand

I was hugely relieved to be back in safe and familiar surroundings, but the feeling didn't last long. I came home with little more than a hundred dollars. The fall semester would commence in a couple of weeks so I didn't see any point in looking for a last-ditch summer job. I'll tell you what I might have done, should have done, but didn't do: I might have gone to the campus and arranged for a part-time "work-study" job for the fall semester that would have enabled me to systematically save money in order to pay off Henry and get my car back. But I didn't do that. I was sunk in futility of my own making, an immature twenty-year-old, with an insufficiently developed judgment region of my brain. None of my friends suggested such a reasonable and practical solution to my problem either, but then they didn't really know what I was struggling with: my missing sense of personal autonomy, failure to recognize that I could take charge of what happened to me and take actions in my own best interests. I was oblivious. It didn't matter that I was poorly prepared by Henry and Muriel, or what I happened to feel about them. I just had a very dim understanding of where I stood and what I needed to get on with my life. And out of that confusion my mind rebelled and broke down.

Anyway, the Woodstock music festival was about to happen and Billy was planning to go there with some of our other friends. After many logistical and legal screwups, the festival promoters finally found a farmer named Max Yasgur in the Catskills town of Bethel, NY, who was willing to rent out his pastures for the event. Yasgur's farm was fifty miles from the actual town of Woodstock. Jumpy and anxious as I was, I had no desire to be in what was shaping up to be an epic mob scene with, possibly, no easy way to get out.

As it happened, Billy needed someone to cover for his summer job, which was picking up bundles of the Rochester newspaper the *Democrat and Chronicle* at the paper's headquarters in the city, and driving the bundles around to country stores in the rural hamlets throughout western Monroe County. By then, Billy had ditched his '57 Thunderbird for a cherry-red Volkswagen Bug convertible — the perfect hippie car — but he was going to Woodstock in another guy's car, so he left me with the keys to the Bug and instructions for dropping off the papers. I drove around the county those four or five days, the radio broadcasting endless tales of the mess that the Woodstock festival had turned into, with its ten-mile-long traffic jams, lack of food, bad drugs circulating through the crowd, and frequent rainstorms that turned the venue into a giant mudhole. I was glad I didn't go.

Soon, the semester started and I resumed sliding back into uncontrollable anxiety and paranoia. Without a car, I had to cadge rides to campus with Billy and Leary. I developed a new phobia about sitting in the passenger seat with no control over a vehicle going fifty miles an hour. It became unendurably stressful. I was sure we'd crash from moment to moment through the whole four-mile trip to town. My roommates began noticing how strangely I was acting, but I was unable to talk to them about what I was going through because all the anxieties and phobias were emotional phantoms abstracted away from the particulars of my life.

I'd registered for my senior year classes, but I started avoiding them too. David Hamilton was mounting a fall production of the Jean Genet extravaganza *The Balcony*. There was no part in it for me. I was no longer his pal. I didn't sign up to work on the crew. It looked like I had washed out in my career as a theater major. To avoid having to snag rides to campus and back, I started staying overnight on the sofa at another friend's house in town. I signed up to see the college shrink Dr. Sandt (yes, spelled differently but eerily close to Dr. Sand, the shrink I saw briefly in the city), who was able to transmit one important concept through my fog of anxiety. *That's how you are these days*, he would say. *There will be other days when you feel differently.* He was low-key and reassuring, but the next day I'd be back in the soup, all phobic and crazy again.

I took up with a girl named Kathy. She was a beautiful blonde sophomore from the Finger Lakes, a fellow theater major, sweet and caring. She stayed with me many nights through October at the friend's house in town, but it was an altogether awkward relationship. I was too freaked out to have sex with her. I doubt we even made out during those weeks. It was yet another thing in life that I couldn't manage. Yet she stuck by me. Then, something really weird happened.

I got a message from Billy out at the barn: Henry wanted me to call him. I'd written perfunctory postcards to him over the summer from Provincetown but hadn't spoken to him. He loomed in my imagination as a gigantic, implacable ogre. I had no idea what he might urgently want to talk to me about. He never called me; it was always my obligation to call him. I caught a ride back to the barn and called him long distance. He said I could come down and get my car back. It threw me. I told him I didn't have the money. He said I could pay him back when I got it, that the car was cluttering up his driveway and if I didn't come get it he'd sell it. I didn't ask him why he changed his mind, and he didn't tell me. I agreed to come down and get the car the following weekend.

Kathy and I took the Greyhound bus down to New York and caught the Long Island Rail Road out to Roslyn. We stayed in a cheap motel on Northern Boulevard on Saturday night and called a taxi for the final leg to Henry and Pauline's house on Sunday morning. Kathy was from a tiny town in the Finger Lakes and suburban Long Island horrified her. Henry was cordial enough — Kathy charmed him — but we didn't talk about anything besides him explaining that he had taken out a temporary insurance policy for me to get the car back upstate, and that after a few weeks I'd be on my own with it. I believe Henry was sincerely cutting me a break, since he could have easily just sold off the Opel, but I felt humiliated because deep down I didn't believe that I deserved a break. I was a bad son and, increasingly, a flop as an adult. The visit couldn't have lasted an hour.

Kathy and I drove seven hours back upstate. The trip consumed all the rest of my money. After that, I just completely fell apart. Days later, my anxiety was so overwhelming that I checked into the campus infirmary and didn't want to leave the place to go anywhere — classes, meals, nothing. Dr. Sandt, the college shrink, was notified. He decided that I needed serious treatment and made arrangements for me to go to a mental hospital. He chose the Payne Whitney Clinic in New York City because that was supposedly my home base. I didn't argue about it or put up a struggle. I was exhausted from feeling scared all the time. I just surrendered to the flow.

Part Four

Welcome to the Laughing Academy

In early November 1969, the college flew me down from Rochester to New York's LaGuardia Airport with a young assistant dean as my minder. He was businesslike but respectful, though I was an obvious mess. The short flight on a Mohawk Airlines twin turboprop plane horrified me. In those days, you could smoke cigarettes absolutely everywhere, even on airplanes, and I must have chain-smoked a pack of Winstons from the time we arrived at the airport to the landing at LaGuardia. Bernie and Muriel met us there and the assistant dean handed me off to them. They had apparently received instructions from Dr. Sandt, so I didn't have to tell them anything. We took a cab into Manhattan. We made small talk, but there was no discussion of the actual situation — why I was in the shape I was in. I was nauseous with horror seeing the skyscrapers of the city rise up as we motored toward the Triborough Bridge — Manhattan was the last place I wanted to be.

It happened that the Payne Whitney Clinic was located two blocks east from the apartment building I grew up in where Bernie and Muriel still lived at 68th and Second Avenue. The eight-story psychiatric hospital — demolished in 1990 — was then attached to the Cornell Medical School at its New York Hospital facility on 68th Street and York Avenue. Many of the windows overlooked the East River. It turned out to be a very posh establishment with distinguished alumni. I'd learn later that it was the place Marilyn Monroe checked into when her marriage to Arthur Miller hit the rocks and she was cracking up. Robert Lowell, author of *The Old Glory* cycle of plays I'd so admired reading on Cape Cod, had been there twice to dry out, and his wife the writer Jean Stafford did a stretch there too.

The Gothic Revival entrance was rather grand, like a collegiate club, the interior lobby all dark, warm wood wainscoting. I was ushered into a comfortable office lined with bookshelves, with a handsome fireplace and leather-covered furniture. A distinguished-looking senior psychiatrist greeted me and interviewed me. Bernie and Muriel waited somewhere outside. I was coherent enough to tell the doctor I'd had problems controlling my anxiety and terror on and off since my introduction to pot smoking four years earlier, and now it was worse than ever. In case he misunderstood, I also said I had done next to zero pot smoking since then — that is, my problem wasn't drugs, but I was fond of drinking. I told him that I'd played a mental patient on stage in *Marat/Sade* a couple of years earlier and I hoped that Payne Whitney was not like the asylum at Charenton. He didn't get the reference. I was briskly admitted and said goodbye awkwardly to Bernie and Muriel out in the hall, who seemed rather dazed by it all, and then was taken upstairs.

I went through the standard admission protocols. An aide watched me get undressed, went through my clothes to make sure I didn't have any contraband on me — drugs, razor blades — and observed me take a shower. He explained the rules and the schedule and showed me the dining room and the TV lounge. I had a perfunctory physical health exam. The fourth-floor ward I was on, apparently dedicated to young adults, was pretty austere, in contrast to the grand rooms downstairs. There was an glassed-in enclosed room called the nursing station halfway down the hall, usually a bustling place with the staff writing their charts, sorting out meds, smoking, and yakking.

My room was not the least bit luxurious — just a single bed, a table with a chair, and a chest of drawers, like a dorm room. The windows were casements, which opened only a few inches so patients could not jump out. There was also a window on the bathroom door, which was a little creepy, but even in my disordered state I could imagine the reasons. There was an ashtray, of course. Practically everyone in the place smoked, patients, staff, doctors. You forget what America was like then. The half dozen or so other patients on the ward seemed quite eager to meet me and I spent much of that first afternoon and evening getting acquainted. In an institutional setting like that, a new person changes the social dynamic of the group. Even people in mental distress seem to sense that and try to suss out how it will affect the order of things.

Across the hall was Carol, a year or two older than me. She was galumphingly big and full-figured with a pleasant full-moon face and bobbed hair, and immediately gregarious, like she was glad to see you, and not at all sexy. Her voice boomed. Nothing about her suggested madness or despair, and that was true for most of the others I met that first day. In fact, it turned out you learned only indirectly what was going on inside the heads of your fellow patients, and then not all that much. We were *not* told to avoid discussing ourselves. Things would come out in the various group therapy sessions, of course, but they didn't necessarily add up to a coherent story line. I'd conclude later on that we were all somewhat embarrassed about being there, and that many of us — certainly myself at the time — might have had a hard time even articulating just what had landed us in *the laughing academy*, as Carol referred to Payne Whitney. It was as if our being in a psych ward called for an extra layer of personal decorum that we all automatically observed.

Carol's room was crammed full of stuff, including extra furniture — a beanbag chair, a bookshelf — and the walls were covered with her therapeutic artwork, like she'd moved in. She told me that she'd been in Payne Whitney for six months. It shocked me but it seemed like bad manners to ask what was keeping her in there so long. I just had to assume that whatever was wrong with her had not been fixed, and it prompted me to worry if I would be there, unfixed, for a long time too.

Sandy, down the hall, was my age, a Queens College student, short and rather chunky. She favored shlumpy clothing that worked against her looks, but she was friendly and sweet. Next door to her was Linda, also early twenties, petite, with long, dark, straight hair and a foxy face, on leave from a Catholic college in New Jersey. She was definitely good-looking, favored tight jeans and cashmere sweaters, and bothered to put on makeup, which the other girls did not. I'd been advised by Mr. B., the aide who admitted me, that sexual fooling around was verboten on the ward, but that didn't mean you wouldn't think about it. Both Sandy and Linda had been in the hospital for months, too, but not as long as Carol. (By the way, the Payne Whitney staff observed a somewhat anachronistic formal decorum, too. All aides and nurses were addressed as Mr., Miss, or Mrs. A, B, C, X, Y, Z. You learned their first names only by accident. I do not remember any of their names, first or last, more than fifty years later.)

Then there was David. He was a Harvard sophomore, red-haired, physically very slight, with a tragic aura. I would learn that, at college in Cambridge, he had come down with irritable bowel syndrome so severe that the doctors had cut out a length of his colon and hook him up to a colostomy bag. What a thing to happen to you before your life even got underway! He had apparently responded to all that by turning suicidal. It was not hard to understand his plight. David had a portable record player, though, and that's how we would get to know each other.

There were two other patients on the ward who were much more visibly far gone than the ones I've already mentioned. The first was, oddly —because it was supposed to be a young adults' ward — a late-middle-aged man I'll call Joe Marino. He was present for a week or so before they transferred him somewhere else, but he rarely came out of his room except for meals, did not speak, and was afflicted with Tourette-like tics. The other was a young man named Randy who was really messed up. Randy, early twenties, with a wild rooster fluff of hair, walked up and down the hallway of our ward hour after hour, very stiffly — he never turned his head to look at anything or spoke to anyone. Actually, he didn't walk so much as glide, as though he were standing on a camera dolly. I asked the others what was wrong with him, and all they said it was *a bad LSD trip*. That's all they knew, and it may or may not have been true. Anyway, he freaked me out because I considered myself to some degree drug damaged too, and my naturally catastrophizing train of thought got me worrying that I'd end up like him, a zombie. Randy was only around for a week or so before they sent him to some mysterious elsewhere, too.

From Bad to a Bit Worse

The first few days in hospital I was hugely relieved just to be taken out of circulation and in a place where, theoretically, I would get some help. I was relieved of all my usual responsibilities and obligations. I didn't have to go anywhere. I felt safe. I began to feel "normal" again. That is, my anxieties retreated and the other parts of my personality that had been subdued by it reemerged rather quickly, including my aggressiveness and my malicious sense of humor.

Those first days were filled with a lot of procedural rigmarole. They sent me to see a social worker on another floor to figure out how Payne Whitney would get paid for my stay there. I'd just turned twenty-one a month earlier, so the social worker finagled me onto Medicaid, the government program for indigents that had been passed by Congress in 1965. The category she put me in was "emancipated adult," meaning, I was not my parents' responsibility anymore, but I was without means of support, and thus qualified for federal aid. I can imagine at some point Muriel had told someone in charge that she was not disposed to foot the bill for this, and I had no idea if Henry even knew I was in the looney bin. Whatever the ethical questions of getting on the government dole, it was a fait accompli. So at least one thing I didn't have to worry about in the hospital was paying to be there.

Next, I met my assigned psychiatrist, Dr. Grodin, in his final training stage, called "resident." (Cornell Med was a teaching hospital.) I can find no record of him on the internet. He was a good-looking, dark-haired guy, about my height, late twenties, soft-spoken, clearly very bright but not very demonstrative. I would see him three times a week while I was there. He put me on medication after that initial interview. The med was Thorazine, a pretty crude chemical hammer that put me in a slight daze, and not a particularly pleasant one. The psychiatric drugs that are familiar now, the SSRIs in the Prozac family, the benzodiazepines such as Xanax, awaited development decades into the future. Thorazine was used promiscuously as an all-purpose tranquilizer for many categories of mental distress. Understand, of course, that all the categories have changed since the 1960s. My problem, which would later be identified as panic disorder or anxiety disorder, barely existed as a discrete category then, though doctors certainly knew a panic attack when they saw one — it had long been one of the most common reasons people show up in emergency rooms.

One more entry detail: I was asked to submit the names of anybody who I wished to be barred from visiting me in the hospital. I suppose this was predicated on the idea that some patients had family members or others in their life who represented a danger to their stability. I didn't have very strong feelings about that, but they seemed to want me to list someone, so I told them Henry, Muriel, and President Nixon, and that's how it stood until close to the end of my sojourn there.

Now that my formal induction was complete, I fell in with the Payne Whitney daily routine, which was frankly pretty dull and a bit lame, considering the place's reputation. Too much of the time you just sat around doing nothing — you watched TV, wrote letters, read books and newspapers, yakked with fellow patients, and smoked cigarettes endlessly. The staff discouraged you from sleeping during the day. At night they often gave me a dose of chloral hydrate to knock me out.

Most weekday mornings we'd have an hour of exercise in the gym on the top floor. It didn't amount to much. They had a volleyball net set up. There were some gym mats on the hardwood floor in case you felt like doing some sit-ups. Patients from other wards were brought up to join us there. That was the only way you could get enough live bodies to form two volleyball teams. Many of those patients, mature adults and older people, were too out of it mentally or physically not able to play. I was among the more athletic patients, and that's where my aggressiveness first came out. I took a certain pleasure in spiking the ball over the net off our opponents' heads. The aides began to notice and warned me to cut it out. There was also a spacious outdoor observation deck up there. It was entirely enclosed with steel fencing, including overhead, like a cage, actually, so that nobody could jump off the roof. It had a million-dollar view of the East River looking south to the Queensboro Bridge and beyond. But I was not all that comfortable with heights — another one of my phobias — so I didn't venture out there much. Besides, it was November, and the wind off the river was cold and harsh.

One luxurious aspect of Payne Whitney was the chow. The dining room on our floor had about five round tables seating six at each, like a restaurant — though there were never close to thirty patients on the ward while I was there. We ate off linen tablecloths and we each received silver napkin rings with our names pasted on with one of those embossed plastic label maker strips. Unlike most hospital meals, ours were at least as good as a first-class highway diner, and I started to pack on the pounds. I never ate three square meals a day at college. During stretches of intense rehearsal, we dined out of the vending machine backstage.

My stepfather Bernie was *not* on the short list of people barred from visiting, and he came to see me fror a few hours most weekends, though we did not really talk about the reasons I was there — probably because I didn't quite know myself, and couldn't have articulated it coherently, being mostly preoccupied solely with my symptoms and phobias. By then, I'd been away from home for more than three years, and he and Muriel remained mystified about what had brought me so low. They'd never visited me in Brockport. We barely knew each other anymore. Anyway, Bernie kindly and dutifully came, and brought me a carton of cigarettes and magazines, and we would sit together in the TV room watching pro football games, not having much to say to each other except comment on the action… a great punt return… a muffed pass. For many weeks, I did not talk to Muriel on the phone, and I had no communication with Henry, my father, nothing by mail, even. Several of my college friends came all the way down and dropped in on me at Payne Whitney. Billy Grant brought my guitar down. Even Janice from Provincetown, with whom I stayed in touch after leaving Cape Cod, visited me. I should have been grateful to have friends who cared enough to come see me, but mostly I was painfully embarrassed to be seen in that milieu, with all the other crazy people.

Soon it was December, Christmastime in New York, which for me invoked plangent memories of loneliness and terror. I grew frustrated about getting anywhere with my misfiring emotions. I'd overhear chatter about intractable patients being sent to Pilgrim State Hospital out on Long Island — a giant repository for hopeless mental cases — and began to worry that I'd end up there if I didn't show some progress. I began to act out on the ward in ways that got the attention of the nurses and aides. In one art therapy session, we were asked to use crayons to join in creating a group Christmas mural for the hallway of the ward — and then talk about it, of course. To me, the exercise seemed childish and lame. My contribution to the mural was a scene of slavering wolves running down a reindeer on a bloody forest trail. It actually revealed quite a bit about my state of mind. Underneath all those phobias and fears I was ferociously angry about something. But the art therapist just scolded me for it, which revealed the limits of their treatment paradigm.

The staff sometimes took us outside the hospital on excursions. The first one I was allowed to go on was an afternoon trip to the Central Park Zoo with half a dozen of my fellow patients. We rode over in two cabs with a couple of aides. There, they set us loose on our own to visit the various houses of the monkeys, lions, and elephants, with instructions to meet up at the seal pool at a certain time. I talked David, the frail kid from Harvard with the colostomy, into getting a beer with me in the cafeteria. One of the aides caught us doing that and when we returned to the hospital I was scolded with extra severity by the head nurse because, she said, David's condition was inflamed by alcohol. If that was so, David must have known and he hadn't protested. We were actually enjoying ourselves for a change. I became snotty about it and a quarrel with the head nurse ensued, and I began yelling, so they called a couple of aides who tossed me in "the quiet room," which was in effect a padded cell. After a few hours, they let me out, and by then it was bedtime.

Another excursion we made was for an evening show at the posh Sutton theater on 57th Street to see the new hit movie *Butch Cassidy and the Sundance Kid*. As you know, I was a movie buff, and that one was perfectly suited to a young man of my tastes. But I couldn't stay in my seat. I kept on getting up and going out to the lobby, and each time, one of the Payne Whitney aides followed me out and stayed with me until I felt I could return, which lasted only a little while and I was up again. Actually, the problem turned out to be chemical. Dr. Grodin had switched me to another of the crude psychoactive drugs, Stelazine (trifluoperazine), which has now, decades later, been discontinued in many countries (but not the USA). Stelazine induces a reaction called *akathisia*, characterized by intense feelings of inner restlessness. It was exhausting. I was on it for maybe two weeks before the nurses recognized the effect it was having me, and Dr. Grodin took me off it. The intense restlessness only magnified my sense of being seriously mentally ill.

One night before Christmas there was a commotion outside my room. I got up to see what was going on. Down the hall, several aides were grappling with a very large man who was rolled in on a gurney. After a while, they succeeded in stuffing him into the quiet room, where he raised hell shrieking all night long. Besides those early encounters with Randy the LSD zombie, this was the first time that Payne Whitney seemed to me like a classic insane asylum. This new mystery patient remained sequestered in the quiet room for another day, though his shrieking and wailing subsided. He was eventually placed in a regular room, locked in, with an aide stationed in a chair outside his door.

After about a week this person emerged. It was George, a twenty-year-old Hofstra College (Long Island) student brought into the hospital because he was hooked on "reds" — Seconal, a barbiturate that was hell to withdraw from. That's what all the shrieking was about. Now, he was off it, and he was not a raving madman but a very likable and gregarious guy, always laughing and joking, a contrast to the otherwise depressive ambience of the place. Carol, Linda, and Sandy especially liked him. He was tall and good-looking, with long black hair. He was a nice addition to the ward and we got along great.

Through those winter weeks, I had little sense of getting anywhere with my shrink, Dr. Grodin. He was pleasant to talk to, a good listener, of course, but parsimonious in his responses. He didn't venture to just state plainly what he thought was wrong with me and what I could do about it. It's possible he didn't know, couldn't figure me out — though I doubt I presented an especially complex picture. I was cooperative, downright voluble, recounting my life to date, my relations with my parents, my various disappointments and sorrows . . . the divorce at age eight, getting yanked out of the suburbs away from my home and friends to the desolation of the city, my awful junior high school years, my lonesome high school career, the incidents around Christmas of 1965 when I damaged my brain smoking pot . . . and then the joy of leaving the city for college in a little Main Street town far far away upstate . . . and finally the events of the past year leading up to my crack-up in Provincetown.

Young Man Blues

I didn't have any dark secrets. I hadn't done anything vile or shameful besides wrecking a car that my father had just flat-out given me in an extravagant and incongruous gesture I never understood, and I was keenly aware of how bad I felt about the whole affair. I wasn't sexually confused, though by that time I was used to the ongoing orgy that was college life in the hippie age and I was sexually frustrated in Payne Whitney. I confessed to jerking off in the shower. Dr. Grodin said it was okay, everybody does.

On New Year's Eve all the wards were invited to a "party" in a fancy suite upstairs that was normally the staff lounge. It had all those trappings of an Ivy League club, leather furniture, oil paintings on the wall of distinguished doctors of yore. I felt I was hitting the bottom — going nowhere, stuck with my stupid problems, getting fat on the hospital food, and hopeless. There wasn't any liquor for us, of course, just soda and snacks. They'd taken me off that dreadful Stelazine, so I could at least sit still. We weren't allowed to stay up until midnight, when the decade would turn and it would be 1970 — the futuristic date that had jangled my mind when I saw it on the marquee of the Strand Theater the first hour I landed in Brockport. Nineteen seventy, the year of flying cars. The future had arrived and I believed I had no future in it.

Surfacing

After New Year's I was put in another room on the same floor with a new patient for a roommate. This was Charlie, early twenties, but with the demeanor of someone much older. He had a heavy five o'clock shadow like Nixon, and the body of a manual laborer. His hair was a very close buzzcut, which, by that point in the hippie years, was quite rare among young men. He was from Huntington, West Virginia. He moved slowly and very deliberately, kind of robotically. He hardly had anything to say, but not in any sort of hostile way. There was no humor in him, I quickly learned, and not much of any other quality either, no joy, sadness, malice. He was an emotionally empty vessel, only half there, a ghost.

Charlie woke me up the first night we were in the room together. I heard some alarming grunts coming from the floor near my bed. Ambient light from the hall glowed through the window of our door and I looked down to see Charlie on the rug between our beds, doing sit-ups. My watch on the night table said 2:30 in the morning. I asked him why he was working out at that hour. He said matter-of-factly, *Anxiety. It helps.* He didn't stop, though. He just kept doing sets until he exhausted himself and went back to bed. I didn't know if it was reliable information, but the patient rumor mill soon put out a story that Charlie had been shot in the head over in Vietnam, and miraculously survived, but had never recovered all his faculties. By then

Charlie's hair had started growing back in and you couldn't really see any scars on his scalp. We never did have much of a conversation. He was unreachable. I began to understand that I was not as messed up as many other people, and I started to develop an intense desire to get out of the hospital and back to life. Something inside of me was changing.

The other patients on my floor, the three girls, Carol, Sandy, and Linda, and George, diverted themselves by starting little wars with the staff, the aides and the nurses (the doctors were above it all). They'd find something to complain about and hold a half-assed "sit-in" outside the nursing station. I didn't join in on that, seeing student politics turn into mental patient politics. Then, a wealthy and handsome young Brazilian guy was admitted to the unit. This was Jose, a manic depressive who was in an extremely gregarious manic phase of his cycle. He had a glass eye from a yachting injury and he liked to take it out to horrify people. The three girls hung around him like remoras following a great white shark. I began spending more time with David and his record player. He was pretty bottled up emotionally, but we didn't have to talk much. We expressed ourselves through the albums we played. He gravitated toward Nick Drake and the Velvet Underground. I played The Band's eponymous brown album over and over, and the Beatles' *Abbey Road*. The song snippet *Boy, you've got to carry that weight* really got me.

In late January, Dr. Grodin said it was time to invite my parents in for some confab sessions. I was okay with that, wasn't afraid. Dr. Grodin made it clear that the object wasn't to put them on trial, so to speak, and I got what he meant. I didn't know what we'd all ascertain, but it seemed a reasonable thing to do. By then I didn't have any particular agenda. After all that time cooling my heels in the hospital, my old grievances and animosities toward them seemed rote and trite, a tired portfolio of complaint. Everybody on the floor had their repertory of beefs with their parents — as probably everybody on planet earth did — and it all boiled down to: so what? Muriel agreed to come. The staff social worker set up a couple of appointments with her, but Henry apparently refused to cooperate. A few days later Muriel arrived.

Nothing hugely dramatic happened, though. At forty-nine, she was still physically very attractive. Years of success in business had made her confident. She actually wasn't on the hot seat, but she acted as if she was and couldn't suppress her flashes of anger. She was mainly concerned about being blamed for my emotional problems, and she made it clear that she wouldn't take the rap for it. Oddly, by that point, I could understand her point of view. I was twenty-one now, legally an adult. My childhood was over and the statute of limitations on my childhood grievances was over too. I'd been out of the house since 1966 and now it was 1970, and it was up to me to steer whatever course I was on, which she was no longer responsible for. It was all true. The sessions didn't leave us feeling any closer or more affectionate, but we knew where things stood, and it was okay with me. I came to the same conclusion about Henry, even though he never came in. In reality, there was nothing to fight about anymore. I could let it be.

Around that time, Dr. Grodin put me on the antidepressant drug Elavil (amitriptyline). The most noticeable effect was that it took me out of my own head — and the usual churn of preoccupations — and got me to focus powerfully on what was happening outside myself, especially what other people were saying. It was quite an exhilarating feeling of liberation. My anxieties dissolved with all that. Next, I was encouraged to venture out of the hospital solo on day passes for a few hours in the afternoons. I took them up on it, and I managed pretty well. I went to the movies and to the Metropolitan Museum of Art and I did fine out on my own, no panic attacks, no freakouts. In early February Dr. Grodin asked if I felt okay about getting discharged. I said yes. I was ready to return to real life. I'd been in there since early November.

Five days later I was released from Payne Whitney. I didn't dawdle in New York. The night before discharge I went out on an evening pass and had dinner with Bernie and Muriel. We met at Maxwell's Plum, one of those "swinging singles" burger bars on First Avenue a few blocks from the hospital. I was in cheerful, relaxed spirits. Muriel seemed relieved and relaxed too, having been able to level with me, and Bernie was his ever phlegmatic self. They understood that I was eager to put this episode behind me and get to the place I now considered home. It was great to just enjoy a good New York burger and watch the pretty girls come and go. The next morning, I packed my bags early, caught a cab from Payne Whitney to the Port Authority Bus Terminal, and took a Greyhound back upstate to Rochester.

Billy and Tim picked me up in Tim's Volvo and drove me back to Adams Basin. First, they brought me over to the post office and general store to say hello to our landlord, "Rich John," as Billy called him. *Back from the dead*, Rich John joked when we marched in. He'd become sort of an uncle to all of us after three years renting his place. It was very cold out, the heart of winter on the Lake Ontario plain, with snow packed deep in the farm fields and orchards, but the cold was stirring and lovely to me after being indoors most of the winter. The barn was warm as ever inside and it was glorious to be back in the place I felt most comfortable. They'd kept my room, with its brass bed, just as I'd left it, the sheets on and my grandfather's heavy sealskin lap robe from the open cars of the 1920s as my bedspread. The car my father gave me, the beige Opel sedan, was sitting in the attached garage, all repaired and waiting for me. That night, I came back to my normal life as easily as slipping between the sheets, with the furnace humming and snow falling softly outside. The tumult and craziness of 1969 seemed a million miles away and I was in the safest place on earth.

Aftermath

I'd missed registration at the college for the spring semester of 1970 by several weeks. It was okay. I'd have to do my whole senior year all over again starting the coming September. The December just past, the government debuted its new draft lottery for the Vietnam War. Everybody in college lost his student deferment and we were all in the same draft pool with the guys on the assembly lines and down in the lube pit. Among the correspondence that had piled up for me at the barn was a notice that I pulled draft number 353. The lottery was based on the 365 days in the year. They were only drafting guys up into the double digits, and never would get much beyond that. Anyway, my friends assured me that three months in the loony bin would disqualify me from military service royally. I would not be drafted. My first day back I checked into the theater department and said hello to everybody. They were glad to see me, but I could tell they were wondering if I was actually okay. They all knew I'd been in a mental hospital.

Within a week I got myself a job on the loading dock of one of the early "big box" chain stores — the Big N (formerly Rochester-based Neisner's), in a new strip mall just built that summer on the edge of town. We clocked in all the new merchandise from the delivery trucks and stashed it on racks for distribution in the back of the store. It was easy and dumb and I was pulling in about eighty bucks a week, which was a fortune by my standards. I hitchhiked there for a month until I had the money for car insurance. My evenings were free. Even though I wasn't enrolled as a student I got a minor role in the theater department's spring main-stage production, *Dark of the Moon*, set in Appalachia of the nineteenth century about witchy doings among the mountain folk. It was a turkey, but I was happy to be back in showbiz.

The wife of Rick Miller, the department's scene design prof, happened to work in a social service agency in Rochester, and she informed me about a state educational grant program called Vocational Rehab. I apparently qualified as a former mental patient over twenty-one. She helped me fill out the paperwork and I eventually got all the money I needed to cover the do-over of my senior year. I would be finally free of that old, destructive quarrel about money with Henry and Muriel. It was a very mellow and enjoyable spring for me, making money and hanging out with everybody. Nobody cared that I was not a registered student. I audited a bunch of classes and didn't have to turn in any papers or take tests. Anyway, in May, the Kent State massacre happened and every campus in America went berserk for week, including Brockport State. Then, most everybody left for the summer.

In June I enrolled in the summer theater program for three credits and performed in a couple of plays directed by Lou Hetler and Dave Hamiliton — *The Night Thoreau Spent in Jail* and *A Scent of Flowers*, a British parlor drama, now forgotten. Muriel and Bernie actually flew upstate to see me onstage for the first and only time in my college career. It was an awkward visit, but I appreciated the effort. I had a summer girlfriend, Adrienne, but I really couldn't give her the attention she deserved. In September we broke up, and she soon fell in love with one of my friends, a fellow theater major.

Then it was fall. My roommates Billy and Tim had graduated and that spelled the end of the barn in Adams Basin. Much as I'd loved it out there I was ready for a change. I moved to town into a two-bedroom apartment in a fine old house with another theater major, Danny Morris, a sophomore. He was a big athletic Jewish kid from Rochester with a very twisted sense of humor. We became good friends. The apartment was right across Utica Street from the big quad in front of the "old main" building, Hartwell Hall, where I'd acted in plays my freshman and sophomore years. Danny and I spent practically every fall afternoon out there tossing a Frisbee in a big open allée between the ranks of towering maple trees.

You could walk to anything on campus in five minutes from my new place so I decided to sell the car that my father had given me two years before. He'd done that as an act of love, I'm sure, but it had brought me a lot of grief, and the car seemed jinxed to me. I sold it, ironically, to the guy who was the new president of the student government. I lived on that money most of my do-over senior year, plus I got regular monthly checks from Vocational Rehab. It more than covered my tuition and fees.

Since Payne Whitney was months behind me and I was no longer officially "a mental case," I tried communicating with my father by letter. I couldn't bring myself to tell him I'd sold the car, but it was registered in my name by then and I knew he'd never visit me anywhere I lived and discover it was gone, so I said nothing more about it. Henry did reply, at least, but the correspondence never got beyond the formal and superficial, just a young man reporting in occasionally to his father out of some dim sense of duty. He showed no curiosity about what my months in Payne Whitney were about. I had to suppose he felt some blame for my landing there, and resented it. I could accept that. I wasn't any more of a good son than he was a good father — something we both probably recognized. As ever, he didn't show much interest in what I was doing, and he had little to say about his own life, except that he was sick and tired of flying to Antwerp every six weeks to buy diamonds. His stepchildren, Pauline's kids, Jonathan and Madge, had their own adolescent difficulties — the details of which I learned only years later from them — which generated friction in his marriage. Jon was floundering in his freshman year at the Kansas City Art Institute (he would drop out). Madge was a troubled teen who would eventually come out as a lesbian.

My do-over senior year was happy and successful. As a theater major, I didn't perform in any more main-stage productions. By then I was more interested in directing plays than in acting — having absorbed a lot by stage managing — and I spent much of that fall directing scenes that my fellow students had to prepare for their acting classes. I wrote a weekly column for the student newspaper, mainly comic riffs on national politics, Nixon and the War in Vietnam. And as winter came on I started playing in a jug band with two other guys I'd known for some time.

A jug band is just a folk music group with some comic instruments — we used a washtub bass, a washboard, kazoos, spoons, a slide whistle, and we all played guitars. Eric Carlson had been the guy who originally leased the barn in Adams Basin and then dropped out. He was back in school and we started playing music together with Jeff Love, a dropout who was working the loading dock at the college receiving department.

We called ourselves the Rocky Mountain Spotted Fever Boys and we practiced in a big attic in the Victorian house Jeff lived in. All of us could sing, and we switched around on the novelty instruments.

As it happened, we got pretty good and began playing at college events and in bars around Rochester. That occupied me into the spring, when I had to prepare my senior project, which was directing a play called *The Great American Desert* by Joel Oppenheimer. It was a burlesque about three cowpoke desperados on the run on the Great Plains, surrounded by hostile Indians, waiting to be picked off and killed. We played it as a very broad comedy. The jug band furnished the incidental music. That was it. In May, I finished my finals and didn't hang around Brockport for graduation. I had no idea what I was going to do. But I was pretty well pasted together psychologically and ready to go out into the world. I did not know that I was not quite done with having to grow up.

Part Five

Into the World

I was twenty-two when I graduated from Brockport State College in the spring of 1971. My do-over senior year was happy and successful — by some miracle I made the dean's list for academic distinction. I had no recurrences of my old struggles with anxiety and panic. I thought I was over all that. But I'd learn that I was still quite a ways from being a full-functioning, psychologically autonomous adult and the next two years would be rough ride ending in revelatory transformation. It's said that the judgment region of a male human being's brain doesn't reach full development until age twenty-four-or-five. My experience confirmed that.

Before graduation, which I didn't intend to stick around for, I packed up all my stuff, shipped boxes of my college books back to New York, said a tearful goodbye to the little college town that I'd felt so at home in, and returned to scary old New York City — on the Amtrak out of Rochester this time, which, bad as it had become, was still luxurious compared to the Greyhound bus. I hadn't a clue where or how to make a start at my adult life. I'd dismissed the idea of graduate school since getting drafted was no longer a threat. I was immediately at loose ends in the city.

I was, of course, profoundly uneasy bunking back in my childhood home. Bernie and Muriel seemed less than thrilled having me there too — they'd turned my old bedroom into a den with a convertible sofa for guests. After a couple of days, Muriel suggested I travel down to Washington, DC, where her brother, my uncle Buddy, the CIA spook, was back from Europe working in the agency's home office over in Virginia, with his family ensconced in a nice Georgetown row house. I had a dim idea about maybe getting an entry job in some federal department, say, the Bureau of Indian Affairs, but once I arrived on the scene I didn't bother inquiring anywhere. It was too intimidating, and I sensed that a life in bureaucracy was not for me. Dashing and charming as he was, Uncle Buddy gave me no help, or introductions, or even advice. I floundered around the museums and mausoleums of the city for a week, went for walks in Dumbarton Oaks Park with my cute seventeen-year-old cousin Jai, and finally vamoosed back to New York to start over.

A friend from Fire Island just my age named Jody — the son of one of Muriel's old pregnancy pals from the summer of 1948 — had an apartment way uptown around Columbia U, where he was a grad student. He was looking to sublet it for the summer and I offered to take it, though I still had painfully ambivalent feelings about even trying to make a life back in my old hometown. The place was a spacious two-bedroom dump facing the air shaft with junk furniture on a strange little two-block-long Street called Tiemann Place between Broadway and Riverside Park, just west of where 125th Street makes a northwest bend. There was nothing Ivy League about the neighborhood — it was Harlem, poor and menacing.

Somehow, I got an old High School of Music and Art friend, Jonathan Fast (son of the novelist and screenwriter Howard Fast who scripted the movie *Spartacus*, etc.), to go in on it with me. Jon had just graduated from Princeton and he wanted to study electronic music with the pioneer composer Milton Babbitt at Columbia. I had enough money left over from the school year to carry me for a couple of months. At least I was out of my childhood home.

Of course, I wanted to become a professional writer — that F. Scott Fitzgerald fantasy still flickered in my brain like an old black-and-white movie — but I had no idea where or how to start. The jejune short stories I'd churned out seemed embarrassing now. I had little experience in the so-called *real world* and I could hardly produce anything an adult would want to read. But I was brash, and as soon I got squared away in Jody's uptown dump I ventured back to midtown, wandered into the editorial offices of *New York* magazine — there were no security obstacles then — and breezed straight into editor in chief Clay Felker's office uninvited, where I presented a folder of my college newspaper column clippings and inquired about a job. Luckily, Mr. Felker was amused by all this. He invited me to have a seat and we chatted for maybe ten minutes. He said he didn't have any jobs at the moment for a person such as myself, but he actually picked up the phone and called a TV producer he knew who was assembling a team of writers for a new show and instructed me to go over to a certain suite at the Plaza Hotel a few blocks away and talk to the guy.

Could it be *this* easy to launch a career, I wondered? Of course not. But I went over to the posh Plaza on 59th and Fifth Avenue with my folder of college clippings and had an interview. The project was the pilot show for an infotainment vehicle to star David Frost, the British TV personality and sometime satirist. I tried to be clever and witty with the producer, name forgotten, and he said, *Thanks, we'll be in touch*. I floated out of there thinking I would start working as a professional TV writer in a few days. I tried really hard to convince myself that I'd like living in New York, fantasized about getting an apartment of my own — though no neighborhood I knew of on the whole island of Manhattan appealed me — and imagined making friends with clever people in TV landlike the types I'd known in childhood from my parents' circle of friends.

That began a nauseating intermezzo up at the Tiemann Place dump just sitting around waiting for the phone to ring. I patiently stood by for a week, and after hearing nothing I called the TV producer. I had to remind him who I was — not a good sign — but he said something like, *Oh, yeah, well, we're still talking to people, but we'll get back to you.* That went on for another week. That Friday I called the Plaza again and the desk informed me that Mr. TV Producer was no longer there, and they couldn't tell me where to reach him. I sadly concluded they'd just jerked me off all that time and I was stunned at the callous cruelty of professionals in the lively arts.

By sheer coincidence, that weekend I got a message from Muriel to call my college friend Al Harmon, who'd tried to get hold of me at 68th Street. Al was running a summer theater upstate in Geneseo, another SUNY college town about forty miles south of Brockport.

He'd acted in the senior project I directed and he offered me a job directing Shakespeare's *A Midsummer Night's Dream*. I jumped at the chance to get out of New York City for the summer, bailed on Jon Fast and the apartment on Tiemann Place, and *rode the dog* (Greyhound bus) back upstate.

For the next month I slept on Al's sofa in Geneseo and worked on the play. They'd rented the college's theater, which would have otherwise sat idle for the summer. Two afternoons a week we toured a children's play, *Rumpelstiltskin*, staring Al, to little towns and institutions around western New York to make money to operate our main shows in Geneseo. I was deliriously happy to be back in a small upstate town focusing diligently on something I loved to do and was pretty good at. The play came together nicely, though I developed a crush on the young woman who played Titania and couldn't get anywhere with her. The actors were all good enough. Then, the night of our technical rehearsal, for setting the light and sound cues, Al announced that the company was broke, box office for the other plays had been disappointing, and he couldn't pay us anymore. He said we could still put on *A Midsummer Night's Dream* because the rent was all prepaid on the use of the theater, but he'd understand if people wanted to leave. Most of them opted to split, so the show did not go on. This turned out to be the end of my career in showbiz.

I didn't know what to do with myself at that point. I called Billy Grant, my old roommate from the Adams Basin barn. He was back in Brockport living in an apartment over a store on Main Street, taking some graduate courses and working over at the college loading dock with Jeff Love, my old bandmate from the Rocky Mountain Spotted

Fever Boys. I told him I was at loose ends. Billy, always sympathetic and generous, invited me to crash at his place. So I retreated back to the town I thought I'd left for good only a few months earlier. It felt like a defeat, but I was not desperate, just conscious of needing to regroup in a comfortable setting.

Billy's apartment had a big front room and I bought a cheap old mattress to sleep on there. I got a job bartending a couple of nights a week at a fraternal lodge in town, making just enough money to feed myself. Days, alone in the apartment, I spent pounding out more short stories on my old Smith-Corona, and sending them to the big magazines that still published fiction. It gave me enough of a sense of purpose to carry on cheerfully. This was pretty much what an aspiring young writer was supposed to do, I thought: work alone in a crummy apartment with barely a few dollars to live on. The life was supposed to be hard and dismal. It would give you something to talk about years later, when you finally had it made in the shade.

I got back a raft of rejection notes, including an encouraging one from a young *Esquire* editor named Amanda "Binky" Urban, who would eventually become a leading literary agent. It was for a short story about a rock and roll star titled "The Nova" that, years later, I would turn into my novel *The Life of Byron Jaynes*. I kept at the writing routine through the fall and into the winter, getting nowhere. Christmas came and went.

At that time, my stepfather Bernie Glaser was working as the East Coast PR rep for the distribution arm of Avco-Embassy Pictures, which had put out hit movies such as *The Graduate*, *The Producers*, and *The Lion in Winter*. He would accompany stars on publicity road trips for interviews with newspapers and TV stations. He knew I was struggling back upstate. I talked on the phone with him more than I did with my actual parents because he had started out after the war with literary ambitions of his own and he took vicarious interest in my travails. He knew the publisher of a successful weekly hippie paper called *Boston After Dark* with whom he'd regularly schmooze for movie publicity, and he'd set up an introduction for me if I would go to Boston. I took him up on it.

Another old college theater crony named Martin Hart was living in Boston and he generously offered to let me crash at his apartment in the Brighton neighborhood. Marty and his roommate Neil, who I didn't know, picked me up at the bus station in downtown Boston in Marty's car. It was early January. Christmas was over but the holiday lights were still strung up everywhere. It was hard otherwise to make anything out in the winter darkness and the journey out Commonwealth Avenue seemed hallucinatory. I knew nothing about the city, had been to Boston only once, in 1957, when the little kids of Camp Annisquam were taken to a Red Sox game at Fenway Park.

I had an appointment with Steve Mindich, the publisher of *Boston After Dark* (known as BAD), the next day. The office was on the grungier side of Back Bay, just south of I-90 on Boylston Street off Mass Avenue. I wore a three-piece chalk-stripe suit, the best outfit I owned. I got it at the Salvation Army store in Rochester the year I was elected student government president, to give me the look of a serious person. Now it helped me make the statement that I was not just another feckless hippie. Mindich himself tried to be a snappy dresser. He was notoriously short and the staff used to make cracks behind his back that his suits were made from his mom's old living room drapes. He was affable enough, but passed me off quickly to an editor named Ben Gerson, a lithe fellow with a bushy Jewish afro, who took me into his cubicle. Ben was BAD's music editor, a very important position, as the long-playing record had become the official art form of our generation. He gave me a copy of Yoko Ono's new solo album, titled *Fly*, and told me write a short review, five hundred words, maximum.

I listened to it at Marty's apartment — it was a pastiche of irritatingly weird noises, hardly musical — and I knocked out a snarky review, summing up the album as "insectile." Ben liked the little item, ran it in the next week's issue, and gave me more records to review. That first professional piece earned me five dollars, which in those days could get you a complete meal at a so-so restaurant. I picked up a little more money subbing for Neil in his night job at a commercial bakery in Allston when he wanted to go to a rock and roll show. The job was a mindless eight-hour shift packing baked goods in boxes as they came off an automated line. But you could stuff yourself all night long on broken blueberry muffins and hermit bars. They were warm, right out of the factory oven.

Otherwise, I didn't hang out with Marty or Neil and it was shaping up to be a pretty lonely existence. One night, after more than a week in town, I ventured into a busy nightspot in Back Bay and managed to schmooze up a stunning redhead named Katherine, or Kitty, who, at six feet, was a couple of inches taller than me. She was a couple of years older, too, divorced, working as a schoolteacher. She took me home to her apartment in Somerville that night and a few days later I moved in.

She was a wonderful girl and, of course, I was completely unprepared to be anyone's regular boyfriend, but that's what I suddenly was.

My existence stabilized overnight. I had a place to come home to. Kitty was a kind and intelligent companion and I didn't have to waste any energy chasing girls in the bars, which allowed me to concentrate on my professional aspirations. Anyway, at that point, I couldn't have made a regular thing of buying anyone drinks. Kitty had a long commute back from her teaching job down in Brockton, and I almost always put dinner on the table — I enjoyed cooking, and was pretty good at it — or else we frequented a cheap Chinese joint off Harvard Square where they served combo plates for a buck and a half, plus all the tea you could drink. I began to understand the value of routines in an otherwise chaotic writer's life.

Within a few weeks of landing in Boston I was promoted, so to speak, to writing feature stories, longer color pieces about Boston lowlife. Most of the regular writers on BAD covered political issues, or politicized whatever they wrote about, including the arts. The *revolution* — the hippie amalgam of sex, drugs, rock and roll, and radical politics — ruled the zeitgeist of Boston and Cambridge, with their huge college-age populations. The Vietnam War was still galumphing along, and the military draft with it, a major sore point with draft-eligible youth (which, it's worth repeating, didn't include me on account of my high lottery number and, as a fallback, the three months I'd spent in a loony bin, making me mentally unfit for the army).

But the *revolution* didn't interest me. I did not believe in overthrowing capitalism — which to me was just people doing business. The revolutionaries of the day wanted to replace that with an idealized, benevolent government taking care of everybody one way or another, so as to banish all inequality and hardship — an odd belief for people who were otherwise antigovernment. As for the Vietnam War, it looked like it would end in its own good time. I liked rock and roll, at least a select range of it. And I had all the sex I required.

Teddy Gross, the editor in chief of BAD, was a few months younger than me, an intellectual prodigy from a high-achieving family of doctors and physicists who was barely out of Brandeis University. But he had an impressive air of authority in his job, as if he were born in a newsroom. He took an interest in what I was churning out for Ben Gerson, and started pitching story ideas to me. The first one was based on an ad he'd seen in a regional law enforcement magazine: someone claiming to be a "Rent-a-Narc" for hire. Narcs were undercover agents, usually freelance private-eye types, hired by local police forces to mix with local hippies and set up drug busts. Teddy told me to go check him out, that there might be a story there.

This character, who actually proclaimed himself to be one "James Bond," after the Ian Fleming hero, ran a phone number in his ad. I called him right up, told him straight out that I was a reporter from BAD, got an address in Waltham, and took a bus and a taxi to a crummy garden apartment where I found him. This was the point where I learned a valuable, basic lesson about journalism. Much of the time, people you seek to write about are completely cooperative, even if they're engaged in shady activities. They're flattered that a newspaper wants a story about them. They think they're going to be a star! They'll tell you all kinds of things, often self-incriminating. This sort of journalism — feature writing — is essentially a hustle. That didn't stop me from pursuing it. I didn't suffer any moral quandaries — getting the story, however you could get it, just came with the territory.

It was clear after about ten minutes with "James Bond," a portly slob about thirty, with an out-of-date Beatles mod haircut, still in his pajamas at one o'clock in the afternoon, that I was in the presence of a colorful whack job. He regaled me with fantastic vignettes of his exploits around New England infiltrating hippie communes and small-town drug scenes, apparently the hero of a movie that was running in his head. I spent several hours interviewing him, recording every crazy utterance as best I could in a reporter's notepad (I didn't have a tape recorder). He even showed me his impressive collection of firearms, including some machine guns, surely illegal in that state, though he claimed to have a special license on account of being a private eye. He waved them around so recklessly that I actually got spooked being in his line of fire. As to his flashy name, he told me he'd changed it officially in the probate court. The story was so extravagant it wrote itself that night, back home in Somerville at Kitty's place.

After it came out, I fell into a routine of hunting down my own stories, not waiting for assignments. I thought of my realm as the freak-show beat. I had the dark underbelly of the city all to myself with everybody else at BAD fixated on politics. It was a marvelous opportunity. Teddy Gross was a fan, but the editorial staff under him generally regarded me with suspicion, as if I was as much of a whack job as the freaks I was writing about. The one person who befriended me was John Koch, the BAD movie critic, who drove an MG sports car and took me along to movies with him some afternoons. We had a similar sense of humor and a disdain for radical poseurs. We were both baseball fans and went to a lot of Red Sox games. Back then, you could get a decent seat in Fenway Park for five bucks.

Day after day, I explored the Boston metro area on foot hunting for more whack jobs to write about, and by some miracle of serendipity I found one after another: a transvestite cabaret performer, a mafia hit man, a loan shark operating out of a sandwich joint under a Southeast Expressway ramp, a rookie charter fishing boat captain who took me out to sea in the backwash of Hurricane Agnes and almost sank us, an elderly couple who had been picketing outside the statehouse for two decades after their home was condemned for the I-90 interstate in the 1950s, a maniac who briefly took me hostage at gunpoint and dragged me down to city hall where he said he was fixing to shoot Mayor Kevin White. (I managed to get loose from him in the lobby and he was apprehended before he could carry out the deed.) BAD paid something like fifty bucks per story I wrote. It made for a marginal existence. I kept waiting for people to notice that I was worth more than that, but I had no way to leverage that wish.

Around Easter time, looking to make more money, I spent three weeks working in an operation called Term Papers Unlimited, with the idea of writing about the experience. (They didn't know that.) The company was located in a crummy suite above a Hayes-Bickford cafeteria on Huntington Avenue, near Northeastern University. We took orders from colleges all over the country. Most of the "work" was churned out by freelancers who picked up assignments from a big ledger book in the hall and wrote their papers at home. I was installed in a big room on the premises called "the tank" with five other writers who did the assignments that the freelancers wouldn't take. The pay was two dollars a page for freshman and sophomore level, two-fifty for junior and senior, three dollars for master's level, three-fifty for a master's thesis, and four bucks a page for doctoral dissertations.

The faster you wrote the more you got paid, of course. The outfit had a "quality control" guy named Dale, who had to approve everything that came out of the tank. But I learned quickly that he almost never rejected a paper unless it had a ketchup stain on it. I made much more money toiling in the tank — sometimes more than two hundred bucks a week — than I'd made covering the freak-show beat for BAD. But on top of being altogether intellectually dishonest, the job was psychologically brutal, like living in a kind of perpetual finals hell week where the studying never ended — and I never was much of a scholar. The tank had a certain warped camaraderie. It was all men, no girls, so that eliminated certain distractions. They considered themselves knights of bullshit, heroically undermining "the system." There was even a guy on staff whose job was to go around to the various college libraries and steal books we needed. (The internet didn't exist in 1972, of course, and we wrote on typewriters.) I tackled a wild array of subjects from *French Attitudes about the American Civil War* to *Race Relations at the University of Kentucky* (the client sent a few copies of the student newspaper for reference, and I made up all sorts of fictional vignettes around the names of people and buildings).

Three weeks was all that I could take of Term Papers Unlimited, and anyway I wanted to get back to my real calling, creative journalism. I quit on a Friday after getting my pay envelope (cash money, no taxes withheld), and handed in my story about the experience to Teddy Gross on Monday. Later that year, the Massachusetts state legislature shut down the term paper industry altogether after holding hearings on the matter. Two Harvard students had handed in identical papers in a class and a dean blew the whistle for the politicians to *do something, dammit!* The owner of Term Papers Unlimited testified that his company "simply sold research materials that came in a form that resembled term papers." Nobody believed that bullshit. The industry was put out of business and, I suppose, went back underground.

It was a huge relief to get back to my routine of hunting for colorful crazy people around town. That summer, I did my one political story of the year: I covered the annual John Birch Society convention at the Park Plaza hotel. Its big meet-up was held in Boston every year because it was convenient for the group's elderly founder, Robert Welch, of the Boston candy company that made Sugar Daddy and Junior Mints, who lived in suburban Arlington, Mass. I ran the idea past Teddy Gross, but he declined it because the paper had covered the annual Bircher jamboree before. So I pitched the story to BAD's competitor *The Phoenix*, another hippie weekly across the Charles River in Cambridge, headquartered off Harvard Square, whose staff was even more rabidly political than BAD's, and, it turned out, humorless too. *The Phoenix* competed with BAD for readers and advertising but had a lesser circulation. By then, I had a load of clippings from my work at BAD, so I was given a green light on the John Birch Society. I turned in a darned good story, but the editors hassled me remorselessly over the gags and ended up surgically excising the comedy so completely that I would have pulled it, except I needed the money. And, ironically, I never did get paid, though the editors ran it.

That summer, *The Phoenix* went through a staff labor rebellion, creating an opportunity for BAD's publisher, Steve Mindich, to swoop in and buy it — not two weeks after my story on the Birchers had come out. As it happened, all he ended up buying was the paper's name, because *The Phoenix* staff moved their entire operation down the street and started up a new rag they peevishly called *The Real Paper*, which actually managed to stay in business a whole decade afterward. I ended up not being able to write anything for it, however, since the editors discovered my heart wasn't in *the revolution*. So I was stuck with BAD.

I came into the BAD office (now calling itself the *Boston Phoenix*) only to drop off my stories and I hardly got to know any of the staff besides Ben and Teddy. And by then John Koch had gone over to the *Boston Globe*. Anyway, I operated on the fringe of the paper in a way that was somewhat analogous to the margins of society inhabited by the characters I wrote about. But I yearned fiercely to get a regular staff job with a salary. As a freelancer, I could produce a major feature story every week, but if it was held over another week for lack of space because not enough ads were sold to run x-number of pages, I wouldn't get paid until the damn thing finally ran. I'd be broke for a week. It was a very discommoding arrangement. It irked and depressed me.

The situation also ate away at my romance with Kitty, because I was unable to contribute equally on the rent and other expenses. It was demeaning. I didn't fool around with other women, or act out in an underhanded way, but I began to resent being tied into a relationship that I was not successful enough, not mature enough, to be worthy of. I found ways of signaling my discontent and in August of '72 I moved out. She was a good sport about it, apparently realizing I was not husband material. I'd already resorted to getting a "real" job working nights, waiting on tables at the Orson Welles theater / restaurant / nightclub complex on Mass Avenue, so I was able to rent a place of my own. I got a studio in a prewar redbrick building on Cambridge Street, a few blocks from Harvard Yard.

I can't say it was a mistake to break up with Kitty — I couldn't stand feeling like a mooch — but I didn't appreciate how stable my life with her was until I sabotaged it, and then I was dreadfully alone in a city that was cold and alienating. Working all night and pounding the pavement for stories days was wearing me out and my nerves started fraying again in the old familiar way: I was getting phobic, anxious, and panicky, much in the same way that I'd begun to crack up in Provincetown three years earlier. It started to interfere with my job at the Orson Welles. One night, I was so freaked out I had to flee the restaurant during the dinner rush and take myself to the Cambridge Hospital ER.

The ER doctor calmed me down and gave me the address of a public mental health service in town where I could talk to a shrink. I went over there the next day and got assigned to a middle-aged lady with a heavy Germanic accent, name forgotten. Dr. Who, let's call her. I told her my story about the Payne Whitney episode, and my further travails the past year in Boston. She wrote out a script for Stelazine, the crude antipsychotic med I'd also been given back in New York.

The following week, perhaps as a result of a pep talk from the shrink Dr. Who, I asked Teddy Gross for a meeting. He lived in over Cambridge too, and he met me in the Orson Welles bar on his way home, before I worked the dinner shift. I made my case for getting a regular staff job on the *Boston Phoenix*. I told him that working nights was preventing me from doing my best to find stories and I really wanted to put all my energy into writing for the paper. He looked across the table for a drawn-out moment, as if I was some kind of hard-to-size-up curiosity, and finally he said he didn't know if I was "a small giant or a tall dwarf" of a writer — which struck me as a dubious compliment. But he agreed to my proposal of an arrangement where I would get paid a weekly retainer of seventy-five bucks a week, whether a story of mine was held over or what. I couldn't have a cubicle at the office, he said, because they were already hard up for space, but I didn't care about that. Teddy said he'd check with Mindich and let me know. I was cosmically relieved and uplifted, like the day that Clay Felker of *New York* magazine sent me to the Plaza Hotel to launch my career as a TV writer that never was, and I felt I was on my way to something stable and consequential.

Mindich okayed the deal, but that new disposition of things didn't last two weeks. There was some kind of uproar at the office — though with no indication it involved bringing me on board, just an awful coincidence — and Teddy Gross quit. His replacement was his assistant, a then new species of hardcore feminist who didn't appreciate my brand of humor one little bit. She made that clear when I ventured into the office looking to pick up a weekly check and see where things stood. That $75-a-week deal, which was strictly a verbal agreement between me and Teddy, had been canceled. Suddenly I was in an even worse position than before, with a new editor who didn't want to publish what I wrote and no other prospects that I could see.

Meanwhile I veered sideways into a weird medical crisis. I was increasingly experiencing a supernatural sense of physical restlessness. I could not sit still, could barely remain in one place, couldn't concentrate. It stole up on me sneakily. This went with a siege of terrible insomnia, which amplified those uncomfortable pangs of restlessness. It was diabolical. Once again, I thought I was going completely crazy. I got fired from my job at the Orson Welles restaurant because the restlessness had driven me to bolt again in the middle of a dinner shift. I was so desperate I went back to the emergency room. There, a canny ER doc figured out what was going on with me and pretty quickly too. The maddening restlessness was a recognized side effect of the tranquilizer Stelazine that Dr. Who put me on. It transpired that Stelazine had to be given with a kind of partner drug, Artane (trihexyphenidyl), that mitigated those side effects.

That very night, with a dose of Artane, all the maddening discomfort ebbed away, just like that, and I finally got a good night's sleep. The next day I felt physically normal again for the first time in weeks. I flushed the Stelazine down the toilet and I quit Dr. Who too, but not before I had a final session where I reamed her out for not knowing what she was doing with pharmaceuticals. It was a tremendous relief to feel okay again. I was, at least, able to address my practical problems, mainly finding some new outfit that would pay me to write for them.

A monthly glossy called *Boston* magazine had started up — kind of a pale imitation of Felker's *New York* mag — and I wangled an assignment (not my idea) to write about the Parker Brothers company up in Salem, Mass, which put out the ever popular Monopoly board game. It was not a good match for my talents. It became obvious quickly enough that *Boston* mag only wanted to publish puff pieces —flattering feel-good stories — and that did not interest me.

I was desperate again. But at least now I could concentrate and sit at a desk for more than five minutes. With no other prospects, I turned to rewriting a bunch of short stories I'd produced over the years about kids at a summer camp, aimed at fashioning it into a novel. The rest of August and into the fall I stuck at that task in my hot studio apartment while a public works crew ran jackhammers outside the window on Cambridge Street for some kind of under-the-sidewalk pipeline job.

I finished the novel in early October when I turned twenty-four and sent a Xerox copy out to the first name on a list of New York literary agents that I'd dug out of the Cambridge library. I did not know enough yet to send out a short and concise letter of inquiry *before* mailing an unsolicited manuscript that was liable to end up lost in a slush pile. And, of course, I had no idea how long I might have to wait for a response. I suppose I thought I might just get lucky, that an agent would read the first page, discover instantly that my novel was a work of comic genius, and, the next thing, I'd be wined and dined at the Four Seasons by some tweedy avuncular editor who would become my Maxwell Perkins.

So I hunkered down to wait for lightning to strike, waiting for that magic life-changing letter, and since I was dead broke, I got a job working the cash register at the Coop, Harvard's huge bookstore on Harvard Square,. The job imprinted in me a deep sympathy for cashiers everywhere and ever since. The Coop gig got more dismal with each passing day as nothing from any New York agent turned up in the day's mail, and my byline was unwanted by the *Phoenix*. My prospects, in Boston, had dimmed to near zero.

One cold, rainy morning after Halloween, leaving the muffin shop on Brattle Street where I always got breakfast, I turned the corner at Mass Avenue, walked past the Harvard Coop instead of clocking in for work, and kept walking through Harvard Yard and all its moiling scholars back to my wretched apartment, where I made a phone call. It was pretty clear that Boston was done with me — actually had been for some time, though I had not gotten the message — and now I surprised myself to realize that I was done with Boston.

Part Six

Everything You Like

The person I called that November day in 1972 when I gave up on Boston was Bob Denning in Brockport, New York. Bob, you might recall, had an important job on the college staff, director of campus planning, at a time when the SUNY system was expanding hugely. We'd been friends since 1966, when he first got hired and, on the side, began acting in and directing plays that I also appeared in. He was a theater nut. He was also an unusually generous and sympathetic person, eager to help his friends, and when I told him I had washed out in Boston and had no place to go, he said, "Come here, we'll get it all sorted out."

I left my few belongings in the Cambridge apartment, which was paid up for the month, and bought a bus ticket — *riding the dawg* again — back to my college town. It was a long ride, probably eight hours with stops in Worcester, Albany, Syracuse, and Rochester. In addition to a suitcase, I was weighed down by a throbbing sense of failure, a mix of shame, anger, despair, and wonder that my career in Boston, which began so brightly, had ended so ignominiously. That cargo of negativity was lightened a little by the yearning I felt about returning to the place where, mostly, I'd lived the happiest years of my life.

When the bus finally dropped me on Main Street in front of Lou's Breakfast Bar — where I'd eaten scrambled eggs and toast a hundred times — it was already dark, and a bitter November wind was cutting across the Lake Ontario flatland. It was a weeknight and few students were out and about. I called Bob from a pay phone on the street and his station wagon pulled up to the curb ten minutes later. He was in his early forties by then, settled and happy, getting a bit burly, with an air of patient humor. He and family had recently sold the raised ranch house they bought on arrival in 1966 and moved into an enormous Victorian farmhouse on several acres a couple of miles west of town. It was an ornately decorated Italianate foursquare with a cupola on top, very grand. Bob informed me on the way home that I could stay as long as I needed to. As we drove past the familiar scenes of my college years, a feeling of immense calm flushed through me, as if this was the first time in a year I could relax.

Bob's new place was quite a scene when we got there. His wife, Margie, a primary school teacher, and his two kids, Scott, ten, and Holly, eight, were on hand. Bob's elderly mother, Grace, was living with them. And Bob's cousin Craig, just back from Vietnam, and one of his war buddies, Richard, were also there. The whole gang was bustling to clean up after dinner, a reassuring whirl of group activity to someone who had been alone for a while. The kitchen smelled like fresh bread — cousin Craig had become a baking freak. Margie put together a plate for me and sat me down at the kitchen table. Nobody doted on me, which was a relief, but the kids were very friendly and curious. I hadn't been around kids since I was a camp counselor, and it was pleasing to rediscover how full of fun they were. Eventually, they were all off to other parts of the huge house, and Bob steered me into a room set up as a den or study.

He knew all about my interlude in the Payne Whitney Clinic in '69, of course, so I didn't have to explain a whole lot about my mental state. He understood I was hurting. He was a better head shrinker than the doctors I knew over the years, and he cut right to the heart of the matter without getting bogged down in side trips down Neurosis Lane. I recounted the events of the year past, and how I'd flopped on the Boston hippie newspaper scene. What did I mean by "flop," he asked. I said, not being able to support myself writing, not getting any recognition, and finally getting bounced off of the *Phoenix* by the new editor. He told me that this was the time in a person's life, when you're young, to get a taste of failure. Most people who ever amounted to anything flopped when they were starting out, sometimes many times. It showed that you had tried to accomplish something, maybe something difficult and meaningful.

I'd gotten myself wound up, so I just reiterated my sob story about how I put out a big effort and got tossed aside like a banana skin. Bob told me that President Kennedy used to say *life is unfair*. He added that maybe JFK knew something about his hometown, Boston. Bob said he personally thought it was snooty, stuck up, and infested with too many college professors. It was famous as a city where plays bombed in their out-of-town tryouts, even some quite good plays. *Maybe*, he said, *it was just the wrong place, the wrong time for you. I'm sure you learned a lot from it, though. It's just too soon to tell.* Maybe, I agreed, but I couldn't think of anything I learned from the past year, except that talent doesn't seem to matter. *Oh, it matters*, he said, *but you're much better off not becoming an overnight sensation. That can really ruin you.*

I was annoyed by how self-pitying I sounded, and both of us were exhausted, so we let it go at that. It left me with a lot to think about, and feeling somewhat relieved, having puked a lot of angst out of my brain. Bob was right: I'd always assumed I would be an overnight sensation as a writer — apparently drawing the wrong lesson from my adolescent infatuation with the career of F. Scott Fitzgerald. Anyway, I was still alive, still somewhat sane, still young, with a future, and at least I came out of Boston with a really nice portfolio of newspaper clippings that showed what I could do, if another opportunity came along. Bob gave me some blankets and a pillow and I sacked out on the sofa there in the den.

It was a Friday when I arrived back in Brockport, and the week ahead was Thanksgiving. I didn't do much, except catch some rides into town and revisit old scenes, take long walks along the canal in the brisk fall weather, so happy to be back in rural, small-town America, away from the expressionist horror movie that Boston had become for me. Naturally, I dropped in on the theater department and said hello to Lou Hetler, the chairman, but when he asked what I was doing back in town I didn't have a good answer, and it depressed me. Dave Hamilton wasn't around, but I never got over the feeling that I'd disappointed him, so it was probably better we didn't run into each other. Anyway, all the students were about to head home for the holiday, and the college was winding down for the break. Something else turned up, though.

Two guys who were townies, Tim and Archie, childhood friends, same age as me, had opened a big bookshop on Main Street in the old Western Auto Parts store. Tim's father was an executive in Rochester, Kodak or Bausch & Lomb, I'm not sure. Tim had been a theater major at Boston University but dropped out. My senior year he sometimes came around our theater department and we got to know each other. Archie's father was the town veterinarian, large animals, dairy cows and horses. They were one of the few Jewish families in Brockport. Archie had graduated from McGill up in Montreal. I also knew Archie's younger brother, David, with whom I had acted in *A Scent of Flowers* during the summer session of 1970, after I got out of the mental hospital. Without a whole lot else to do, I gravitated to the bookstore that idle week and became reacquainted with Tim and Archie. Their business was instantly successful because they made a deal with the college to sell textbooks. They were both single and lived in a rented three-bedroom house along the Erie Canal east of town and it happened that their third roommate Geoff was about to move to another part of the country. They asked if I was interested in taking his place. I said, yes, I was.

Thanksgiving was festive at Bob and Margie Denning's house, with that extended family and the kids, and a big rumpus in the kitchen, everybody assigned to some task. I got a lesson in bread making from cousin Craig. It was gratifying to be part of a family for a normal holiday.

I had another one-on-one session with Bob in the den that weekend. He was just checking in to see how I was doing. I was, of course, still pretty fuzzy about the immediate future, but I wasn't freefalling anymore. He asked me to draw up a list of *"everything you like,"* and to keep it with me and read it over at least three times a day. I didn't think much of the exercise at the time, but I kept a slip of paper in my wallet with the top ten items, and I reread it faithfully for weeks to come in a sort of obsessive-compulsive way, like a repeating a prayer. I believe it had a subtle and favorable effect on my mind. Early the week after the holiday Bob came home from his office at the college and said he had a tip on a job I might be interested in. A local newspaper operation in neighboring Spencerport was looking for an employee — editorial, with some other duties.

I called the place the next day and was asked to come in for an interview. Cousin Craig lent me his beater Chevy Impala. I wore a corduroy jacket with leather elbow patches and a rep tie, presenting myself as a mature professional. The outfit was called the *Suburban News*, situated in a homely cinder-block building built purely for functionality, on the edge of Spencerport, another little main street canal town a little closer to Rochester. The *Suburban News* was actually a chain of four small-town papers, identical except for a different front page and centerfold for each town. The publisher, let's call him Edgar McPhail, was a gentleman in his mid-sixties with a strikingly scrofulous red bulbous nose that suggested alcoholism. He didn't say much. His wife, Pat, apparently the driving wheel of the outfit, did most of the talking, all business, rather fierce in demeanor, like a bird of prey.

They were looking for a writer / editor, she said, someone to fill the pages with copy, much of which came in the form of press releases from all the local town offices, fraternal organizations, clubs, schools. I'd have to rewrite them, make them coherent. I would also have to pick up advertisements from the various businesses in the four towns scattered around Monroe County and, incidentally, pick up news items from them that could be developed into stories. I could do that, I said. I brought along my folder of clippings from Boston in the Mark Cross leather portfolio that was my college graduation present from Muriel. They just flipped through the clips without reading anything, apparently impressed that my byline was sure enough right there on the page — but not interested in the stories. They said the pay would be eighty dollars a week. *That your car out there?* Pat asked, pointing through the front window at the Impala, with rust all along the wheel wells and rocker panel and the outside mirror on the driver's side missing. I told them it was borrowed from friend. Pat looked me up and down, as if trying figure out an actuarial equation, and eventually she said there was a lot of driving involved in the job, and I'd have the use of a company car that I could take home with me. That was electrifying. It solved so many problems instantly. They asked if I could start the next day. I said sure.

I worked the rest of that week learning the ropes. Edgar gave me the keys to the company car with a warning about using it for "joyriding." It was a 1969 gold Dodge Dart with about forty-odd thousand miles on it. The car had an automatic transmission, an AM radio that worked well, an engine that started reliably, and no apparent problems. The tire treads looked good enough. The interior was tidy but hardly spotless. I never did find out who my predecessor was, but he smoked unfiltered cigarettes, which the ashtray was still full of. I was thrilled to have a car at my disposal.

Young Man Blues

Edgar rode around the county with me two of those days that week, introducing me to his advertisers in each of the towns — car dealers, insurance companies, the little main street shops and eateries — showing me how to schmooze them up and book ad sales. It turned out I was obliged to work a half day Saturdays too. The first Saturday afternoon after work at noon I cut out and drove all the way to Boston. I got there well after dark. December had only just started so my stuff hadn't been carted off for not paying the rent. It was just some books, a guitar, my typewriter, and a wok I'd acquired. I left behind the secondhand mattress and the desk I'd set up made of a hollow-core door on some screw-in legs. I left Cambridge at dawn Sunday morning, with few other cars cluttering up the confusing tangle of roads and ramps to the Massachusetts Turnpike, I-90. It was close to a thousand-mile round-trip. I didn't know if Edgar would check the odometer, but I never did hear anything about it, and I took no other long-distance trips in it ever again. I would put an average of three hundred miles a week on the car in the months ahead, driving all over Monroe County. The McPhails had their own private gas pump at the back of the parking lot. Pat could unlock it from the office. I just had to ask and I could fill up the tank.

By the second week I was on my own, without Edgar tagging along. I also moved from Bob Denning's sofa to Tim and Archie's house on the Erie Canal after their roommate Geoff took off. He left a bed and a chest of drawers behind. It was perfect.

My new roommates were good company. Archie was a quiet intellectual. Tim was theatrical, a comedian who specialized in sex jokes. They both worked long days at their new bookshop, and some evenings, too, but we had dinner together once or twice a week. I had the luxury of a room of my own again. These sudden changes in my circumstances quickly flushed the anxiety and depression out of me. Even though my new job called for no literary artistry I was glad to have it. I'd landed back on my feet after a big stumble, and that was enough for time being.

I quickly got the hang of the job. My duties were mostly rote and undemanding, but the hours were very long. There were two other employees besides me and the owners. One was a young part-time gal who sat at the keyboard of a big new typesetting machine the size of a food freezer that spat out columns of justified layout-ready copy she had entered. It was one of the first such computerized newsroom devices, pretty rudimentary, but a big improvement over the clunky old linotype machine. The other employee was Randy the layout man. The typesetting may have been automated but everything else about putting the papers together was manual, old-school labor. Randy did it all. He laid out all the pages by pasting up those columns of news and ad copy, along with the Polaroid photos that I shot — of new car models, businessmen receiving awards, high school sports events — and ads that he composed using "press-type" lettering and "art" from a gigantic book of camera-ready cartoons and illustrations for every product on God's green earth, plus insignia and pictures for all holiday occasions and renderings of every imaginable type of human being in a thousand different demeanors.

I made the rounds in my company car, tidied up the press releases into coherent items, wrote a few puff pieces about the local car dealers and Rotary officers, and quickly learned the routine. Soon, snow flew and I spent long afternoons plying the dead-flat landscape between the four towns, happily alone in the car on the desolate country roads, singing along with the radio. It got so I spent only an hour or two a day in the office itself. But I did what was required to keep the papers stuffed with items and plenty of ads. I was gregarious and got along well with business owners of all kinds, and, it turned out, I was pretty good at selling ads. Edgar and Pat seemed happy with how I was working out.

Tuesdays were an absolute killer, though. That was the day we put the week's issue of the papers to bed. Randy had all the pages pasted up by midafternoon. Edgar had a room in the building that served as a giant camera. It was painted all black inside. The back wall had a rack for the laid-out pages. Randy photographed each page setup with a special large-format camera and by five o'clock he had them all converted into large negatives sized to the broadsheet printing format and loaded into a big flat box. I then had to drive to the printer about thirty miles east on the far side of Rochester and deliver the page negatives. Edgar gave me a ten-dollar bill for dinner. There was a steak joint Edgar recommended in a brand-new shopping mall — one of the first of its kind — a few miles from the printing plant. You could load up at the salad bar waiting for your steak to arrive. It was a fabulous luxury to me. Then, I'd wander around the mall awhile.

Around nine o'clock I returned to the printer and picked up the finished papers. They were all tied up in bundles, and, when I pulled out of there, the entire car from the trunk to the passenger seat was stuffed with bundles of newspapers. I'd get back to the office around ten o'clock. Edgar and Pat would be waiting for me. We took all the bundles of newspapers inside and ran each paper through a device called an Addressograph machine, a mechanical wonder of the mid-twentieth century. It was about the size of a pedal steel guitar. On one end, you loaded a metal magazine, like something you'd see on a machine gun, with dozens of dog tag–sized metal plates, each one with the name and address of a subscriber. The process of running papers for every single subscriber in the four towns (the four editions of the paper) through the Addressograph took around two hours. Then, Edgar and Pat would rebundle the papers for each town using another marvelous machine that tied them in up twine. Finally, they'd help me reload the Dodge Dart with all the bundles. Then they'd say good night and head home. Now it was after midnight. I would have to drive about sixty miles around the county to the four towns and drop off the bundles at each post office — they were closed for the night, of course, so I left the bundles on the loading dock, as much out of the weather as possible. I'd get home after two o'clock in the morning. That's what my Tuesdays were like, week after week: an eighteen-hour day. Looking back, my stamina amazes me.

Otherwise, I was having a pretty good time back in my college town. Christmas came and went, and I had a big dinner at the Dennings' house with the usual happy commotion. I avoided going to New York City — an eight-hour train ride from Rochester, if you were lucky and the Amtrak didn't break down — and I was barely in touch with Muriel and Henry. I called my mother maybe once a month and my father even less frequently. I knew Muriel and Bernie were mystified by this retreat back to my college town, but they were busy enough with their own lives in their early fifties. So I didn't try to explain. I just told them I had a job, was living with friends, and was happy.

Young Man Blues

Lyndon Johnson dropped dead in January 1973. That sure seemed like the end of an era. Richard Nixon was just beginning to enter the ordeal of the Senate Watergate hearings. The Vietnam War still chugged along, but the national mood had definitely swung against it. The high-pop phase of rock and roll music was going strong and there were good songs to sing along with on the radio during my long solitary drives around the wintry countryside: "Dancing in the Moonlight," by King Harvest, "Superstition," by Stevie Wonder, "You Turn Me On, I'm a Radio," by Joni Mitchell, "Peaceful Easy Feeling," by the Eagles. Meanwhile, our country had stealthily left behind the era of its greatest general prosperity and global influence, but it would be some time before the troubles of the mid-seventies really hit.

I had miraculously settled into my own *peaceful easy feeling*, a few months after being trapped in a globe of anxious despair. Life at the house on Canal Road in the winter of 1973 was lively and happy. The three of us got along really well and often threw parties on Saturday nights. As a SUNY alum, I had privileges to use the college gym and the pool for free. I started working out in the weight room three or four nights a week and swimming laps, a habit that I would keep up for more than thirty years afterward. I had a few serial romances with girls I met, but I had no illusions about getting into a serious relationship that might lead to matrimony. I still aspired to get on with a real writing career. Fortunately for me at that time, the sexual revolution was still evolving, despite its demoralizing effect on relations between the sexes. Women were experimenting with the *liberation* of birth control, and that was all right with me.

I still had a network of college friends in Brockport, fellow veterans of the hippie halcyon days who never left town after graduating and took up hippie occupations there — a leather shop, a guitar maker, a natural foods restaurant, and so on. There was plenty to do when I wasn't working. The college hosted interesting free cultural events. The Strand Theater got a new movie every week. Tim and Archie always had the latest new books around the house. I was happy to be part of that community, and I truly loved small-town living after the purgatory of Boston. The job got to be so routine and easy, despite the long hours, that my prankish nature prompted me to liven it up. I'd noticed that Edgar and Pat didn't pay much attention to what went into the paper apart from the ads, so I decided to have some fun with it.

I started by making up fake news stories and quietly planting them in the papers. The first was a Bigfoot sighting in the town of Hamlin, up by the Ontario lakeshore, a short item, reported skeptically, just someone who thought they saw something "out there" one night, "something like a human, but much bigger." Edgar and Pat didn't say anything about it the week the story came out. So the next week I ran a story about a farmer who was eating dinner with his family when a meteor crashed through the roof of his house, clear through the kitchen table, and down into the basement. I had the office-issue polaroid camera with me in the car, so I took a shot of my roommate Tim in a straw hat, holding a rock the size of a softball, the fateful "meteor." My network of friends in Brockport were catching on to *The Suburban News* turning into a kind of local *National Enquirer*. It was getting laughs. That spurred me on. Edgar and Pat still said nothing. There was virtually no reader mail about the weird stories — and I saw all the "letters to the editor"— which reinforced my conviction that the papers were mainly used for lining cat-litter boxes.

I enlisted Randy the layout man in my pranks. It turned out that his giant book of cut-and-paste advertisement illustrations was a gold mine of material. I wrote a story about an army enlisted man returned from Vietnam who had acquired "a rare tropical disease there that was turning him slowly into a T-bone steak." I had taken some photos of Vietnam returnees in their uniforms at a VFW function some weeks earlier, and I got Randy to paste up an illustration of a steak as if it was coming out of his shirt collar, where his head should be. He did a great job.

At that point, I started a couple of regular features: a horoscope attributed to the "world-famous astrologist" Dr. Otto C. Cragg, and an advice to the lovelorn column titled "Ask Mable Sage," for which I wrote all the questions and answers, of course. I used a drawing from the big ad book of a man with x-ray eyes for Dr. Cragg, and a picture of a grandmother hovering over a Thanksgiving turkey (with the turkey cut out) for Mabel. Among the twelve zodiac predictions each week were always two or three designed to be horrifying. For example: *Taurus, Pets can be tricksters. They hide their true feelings. Your cocker spaniel doesn't like you very much. Now might be a good time to get rid of him. Blue is your lucky color this week* . . . Or *Virgo, Sometimes, we must face the fact that we're just bad people. You can make the best of this by always wearing a smile around others, so it will be harder for them to tell. Thursday is your lucky day for bargain hunting* . . .

Old Edgar was often soused when he happened to come to the office, and he appeared less frequently as the weeks went by. Once, because I was doing such a good job (that is, selling a lot of ads), he invited me out to a fancy lunch at the steak house in Spencerport, a two-minute ride from the office. He knocked back at least two rye and sodas with lunch and on the way back to the office in his car he put his hand on my thigh. I removed it, and didn't say anything to him about it either at the time or ever after, but we knew where things stood. That was the last time we had lunch together. Or went anywhere together in his car.

One day in late winter, Pat gave me special instructions to go to one of the car dealerships in Brockport on Saturday and take Polaroids for a big centerfold layout of a promotional event there. It was the debut of a sensational new product they'd gotten a franchise to sell: the snowmobile. Looking over the photos back in the office, they struck me as a capital opportunity for comedy. I wrote a series of elaborate captions for the layout that told the story of how a local militia group was training to defend Monroe County from a Red Chinese invasion, expected imminently, using a newfangled kind of winter combat sled. Randy, the layout man, went along with the gag and assembled the layout just as I directed him to.

I'd gone too far, of course, and pretty much on purpose. On Wednesday, when the papers came out, the owner of the snowmobile dealership complained to Pat and Edgar. They were steaming. They made me apologize to the guy, which I dutifully did, just to be a gentleman about it. (He admitted the spread cracked him up, and, anyway they hadn't charged him any money because it was a free puff piece.) The owners did everything but fire me, at least not right away, for the obvious reason that they would have to search for someone to replace me, which meant probably weeks of drudgery for them doing all my chores, including the gruesome Tuesday night trip to the printer and then the rounds to the little village post offices after midnight. They heaped abuse on poor Randy, the layout man, but he was even less replaceable than I was, and they knew it. The excuse he gave them, though, was rich. He told them he thought folks really *were* training locally for some kind of trouble with Red China.

Pat pretended I was "on probation," but the next week there was a two-inch display ad in the paper: "Wanted: Executive Editor." The only thing that surprised me was that my position carried such an exalted title. I quit writing fake news stories, but as long as I was still the sole editorial employee of the *Suburban News,* I kept the two columns by Dr. Cragg and Mable Sage going, and, amazingly, nobody complained about them. They stopped giving me dinner money for the Tuesday night marathon, though, to let me know I was in the doghouse.

Then, the first really nice spring Wednesday in mid-April, Pat finally cashiered me. Edgar was staying away from the office, drinking more, I suspected. She paid me an additional week's salary to stick around and train my replacement, a geeky English major from Spencerport who was about to graduate from SUNY Geneseo. I drove around the county with him in beautiful spring weather, introduced him to the advertisers, and bragged about how I'd customized the paper for my own amusement. He said he'd never do anything like that, and I believed him.

My friends were a little sad because they'd been enjoying the transformation of the paper into a comedy sheet.

James Howard Kunstler

I had no idea what I was going to do next but I didn't freak out about it. Staying calm under pressure was a new thing for me. I had a strange confidence that everything would work out. I did not feel exactly like the same emotional cripple who had skulked away from Boston in defeat six months earlier. I was physically much healthier. Months of lifting weights and swimming laps had hardened me up.

The worst part of getting fired was that I had to surrender the company car. But I'd saved a bit of money and a friendly used-car dealer I'd sold ads to found me a beater 1966 white Chevrolet Impala convertible for two hundred dollars. It was my first car since the doomed Opel that Henry bought me in 1968, and I was hugely proud of having gotten it for myself, by myself. It had surely been a peach when it was new, with a snazzy red vinyl interior and the ragtop, but now it had a scrofulous collar of rust around the wheel wells and the tires were nearly bald — and that was only what was immediately apparent. But it did what you basically needed a car to do: take you from point A to point B. The ragtop went up and down (it leaked a little) and the radio worked.

My first trip in it was to the Monroe County unemployment office in Rochester, the same building where I'd signed up for vocational rehab when I go out of Payne Whitney three years earlier. So I was not taken aback by the seedy bureaucracy, and my application sailed through. Within a couple of weeks I was receiving a regular check for not working. I also paid a visit to the office of the *Democrat and Chronicle*, Rochester's big daily paper, a cold call, the same way I had waltzed into Clay Felker's office at *New York* magazine years before, without an appointment. I brought my portfolio of *Boston After Dark* clips and hit it off with an editor I approached in the big newsroom.

She was the Sunday editor, probably twenty years older than me, with an air of professional authority and competence. She actually read a few of my stories while I sat there and she invited me to submit pieces to her on a trial basis. She said the paper could "use a little color."

Two weeks later, my first story came out in the *D & C*. It was about the old man who sat in a little booth at the lift bridge over the Erie Canal in Brockport and raised and lowered the bridge for passing barges. He was not an electrifying character, but I jazzed up the piece with a lot of Erie Canal lore and history. The editor liked it a lot. Then, I wrote one about a colorful and charismatic young evangelical grifter who had landed in town and assembled a bit of a cult around himself. Then one about the trout-fishing scene on Oatka Creek. I was becoming a regular contributor, writing about whatever interested me or serendipitously entered my life bubble. I still collected unemployment and I sweated that someone in the county office might spot my byline in the paper, but no one ever did. I was gambling that before long the *D & C* would put me on the regular payroll with an actual job.

For the time being, though, my life was very agreeable and I just wanted to remain in that sweet spot. I could knock out a newspaper feature in a couple days. I was pulling in more money now than I did working six days a week at the *Suburban News*. I was playing tennis about twenty hours a week, working on my tan. I bought a cheap fly rod and explored the lazy creeks south of town where there was a little more topography to the landscape. One sly benefit of those months I put in at the *Suburban News* was that driving all those hours on the back roads through the rural landscape I had learned to enjoy my own company. And I acquired a sense of finally being in charge of my own life.

JHK, 1973

When summer came on, I discovered that there was quite a scene at one of the rock quarries west of town, which had filled with water and made a huge and fabulous swimming hole, really a small lake. A mob of hippies hung out there with music blasting, coolers of beer, and marijuana smoke wafting over the rock ledges. For some mysterious reason the police never busted the place the summer I hung out there. During this peaceful interlude, I chanced upon a book in Tim and Archie's store that made a huge impression on me. I was the right reader for it at the right time.

It was called *How I Found Freedom in an Unfree World*, by one Harry Browne, a journalist and financial writer who decades later on would run for president on the libertarian line in the 1996 and 2000 elections. At the time Browne was beginning a new career as an investment adviser. He had published his first book in 1970 titled *How You Can Profit from the Coming Devaluation*, which shrewdly anticipated the monetary inflation of the 1970s caused by blowback from the enormous government spending on the Vietnam War and Lyndon Johnson's Great Society programs.

Browne's book — an early entry among many books in the new so-called self-help vein — was essentially a set of principles for recognizing the power of one's personal responsibility, of making choices to act free of delusions, assumptions, and false obligations to other people's beliefs and needs. He presented an interesting framework for understanding the various traps we fall into, which prompt people to act out role-playing scripts against their own interests. It was a similar approach to becoming a better functioning autonomous adult as the est program Werner Erhard (a.k.a. Jack Rosenberg) developed around the very same time. (As it happened, I would meet the charismatic Erhard two years later when I worked for *Rolling Stone* in San Francisco, but I never took the est training.) Browne's book was a practical manual for assessing what is real in human relations and acting accordingly. He was strongly opposed to magical thinking. Browne wrote, "One of the greatest encouragements to wasted effort is the concept of positive thinking. To say, 'You can do it if you'll just believe you can' is to try to wish away reality."

Browne's point of view grounded me like nothing I'd encountered before, no head shrinker, or father figure, or big brother substitute. I think it affected me so strongly because, at age twenty-four, I came upon him at exactly the time in my own life when the judgment region of my brain was finally completing its long and painful development. (It happens surprisingly late in young men.) I was ready to receive Browne's message. Another important module of his ideology was to treat the world as a gigantic marketplace, and to understand that it is filled with opportunities. There is a place for you if you seek it out. Some people, companies, institutions, clubs might not want what you have to offer, but others will, probably plenty of others. And don't take it so personally. Instead of falling into the *despair trap* in the face of rejection — as I had in Boston on my entry into "the real world" — one can just say "next." Move along to the next possibility, the next opportunity. Don't fall for getting stuck. Instead of *positive thinking* try perseverance, discipline, and dedication to what matters to you.

I experienced all this as a kind of awakening. From it I would eventually develop some of my own principles of human relations. My first principle states: Out of every room of a hundred people, ninety-nine of them think that they're the *only one* who doesn't have their shit together. Just about everyone is secretly insecure, so don't worry about what people might think about you; they're probably preoccupied worrying about themselves. If you're in that room, get out of your own head and find out what other people think and feel. They'll probably tell you and reveal as much as you want to know about them. If people ask about you, remember that you already know about yourself, so keep it short. Get out of your own skull and you'll find out how universal human experience actually is.

My life didn't change overnight. At that point, June 1973, I was content to keep enjoying the scaffold I had set up for myself: playing tennis, fishing, swimming, going to the gym. It was certainly the best summer I'd had in years. I still thought there was a good chance that the Rochester *Democrat and Chronicle* would put me on staff after a while. I kept churning out feature stories for the Sunday editor. I was independent, productive, and able to pay my way. I began spending time with a young woman, Laura, twenty, who was the daughter of a popular poly sci prof at the college. I'd taken a course from him back in 1970, in my do-over senior year. His daughter was back from college elsewhere for the summer. A slim brunette, with a kind of feral intelligence, she had a keen interest in sex, and most of the time we spent together was in bed. I began to think of her as my girlfriend. In fact, she was a genuine *femme fatale*.

One Saturday night, Tim and Archie and I threw one of our parties and at some point I happened upstairs and found Archie in his room making out with Laura. Weirdly, the door was open. I was pissed off about it and interrupted them, demanding that Laura get out of the house. Archie pretended to be indignant but he didn't stop me from yanking her up and out of the room and out the door.

Evidently, I was more emotionally invested than I'd realized. Of course, I stopped keeping company with her after that and I was still pissed off enough at Archie to make arrangements to move somewhere else. I found a fine two-bedroom apartment in town on the third floor of a grand Italianate Victorian two blocks from Main Street. Part of the third floor was actually a ballroom. I didn't have any furniture to put in it, but it was a magnificent space. I built myself a table out of plywood and two-by-fours for legs and got a secondhand mattress for the bedroom floor. One of my tennis buddies, John McGuire, a Vietnam vet and a grad student, happened to be looking for a new place and he took the other bedroom.

Not many years later, I learned that Laura was murdered in Washington, DC, in what sounded like a classic crime of passion that made the national news. I was not so surprised to read about it. She apparently had a thing about recklessly playing games with men's emotions and she finally laid her trip on a truly dangerous character, a *femme fatale* for real, and not the last of her type I would run into.

I kept up my summer routines, but in late July I was surprised to get a letter on good rag stationery embossed with the address of the *Louisville Courier-Journal*, a newspaper of better than average repute. The gal at the Rochester *D & C* handed it to me. It was from a gentleman named Jack Pease, saying that he was about to take a new job as managing editor of the Albany, New York, evening paper the *Knickerbocker News*, owned by the Hearst Corporation. He said he'd encountered my articles and he was assembling a staff for himself and would I care to interview for a job on the paper? I was astounded that my articles got around on their own to anybody out there in the world of bigtime daily newspapers.

I was thrilled at the prospect of getting a job as a reporter on a real metro daily. I wrote back at once and, sometime in August, when Jack Pease had moved east and settled in, I drove to Albany in my clunker Chevy Impala convertible and met him at the paper's headquarters to be interviewed. The building was a brand-new modernist box at the end of a heroic, brand-new, six-lane boulevard, Wolf Road, lined by shopping malls and chain stores halfway between the cities of Albany and Schenectady. This pop-up suburb had the ominous look of *the coming thing*, in terms of American urban design, exactly the template of office parks and strip retail that would be followed all over the country the next fifty years as cities decanted their contents and spewed them out over the countryside. It made me a little queasy.

Right on the spot, though, Jack offered me that job and I accepted. I was about to cross a major threshold out of my protracted post-adolescence into autonomous adulthood: a grown man with a real job, a paycheck, a place to live, a set of wheels, and something to aspire to. I was finally accepted into the daily newspaper world of one of my heroes, H. L. Mencken, the epitome of the twentieth-century American newspaperman, and I intended to become the same sort of public gadfly that he'd been. My apprenticeship was over and I was on my way.

For years afterward, I kept in my wallet the list I'd made of *everything you like* that Bob Denning asked me to compose and took it out and reread it often, until it finally fell apart at the folds, and I felt safe enough to throw it away.

Part Seven

A Professional

I did not leave my anxiety problems behind me even after I began to operate as a confident autonomous adult. I continued to have panic attacks on and off through the rest of my life, though the intensity and frequency depended on what I was going through at any particular time. By then, I knew what they were and I learned to manage these episodes. Something surely had happened to my cerebral wiring that first experience smoking marijuana Christmastime of 1965. That panic response was incorporated into the architecture of my brain, like a software code module that keeps spinning as long as the computer is switched on. I could never completely rewire myself.

One thing slowly became apparent: an emotional linkage between my feelings of anger and panic attacks that often ensued. My stock response to adversity was to get angry and that threw a toggle that would set off a panic attack, not always right away. Getting angry scared me. It took me many more years to learn how to manage my anger as I continued on a difficult chosen path in life — a career in writing.

Young Man Blues

As it happened, I didn't see much of my two sets of parents anymore. In my twenties, I kept a safe distance geographically from Henry and Muriel. I moved around the USA, but I never lived in New York City again, and I didn't visit much. My mother was preoccupied with her thriving business, but at that time she was having trouble with my stepfather, Bernie, who had was tracking a quiet descent into alcoholism and depression.

In his mid-fifties, his career aspirations were pretty much dashed. He was fed up with being a public relations executive. But he didn't have that proverbial fire in his belly to impose his doings and makings on the world. Bernie had those friends from years back after the war who did become successful TV writers, ambitious, mercurial, unstable men, who weren't necessarily doing any better. Something about being a teenager in the final years of Prohibition had inclined them to hard liquor, a generation of whiskey drinkers. They, too, developed problems with alcohol, and their careers went off the rails around the same time Bernie was skidding. Perhaps they also had higher aspirations than writing gags for *The Tonight Show* — it was hardly a higher calling than being a PR flak — and none of them became a Saul Bellow, a Joe Heller, or a Don DeLillo — their heroes.

Bernie's experience in some of the worst battles of World War Two might have broken something inside him — he rarely talked about the war. But in 1973 he quit working for Avco-Embassy, the movie company, and for the better part of a year he was jobless. He appeared unable to mount a fresh start. So I stayed away from New York City and spoke maybe once a month with Muriel and Bernie on the phone. Bernie took some vicarious pleasure in my doings as a newspaper reporter. I sent them clippings that I thought were pretty good. They never threatened to come and see me, and that was probably a good thing.

My actual father, Henry, had little to say to me in those years. I suppose he was just glad I was fully out on my own, disburdening him. His work routine of flying to Antwerp every six weeks to pick up diamonds stultified him, but I doubt he gave a moment's thought to doing anything else with his life. He was having matrimonial problems with his wife Pauline, who had begun to stray into a romance with a wealthy trucking executive she'd met at a party – eventually her next husband. Her children were out of the Roslyn Heights house, off to college. Troubled as their relations with Henry had been, Jon and Madge must have been the glue that held that family together. Henry didn't show any interest in the newspaper adventures I'd been having. It never occurred to him either to drive up to Albany to visit, go out for dinner, or see the world I was living in. I didn't dwell on any of that, though. I was busy.

At Albany's *Knickerbocker News*, I functioned briefly as a general assignment reporter. I couldn't have been less interested in zoning board meetings and it showed. Then, just weeks after I came on board, the oil crisis of 1973 happened. Every reporter in the newsroom covered the story from one angle or another. It was an epic disruption in American life through the weeks it lasted. It really turned the daily order of things upside down with gasoline shortages and long lines at the service stations, where fights broke out. It crushed many businesses. Eventually, the price of oil found a new, much higher, floor, and that ushered in the great inflation of the 1970s. The OPEC Oil Embargo reinforced my recognition that the way our national life had arranged itself on the landscape, the relentless suburbanization, with its deep car dependency, was a civilization-crashing problem — something that became the subject of several books I would later write.

When that died down, Jack Pease, the managing editor, put me to better use. For about six months, I was the arts reporter and I got to review all the movies I wanted to see. It was a great time for Hollywood, a new wave of directors coming on the scene: Scorsese with *Mean Streets,* Terrence Malik, *Badlands,* George Lucas, *American Graffiti,* Polanski's *Chinatown,* Altman's *Thieves Like Us.* I loved writing about movies and the editors didn't try to tune down my prose. I also got into all the big rock concerts for free and could get backstage to drum up interviews. A press card really was a kind of magic pass into anything. I covered what live theater there was. All of that lent itself to tour de force writing. I traded in my white Chevy Impala convertible for another slightly younger, bright yellow '68 Chevy as big as a ferry boat. It was hard to park but it never broke down on me.

I was not crazy about Albany, New York's capital, which was well into a long, agonizing decline. The two daily Hearst newspapers (morning and evening) were a part of that slide, having moved their headquarters from downtown near the state capitol building to that giant concrete box building on a suburban boulevard five miles outside town. The nearby cities of Schenectady and Troy were equally dismal (though both still had their own daily papers). The office scene at Capital Newspapers was not exactly a scene out of *The Front Page.* My fellow reporters on *The Knick* were mostly schlubs, grinds, and burnt-out cases. I made only one friend there, a crime reporter named Tim, my age, who had a wild streak, was a devoted trout fisherman, and had a New York handgun license. For about six months we shared a pretty grand brownstone apartment on State Street. Tim's motto as a reporter was "There are a lot of people in this world who need a good fucking over, and I'm just the one to do it!"

I found a girlfriend on our morning-side paper, the *Times Union*, a fellow reporter, a half-Filipino beauty named Debbie, petite, very smart, sweet-natured, and sexually dreamy. We never lived together and we were both very busy, and I still had no intention of getting onto the marriage track with anyone. It was that simple. The 1970s were not a good time for courtship behavior. All the old guardrails were gone. The birth control bill had changed the equation drastically. It was simply easier for a man to evade commitment, and I did.

In the early summer of 1974, the management made me a three-days-a-week columnist. It was a lot of work pumping out those three weekly pieces, which usually required legwork and interviewing, but I could write about whatever I wanted to, come and go as I pleased, and was barely subject to any supervision. After a year on a metro daily, I felt secure in a budding career. The Watergate scandal was creeping to its tragicomic ending just then. Journalism had taken on a romantic tinge in the 1970s order of things. A lot of young people wanted to become Woodward and Bernstein. We were not mouthpieces for a reviled, sinister *establishment*.

Capital Newspapers had instituted a new computerized typesetting system — getting rid of the old-school hot lead linotype machines down in the basement press room. Now you'd write your stories on a particular type of paper with red ink borders using an IBM Selectric

255

typewriter equipped with a special type ball that had about eight additional non-Roman characters — omega, delta, theta, etc. — and these were read by an optical scanner to signify *new paragraph*, *italic*, et cetera, which was then converted by a machine into pasteup-ready columns of copy. The old union hacks on the copy desk, however, were resistant to learning how to edit using the new system. The net result was that they did very little actual editing during the roughly year that I worked there, which made my job extra gratifying — because there is one thing almost all professional editors are good at: removing humor from your copy. That whole year they pretty much kept their paws off my prose.

I developed a following, a readership. It was what I had hoped would have happened in Boston and hadn't. I was a star writer in a bush league newspaper market. I used

the methods I'd developed for hustling stories in Boston, hunting down weirdos, lowlifes, evangelists, hustlers, and other assorted colorful characters to write about. There was an infinite supply of them, and if I ever came up empty the police always had someone on offer, such as the homicidal maniac Robert Garrow, who went on a spree killing campers in the Adirondack Mountains that summer. I could also concoct an interesting column out of the sheerest banalities, such as the ennui of the motor vehicle bureau and the semiology of shopping malls. One time, a press agent came around with a wrestling bear act to promote something or other and I volunteered to face off against him — he pinned me in about three seconds flat, and his fur stank ferociously. But I was having some fun on the job.

JHK, 1973

That June, I got a letter from the National Desk editor at the *New York Times*, one David R. Jones, asking me to come down to the city to discuss a possible job. I guess someone at *The Times* state capital bureau had shown him some of my clips. It was flattering, but I had very mixed feelings about it, especially about having to live in New York City. But I took the train down and met up with Mr. Jones, a dashing Cary Grant–type figure who toured me through the various newsrooms — impressive for sure — and then, over lunch in the executive dining room, offered me a job . . . in the paper's Detroit bureau. Detroit was well on its way to becoming a pitifully failed city in 1974, and that might have been interesting, but I just did not want to go back to being a common reporter in a giant mid-western dump. I was not interested in news per say, rather in fashioning colorful prose. So, I did not jump at the opportunity to gain entry on the country's leading newspaper. And while I pretended to "think it over" for a couple of weeks, Mr. Jones found somebody else more avid for the position.

Despite my privileged situation on *The Knick*, though, I was growing restless there. A big part was that living in downtown Albany was a drag. So, in August, not long after President Nixon resigned and waved goodbye from his helicopter, I found a charming apartment in Saratoga Springs, thirty miles north of Albany, a wonderful old resort town, way past its prime, but filled with fabulous Victorian architecture and a lively cultural and social scene due to Skidmore College being there. It was an improvement but I was feeling trapped in the job. My anxiety was trying to tell me something. Someone, I forget who, recommended a head shrinker who practiced a new brand of pop psychotherapy called Transactional Analysis (TA).

TA was pioneered by Dr. Eric Berne, author of the bestselling book *Games People Play*. As the title suggests, TA was much more of a practical, interpersonal approach to daily life than standard psychiatry, affording a lot of insight into where people were coming from in particular stock situations. You learned a lot about your own habitual games, and the positions you fell into mindlessly. It was a very good supplement to Harry Browne's practical approach to navigating through life, which had so electrified me the year before.

The basic TA theory was that people always positioned themselves in some iteration of a child, parent, or adult role when acting out common situational "scripts" — the adult being an autonomous executive function able to steer you through the various emotional traps that largely resided in the child and parent roles. These scripts were Eric Berne's *games people played*. He gave them snarky, incisive names: "Let's You and Him Fight"; "Poor Me"; "Wooden Leg"; "Kick Me"; "I'm Only Trying to Help"; and so on. You could accuse TA of reducing complex human transactions to cartoons, but the truth is that an awful lot of the problems people cause for themselves and those around them are stereotypical. We're different, but not all that different, and similarly equipped with emotions, minds, and decision-making power. The TA sessions were a group meet-up, five or six of us in the room, presided over by a bawdy Scotsman, Dr. Bob Mitchell, and I was getting a lot out of it when another significant opportunity presented itself.

Sometime in October 1974 I got a message at the office to call a woman named Anne Wexler, a Democratic Party activist who had managed Senator Ed Muskie's campaign in the 1972 presidential primaries (he dropped out after losing New Hampshire). After that she was hired by *Rolling Stone* owner and editor Jann Wenner to upgrade the magazine's political coverage. Wenner was ambitious to develop the magazine's political clout. Gerald Ford had replaced Nixon by then after the disgrace of Watergate, so 1976 looked like an excellent moment for the Democrats to sweep back into power. Wenner wanted to play a part in that effort and lead his generation of readers out of its utopian wool-gathering into big league hardball party politics. Until then, his main political instrument was the unstable character Hunter Thompson, a comic metajournalist who always put himself — and his increasingly reckless antics with drugs — at the center of every story. Jann needed something more solid than that to be taken seriously by the political establishment. That fall of '74 Wenner was going around the country with Ms. Wexler ostensibly offering himself up for interviews at one metro daily after another. He was coming to Albany, Ms. Wexler said. Would I like to do a story on him?

Well, sure. Like many people in their twenties then, I was a *Rolling Stone* reader. Wenner, two years older than me, was a college dropout who'd started the magazine in 1967, when I was a sophomore at SUNY Brockport. His timing with that start-up was perfect. There was nothing else like it that spoke directly to our generation. It was determined to be taken seriously. It cast a wide net on the counterculture scene but sidestepped the more juvenile backwaters of radicalism. I admired it, thought of it as the apex of hippie journalism, a level above regional rags like the *Boston Phoenix*. I was immersed in rock music too. For all that, I didn't think of writing a column on Wenner as anything more than any another celebrity meet-up. I'd interviewed movie stars and rock stars on their publicity tours before.

I met Jann and Ms. Wexler at the Cranberry Bog, a faux-fancy lunch spot off Wolf Road, that six-lane suburban boulevard that terminated at the Capital Newspapers building. Wenner was chubby and short, wearing a wide, flowery tie, still sort of a kid, but obviously charismatic, in charge. Ms. Wexler was a middle-aged professional who reminded me of a high school math teacher. We spent about an hour yakking, me taking notes furiously the whole time in my standard-issue reporter's notebook. I wrote up a column about him and where his magazine was going now that *the sixties* were well over and our generation was growing up.

What I didn't realize at the time was that I was as much an interview subject as Wenner. He was hitting all these newspapers around the country looking for young people with some professional experience to beef up his staff while cutting loose some of the stoned hippie deadweights who were cluttering up the office. A week after my column on Jann came out, I got a letter on *Rolling Stone* stationery from the editor of the music section named David Hamilton (no relation to the theater prof of the same name who'd influenced me in college). In his letter he asked how much Capital Newspapers was paying me and would I be interested in coming to San Francisco to work at the magazine? Of course, I wrote back at once, saying, "About $8,500 a year . . . and yes."

Hamilton offered me $14,000 a year and then it was just a matter of me giving notice to Jack Pease, *The Knick*'s managing editor, and making arrangements to move to California. I was sorry to say goodbye to my girlfriend Debbie, but this was exactly the circumstance that had inclined me to behave the way I did with the young women in my life. Debbie had a good job and she liked it. She was staying. We were not living together. I was ambitious. I was open to opportunity, but I was waiting for the right opportunity. I hadn't wanted to go to the Detroit bureau of *The New York Times*, but I definitely did want to go to work at *Rolling Stone* in San Francisco. So, I was on the move again.

The End of the Road

Rolling Stone was a glamour job, for sure, and I was walking on air those last weeks at *The Knick*. My fellow reporters were stunned to hear that I was going to Counterculture Central. I declined Jann's offer to fly me out — terrified of airplanes ever since my trip to the Payne Whitney Clinic — and instead I took the three-day-and-night cross-country Amtrak train, which by then had devolved to a Soviet level of service, with many unexplained delays, greasy upholstery, and horrible food. Chris Dunworth, my old friend from Fire Island, summer of 1966, was living in San Francisco with his girlfriend and invited me to crash at his apartment until I found a place. The little stuff I'd accumulated, mainly my books and my stereo system, came west in a Mayflower van and was waiting for me in a warehouse somewhere out there. I'd sold my big yellow '68 Chevy to a fellow *Knick* reporter for a few hundred bucks.

The *Rolling Stone* office was in an old four-story building south of Market Street on Third Street off Brannon, then a run-down, gone-by, light-industrial district awaiting the city's next incarnation — it wasn't clear yet that it would be computer tech. Jann had done a nice renovation on the two floors he occupied, with the magazine's editorial office on one floor and the business staff and his Straight Arrow Books operation on the other. He put me to work at once writing the magazine's gossip column, "Random Notes," a grunt job. My predecessor, a gal named Cindy, was a sort of utility infielder around the place and was moved on to other duties. I inherited her Rolodex, stuffed with phone numbers of music industry flaks and executives and quite a few rock and roll stars. Writing "Random Notes" entailed me calling around and chatting up these people for "items," tidbits of gossip. These were often publicity opportunities for the record companies, so it was easy to get material for the page. I also went around to the many clubs and rock music arenas in town at night and easily got in backstage to chat up the headliners.

These were the last years that *Rolling Stone* would remain out west — Jann moved the whole outfit to New York in 1977 — as San Francisco was increasingly an inconvenient home base. Its heyday of being the epicenter of hippiedom was well over when I got there in 1974. The days of the Jefferson Airplane all living in a "painted lady" Victorian house in the Haight-Ashbury district, and Janis Joplin hooking up with Big Brother and the Holding Company, and all the "Love-in" events that took place in Golden Gate Park with Timothy Leary and the LSD-for-lunch bunch . . . that scene was finished. There were a handful of celebrity musicians left in and around town. Boz Scaggs's star was rising and he was a close friend of Jann's. He invited the whole office to his Christmas Party. Mike Bloomfield, the guitarist on Bob Dylan's classic mid-sixties electric opuses, lived up in Marin County, across the Golden Gate Bridge, as did the Grateful Dead and their entourage. And Joan Baez and her sister Mimi Fariña had a little scene around them. But bigtime rock and roll otherwise was split between New York and Los Angeles and I mostly worked the phones to do my reporting.

Being stuck in the office was not fun after being very much on my own at a metro daily. My job was lodged in the magazine's music department. David Hamilton was in charge of it. The only other full-timers there at the time were Ben Fong-Torres and David Felton. Hamilton had been hired off of *Long Island Newsday* where he'd been the right-hand man of publisher Bill Moyers (who'd previously been President Johnson's press secretary). Hamilton, who'd recommended hiring me, was a very sympatico guy, but he quit *Rolling Stone* suddenly only a few weeks after I got there and went back to *Newsday*, apparently very disenchanted with the counterculture press. He was replaced by a guy named Abe Peck, off an "underground" weekly called *The Chicago Seed*. Peck and I never did get along. He was super-serious about radical left politics and I, as ever, considered all that a ridiculous waste of time. We could barely stand each other.

Ben Fong-Torres, a hometown San Francisco kid who had jumped into *Rolling Stone* near its launch in 1967, was the established pasha of rock and roll journalism by 1974. He'd mapped off his own domain in the rock world and was efficiently grinding out celebrity profiles on an assembly-line basis, in great demand from what had become a dynamic relationship between the record labels, their "product" (the bands), and *Rolling Stone*'s command of public opinion about music, meaning its ability to juice sales tremendously with favorable coverage and rave reviews of albums. Ben was diligent and ambitious and he knew how to work the system. When he wasn't on the road, we had lunch together several times a week at the Doggie Diner, a greasy spoon down the block in the old Southern Pacific rail terminal. I enjoyed Ben's colorful travelogues with rock royalty over a plate of enchiladas, but he couldn't help condescending as if I were born the night before last.

David Felton, on the other hand, was a more kindred spirit. He'd come off *The Los Angeles Times* and done some knockout reporting about the Charles Manson "family," and then a lesser-known outfit that surrounded Mel Lyman, the banjo player in Jim Kweskin's jug band who became a master of controlling people around him, specializing in attracting heiresses to his personality cult. I also had an abiding interest in cults, of which there were many then because so many aimless young people needed someone to tell them what to do, give some structure to their lives. Felton's duties in the music department remained mysterious while I was there. He edited stories assigned to various freelancers around the country, as I would do too, and he worked on Big Stories that somehow never saw the light of day. But he was affable and humorous. You could go into his cubicle next to Ben's and yak with him pretty much any old time. He later went on to a career at MTV and helped create the *Beavis and Butt-Head* cartoon series there.

One special chore assigned to Felton was to serve as Hunter Thompson's babysitter when that lunatic came into the office, which was only a few times a year. Thompson did not work at our headquarters as many fans imagined he did. He lived outside Aspen, Colorado, where he was able to play with guns, blow things up, and take every drug he could get his hands on. The first time he showed up after I came aboard he disrupted the office for three days. He arrived in a state of florid intoxication and made a big commotion. After huddling with Jann for an hour or so over a late assignment he'd barely started, Hunter realized he had no idea where he'd parked the rental car he picked up at the airport. Somehow, the police got called in to help find it and next thing there were half a dozen cops rambling around the office at a time when there actually was a marijuana haze in there — because Hunter was toking up all day — and more complications ensued that fortunately did not lead to any arrests.

Around six o'clock, Felton invited me to tag along for dinner with Hunter and Felton's girlfriend Kathy, who was Wenner's editorial assistant. I think David simply wanted a little social cushioning at the table, but I looked forward to spending a few hours up close with the Great Man. We drove down to a rootsy Mexican joint in the Mission District. There, Hunter managed to consume several giant margaritas and half a dozen Carta Blanca beers, on top of slipping off to the men's room to toke up or do bumps of coke. His appetite was awesome. Apparently, he hadn't eaten all day and as soon as he finished one burrito dinner complete with rice-and-bean sides he ordered a second dinner and finished that one too. Physically, he was over six feet tall and barrel-chested and whatever space he happened to occupy — a chair at the table, a slot of air standing up — his body had a weird way of overspilling its boundaries, and rather aggressively so, that made him appear to be an agent of chaos. You didn't want to get too close to him.

We all left the restaurant pretty ripped and proceeded to Felton's place, a walkup in the seedy Mission District nearby with almost no furniture in the large living room — who needs furniture? — except for a secondhand dentist's chair. Hunter and David commenced drinking Jack Daniel's and doing hits of nitrous oxide, laughing gas, which was a fad drug that was turning up at parties in the city. There was a tank of it next to the dentist's chair. I just did not want to get any more intoxicated than I already was and made excuses to split the scene.

You could see that Hunter Thompson was already well on his way to destroying his talent as a writer. The following spring of 1975, he would botch an assignment on the fall of Saigon with self-dramatizing histrionics and he would see only limited service in the 1976 election — an interview with candidate Jimmy Carter.

Grunt Work

Putting out each issue of *Rolling Stone* was a terrible grind because it came out twice a month then, unlike most other once-a-month magazines, so we actually did twice the work of the average magazine staff, and each twice-a-month *closing* — preparing to go to print — was a horror show of incessant last-minute changes, desperate rewrites, frantic meetings, and a lot of concocted melodrama. Drugs certainly had something to do with the last-minute histrionics. But I was not a druggie and didn't smoke weed in those days or do any cocaine. I was never invited to do coke with anyone there. They kept that very much on the down low.

In his push to professionalize the staff by hiring young newspaper and magazine veterans, Jann had, ironically, acquired a number of rather heavy drinkers. Joe Eszterhas came out of *The Cleveland Plain Dealer*, a very rough character who carried a folding Buck knife on his belt and used to take it out and stab the table at editorial meetings when he wanted to make a point. Paul Scanlon, the managing editor, used to take afternoon breaks with Eszterhas and general assignment reporter Tim Cahill at a nearby dive bar called Jerry's (with the hallmark neon martini glass in the window). The young diva photographer Annie Leibovitz was rumored to have a hard drug problem (though she was always very nice to me when she was not on the road with some hot band, which was more often than not).

The office was just not a very friendly place. Jann was AWOL half the time. At that point in his life he was off socializing with now very wealthy rock stars on Caribbean Islands and other glamour spots. The magazine was increasingly being run by Scanlon and Marianne Partridge, gang boss for the support squad of female copy editors and fact-checkers who all came to the magazine just before I did — Sarah Lazin, Harriet Fier, and Christine Doudna. Marianne knew that I was unhappy writing the gossip column, and she met me one evening at a bar called the Old Waldorf to listen to me complain, but I was stuck there with no apparent way out. Around the same time, David R. Jones of *The New York Times* turned up again. He flew into San Francisco to host a meet-up of the National Desk staff, guys posted all around the country. Somehow, he found out that I was at *Rolling Stone* and he invited me up for a drink with his gang at his hotel. When I got there, I discovered that his suite was on one of the upper floors. I couldn't make myself go up there. I'd developed a new phobia in San Francisco.

I'd been at Chris Dunworth's brother Joe's house in the Mission on Thanksgiving shortly after I started the job, and there was an earthquake that day, centered in the town of Hollister, not a big one that caused much damage but you could sure feel it. The old wooden house swayed and creaked like an ancient Spanish galleon at sea. It made an impression on me, kind of freaked me out. After that, I made a point to avoid walking anywhere near the only two giant skyscrapers downtown: the Bank of America building and the Transamerica Pyramid. I'd walk five blocks out of my way if I had to. Fear of heights was also, of course, one of my old entrenched neurotic phobias. So I couldn't make myself get in that elevator to schmooze with the *New*

York Times National Desk gang — and thus probably missed another job offer at some bureau more appealing than Detroit. I left Mr. Jones a note at the hotel desk saying I was sorry but I was suddenly feeling ill.

Outside the *Rolling Stone* office bubble I was dissatisfied with life in San Francisco. The city had its renowned charms, of course: the rugged hills with their great views; the waterfront and the beach; the snowless winters and cool (foggy!) summers; the palm trees, the surviving Victorian architecture, and the cute cable cars. But the place was also run-down then. The Haight-Ashbury hippie scene, which started so colorfully around 1966, had turned seedy and low by 1975, with Charlie Manson types and lost girls with dirty bare feet, strung out on bad drugs, infesting the streets. I first took an apartment on Page Street in the Haight in November but lasted there only a month. It was depressing. So, after Christmas, I answered a "roommate wanted" ad in *The San Francisco Chronicle* and moved into a luxurious four-bedroom triplex flat off Jackson Street in the town's poshest neighborhood, Pacific Heights. My new trio of roommates were all young bachelor accountants working for the Bechtel Corporation, a global engineering firm. (One was a Brit.) They thought having a *Rolling Stone* staffer on board was hip and exotic.

The flat was huge and beautiful, and it improved my state of mind a lot. The rent was just $600 a month for all of us ($150 each) — which tells you something about San Francisco's economy in the mid-1970s, the years bookended between two oil crises. The city then was primarily a banking center with a tourism overlay. Banking was getting clobbered by inflation and soaring interest rates. After the Summer of Love fizzled out the arts community that remained was the old beatnik contingent in North Beach surrounding poet Lawrence Ferlinghetti's City Lights bookstore, and of course the beatnik scene was way more over than the hippie scene. The whole computer and software industry that would later transform San Francisco was hardly born yet.

The three accountants I lived with were *regular guys*, flamboyantly unhip, a nice contrast to the self-consciously superhip *Rolling Stone* crew. We went to a lot of ball games together over in Oakland, where the A's were in their prime World Series–winning years, with Reggie Jackson, Joe Rudi, Bert Campaneris, Sal Bando, and Gene Tenace for offense, and their superb pitching staff of Catfish Hunter, Rollie Fingers, Blue Moon Odom, and Vida Blue. I acquired a beater car from the receptionist at the office, a godawful old Mercury Comet with a leaky roof (February and March was the monsoon season there) but I ditched it after getting towed a couple times at $200 a pop. Instead, I bought a used Honda-350 motorcycle from a colonel in the Presidio military base just downhill from Pacific Heights. By that time, the rain had stopped and the bike proved to be an ideal way to get around the city. Riding it was a thrill, of course, but the best part was I could chain it up to a lamppost wherever I went, so there was no parking problem, and I never got towed or hassled by the authorities.

As for romance, I had the usual tomcat promptings of any young man in his mid-twenties, but I was not looking to get serious, and so I played it that way. The young ladies at the office were basically off-limits. I developed a crush on one of them, but she had a boyfriend. I met some women at events I covered, rock shows at Winterland and the Boarding House, an old church converted into a comfortable cabaret theater that I frequented to interview musicians coming through town. For a while I dated a girl who waitressed at my favorite Indian restaurant, but we had nothing in common except youthful libidos. And that flat I moved into in Pacific Heights had an identical mirror-image triplex apartment in the other half of the building, only with four young women. I spent some time in bed with one of them. But nothing and no one captured my restless heart, and for the same reason as ever: I felt another move coming on. I wasn't going to stick around.

Dropping Out

Over the winter and spring, I developed a growing sense that I had gotten about as far as I would go in corporate journalism with *Rolling Stone*, and logically I had to move on to the next thing. That next thing would be writing novels. The cultural programming for young men with literary aspirations in the 1970s was to become the next J. D. Salinger, Joseph Heller, or Philip Roth, a serious writer, a literary artist, a heavyweight. Journalism was mere preparation for that. It was lightweight. Even Tom Wolfe, the journalist's journalist, in his prime in the 1980s, eventually ditched his very successful nonfiction career — book-length journalism — to write *big* novels of the *Vanity Fair* type.

It was also becoming clear that I didn't operate well in the office ecosystem. I wasn't a team player. I didn't enjoy editorial meetings or the frantic closings every other week. I was averse to office politics — which had gotten more complex with women coming into power jobs. And I didn't like getting pushed around by fact-checkers, who made me call back all the people I'd interviewed, to confirm that they said what I said they'd said, which annoyed them, too, and spoiled them as sources. Finally, the rock music scene itself had degenerated and was now sinking into a morass of disco and other crap. Getting to *Rolling Stone* had been a fortuitous accomplishment for me but I just didn't like working there one little bit.

For another thing, I'd joined another Transactional Analysis group run by Jack (John M.) Dusay, a psychiatrist who had been a colleague of Eric Berne's, the originator of TA. Most of the other five or six in the group were older than me, mature people, with good jobs and more life experience, and through these conversations I began to realize that hanging on to a glamour job any longer than necessary was a bad bargain, even if it meant stepping out into the scary unknown.

I'd started and stopped writing half a dozen novels in the years after college, including the stitched-together set of short stories about summer camp that I finished just before I fled Boston in 1972. The other false starts were all, in one way or another, jejune scenarios about a young man trying to kill his father — which, given my personal history, seemed like a subject of literary heft to me — but I always stumbled on setting up a plot more dramatically acute than one based on the petty quarrels I had with my own father. They all collapsed around page fifty. TA helped me see beyond that preoccupation. It prompted me to incorporate other parts of my limited experience in the world, namely my complex feelings about the various older brother figures I'd known. I also decided to take a tactical approach to the task of writing a publishable novel: to cook up a rip-roaring commercial horror story that would make enough money to set me up for years to come — when I could get down to more highbrow material, maybe even a Dostoyevskian behemoth about a boy who kills his father. And, even so, there was no reason that a commercial novel couldn't also be a bravura writing performance.

I embarked on this new project methodically during the rainy season that late winter of 1975. Peter Benchley's novel *Jaws* had come out, and would spend all year on the best seller lists. I bought it and studied it. It was sturdy enough, with adequate dramatic velocity, but it was stylistically *blah*. I wanted to write a horror novel with the panache of the young novelists then on the scene who I admired: Thomas McGuane (*The Bushwhacked Piano*, 1971) and Ishmael Reed (*Mumbo Jumbo*, 1972). These guys were dazzling on the page, whatever they wrote about, and I wanted to dazzle, too, not just spin a yarn.

I got the idea for my novel one rainy afternoon in Eddie Bauer's outdoor adventure store downtown, its original headquarters before it became a national chain, a multifloor emporium packed with state-of-the-art camping equipment, fine expeditionary clothing, and firearms. There was a big geographical survey map of California on one wall and I found myself studying the vast national forest tracts in California's northern coast mountains. This got me thinking about Sasquatch (a.k.a. Bigfoot), the legendary giant apeman of the Pacific Northwest. One of the first books that had excited my eleven-year-old imagination back in New York City was *On the Track of Unknown Animals* by the French "cryptozoologist" Bernard Heuvelmans, which contained a lengthy chapter about Bigfoot's cousin, the Abominable Snowman of the Himalayas.

The story for my novel came to me pretty quickly. Two old college buddies, former roommates, are reunited in San Francisco in their mid-twenties. Nichols is a photographer, psychologically edgy, brooding, and intense. His old pal Traveal is rich kid, vocationally aimless, athletic, but a goofball. The catch is, back in their senior year of school, Traveal ended up birddogging Nichols out of his then-girlfriend, Diana, breaking Nichols's heart. The two supposedly get over that (ha!)

and manage to remain friends. But then they must graduate, go out into the world, and lead their lives. So a few years later in the then present day of the mid-1970s, Traveal, still aimless and bored, shows up in San Francisco, having moved there with his now-wife Diana. Nichols's old grudge is rekindled. A bit at loose ends himself, Nichols proposes going on an outdoor adventure with his old pal Traveal, who has nothing better to do. The idea is to venture into the northern California wilderness, kill a Bigfoot, and bring it back to civilization where glory and fame await. The catch is that it kind of looks like the brooding Nichols is fixing to kill his old friend in the process. Diana senses something not being right and tries to talk her husband out of it but fails. The two men outfit themselves with camping equipment and forty-four magnum pistols (at Eddie Bauer) and head up north to their jumping-off-place, the town of Willow Creek, to hire a couple of horses and a mule for the equipment. The working title of this opus was *Bagging Bigfoot*. It seemed destined to be a gigantic best seller before I finished typing the first paragraph.

I liked to come into the *Rolling Stone* office early, around seven a.m., before anyone else got there, so I could work the phones to New York City before my sources at the record labels went out for their three-hour lunches at nine o'clock Pacific time (when my fellow staffers began to show up). With my new project underway, I started getting up at four in the morning to write before leaving for work. I forged ahead steadily and by the time I got to page fifty the story was moving very nicely. I was sure I'd broken through that old mental barrier and would finish the darn thing in a few months. Like the many novels I would write in the years ahead, the story took on a life of its own. It became a self-informing process. Each sentence, each scene, instructed me where to go next. All I had to do was show up at my writing table and type. It was hard work — McGuane once said of writing, "it's like loading cinder-blocks on a truck" and it really is a sort of mental heavy-lifting — but I was fully engaged in the task and quite satisfied with the result, feeling surefooted and optimistic.

As the weeks went on, and my confidence about my project grew, I got a little cheeky with the "Random Notes" column. The reality was, I'd stopped giving a shit about my future at the magazine. The column was making Jann nervous. In April, I ran an item with the subhead "Frozen Fruits" about a fire emergency in a New York City gay bathhouse that sent many of the customers fleeing out into the frigid streets with hardly any clothes on. It disturbed Jann, who at the time was still in the sexual identity closet, and wouldn't come out as gay for a couple more decades. At the time I had no idea. He was married then to Jane Schindelheim, whose family had loaned Jann money to start the magazine in 1967. By the mid-1970s they were a glamorous international *power couple*. Everyone thought they were solid. Otherwise, Jann always acted like he was *one of the guys*, surrounded, as he was in the office, by the overtly macho praetorian guard of Eszterhas, Scanlon, Cahill, Felton, and Fong-Torres.

But he obviously sensed that I was a loose cannon on the deck, a more antic personality than he'd bargained for. In staff meetings, he nicknamed me Nox. (I thought it was "Knox," and didn't get that it was short for *obnoxious* — ironically, I would learn many years later in Joe Hagan's biography of Wenner, *Sticky Fingers* [2017], that Wenner himself had been nicknamed Nox back in college.) Thus, when he was around that winter and spring— which was maybe half the time — Jann started insisting that I run all my "Random Notes" leads by him before I looked deeper into them, especially before I phoned any of the rock stars he was lately consorting with, apparently worried that I'd spoil his social life. Paradoxically, he'd also nagged me to get "juicier" items into the column — cognitive dissonance due, perhaps, to the various drugs he was using at the time?

Sometime in May I got a blind call from an LA party girl who often passed on interesting tidbits of gossip to me, which usually checked out. She was a reliable source, even if a person of dubious character. She said she'd been hanging out at the Record Plant where Paul McCartney was remixing his *Venus and Mars* album (with his band Wings). "Paul is broke," she said, "and his wife is fucking everyone in West LA." That was pretty juicy, all right, I thought . . . a Beatle and all. I'd interviewed McCartney over the phone that winter because I had to rewrite a botched story that a stringer had filed about Paul initially recording his *Venus and Mars* album down in New Orleans. So that day in May when the tidbit came in Jann happened to be around. I went into his office and ran it past him, exactly as the party girl had transmitted it. He mulled it over a few moments and finally said I should check it out. I asked if he was sure. It was pretty lowdown stuff. He said, yeah, go ahead. A little later, I called the Record Plant in Hollywood, and got Paul on the phone — he remembered that I was a *Rolling Stone* editor who'd interviewed him and he took the call.

We chatted about the album for a few minutes, and then I told him that there was some vicious chatter going around about him. He asked what it was. I apologized and explained that it was my job to write the "Random Notes" column and, unfortunately, that I'd gotten some salacious gossip I was told to check out. What was it? Paul insisted. I asked him if his marriage to Linda Eastman was on the rocks. He was shocked and angry that anyone would insinuate that. *Not in the least bit!* he said. I didn't get to the other part about him being broke because he started yelling at me, saying that *Rolling Stone* had become a disgusting rag, and a moment later Linda picked up an extension in the studio control booth and when she got the drift of what we were talking about she joined in the yelling.

I took it all to be a firm denial that any of it was true, and after Paul and Linda had finished ventilating, and had hung up on me, I wrote a note and gave it to Jann's assistant, saying I'd spoken to the McCartneys and that the tidbit didn't check out. Later that afternoon I was summoned into Jann's corner power office. He said that Paul and Linda had called him in a rage complaining about me. What had I asked them? I told Jann how it went down, and reminded him that I'd run the lead past him, as instructed, and was told to go ahead. I'd gone directly to the source. It must have been too much for Jann's brain, sore beset as it was with responsibilities, anxieties, and probably some mind-altering substances. He just pointed to the door, which I took as meaning *this meeting is over*.

A couple of days later I was back in Jann's office listening to him tell me that our arrangement wasn't working out. He seemed surprised when I agreed. I was not very happy writing the magazine's gossip page, I said. It was way more unserious than anything I'd been doing before, working on a regular newspaper. I also said that Hunter Thompson was doing a piss-poor job and I could probably handle his assignments better. This was a few weeks after Hunter botched the fall of Saigon story. Jann looked at me as if I was nuts — offering to replace his star writer, his crown jewel? If he couldn't give me something serious to do at the magazine, I said, then maybe I should figure something else out. He said he'd think about it. He didn't know that I had a side project writing a sure-thing bestselling horror novel, and I didn't tell him. Before the end of the week Jann gave me a few thousand dollars to go away and figure out that something else. It was quite generous of him. I was hugely relieved. I put one final "Random Notes" page together for the next issue so he could have time to find a replacement, and then I stopped coming into the office.

I was quite satisfied with that outcome, though it was a little hard to explain to friends and family that I'd bailed out of such a fabulous glamour job. (How could I *not* be happy there?) I filed for unemployment right away and in a couple of weeks the checks started coming in. Meanwhile, I had whole days to work on *Bagging Bigfoot* and I raced ahead with the story. In my mind, I'd already transitioned from a journalist to a novelist. I didn't work around the clock, though. No longer a corporate serf, I started to actually enjoy living in San Francisco a little bit. I had the motorcycle, which was all paid for. I bought a cheap fiberglass fly rod and started showing up at dawn at the fly-casting pools in Golden Gate Park to practice casting under the towering, fragrant eucalyptus trees, a pretty cosmic experience. I joined the Jewish Community Center down the block from the big flat on Presidio and started swimming laps every day around lunchtime after putting in a morning shift at the typewriter.

In June, I triumphantly finished *Bagging Bigfoot*, got a list of New York literary agents from the library, and fired Xeroxed copies of the novel to several of them. In early July I got a reply in the mail from one Virginia Barber (1935–2016), who'd started her own agency the previous year and was building a client list. She wrote that she'd be pleased to represent my novel to publishers, which she termed "exciting and accomplished for a newcomer," and asked me to call right away, signing her name "Ginger." All of a sudden, I had an agent. I phoned her at once and had an intoxicating conversation that convinced me I would shortly be an overnight sensation. She rattled off the names of a dozen New York editors she knew who would be as excited as she was to discover a new talent. She was eager to meet in person, and just then I realized I would be leaving San Francisco even sooner than I'd imagined.

I decided to ride my motorcycle across the USA, with the eventual goal of resettling in Saratoga Springs, the upstate town I'd enjoyed living in my last few months working for Albany's *Knick News*. It struck me as the perfect place to hunker down into my new life as a bestselling novelist: a fine small town surrounded by lovely countryside, and the Adirondack wilderness. Of course, I went down to Eddie Bauer to get the outdoor equipment I needed for camping out cross-country — a small tent and sleeping bag, a first-rate rain jacket and matching pants, a compact white gas stove and mess kit. I found a set of panniers to go over the rear rack of the bike for carrying all this stuff. I sold off my bed and my stereo, packed my books in boxes, and brought them over to Chris Dunworth's brother Tom's house, to be shipped later. I left my typewriter with one of my Bechtel accountant roommates — a reliable fellow — to be sent east as soon as I got a foothold back east.

In my extended state of elation, I spent one of my final afternoons in San Francisco at a foreign car dealer on Van Ness Avenue checking out the hugely expensive English cars on display — Rolls-Royces, Bentleys, Aston Martins, Jaguars, the legendary Jensen Interceptor. The salesman gave me a lot of attention. In those days, young, suddenly rich rock musicians, or drug entrepreneurs, would walk into a place like that and buy a thirty-thousand-dollar car with a wad of cash money. I was a pretty deluded, of course. Then, one bright morning in early August, I loaded up the bike, said farewell to my three roomies out on the sidewalk, and rolled out of San Francisco into the midst of life. I was twenty-six years old, a grown man on an archetypal quest. I didn't know how it would go from there, of course, but I was dead certain I was headed in the right direction.

Epilogue

Into the Unknown

The way I figured it, by the time I finished a leisurely motorcycle trip across the USA, Ginger Barber would have found a publisher avid for my boffo novel *Bagging Bigfoot*, and my worries would be over — movie rights to follow about eleven minutes later, like with Peter Benchley and his boffo novel *Jaws*. (I saw the movie, by the way, before I left San Francisco. It was better than the book.)

That bundle of expectations was perhaps a bit delusional, but the overall plan wasn't. It was a deliberate commitment to step boldly into the unknown. I was confident that I had the skill and fortitude to be a novelist — hadn't I just turned one out by sheer force of will and found an agent who liked it? — and it seemed to me there would never be a riper time to make my move . . . to bail on the world of bosses and jive corporations . . . to drop out! Like many inexperienced adventurers, it would turn out I had no idea how tough a slog the adventure would be. But just then, setting out, I was ready for anything.

The cross-country ride was not so leisurely. Nevada was a stupefying repetition of basin and range, and I couldn't wait to get out the other side. I crossed the Utah salt flats at dawn (bad decision) so that the rising sun blinded me reflecting off the salt pan as I raced east toward the army's Dugway Proving Ground (where they had recently killed a bunch of sheep testing nerve gas). Camping out had its charms but I had no desire to stick around any of my camping spots. Somewhere outside of Tabernash, Colorado, on Route 40, a state trooper had the road blocked off. He told me that a truck had spilled radioactive waste on Interstate 70, where I was going, and when I told him my destination was Boulder he advised me to take the nearby Rollins Pass as a detour. He said it was "a nice shortcut."

After about a mile of asphalt, the Rollins Pass road turned into a mule trail, going up over the Continental Divide. I didn't get out of first gear for more than an hour as I followed the switchbacks up, up, up. Somewhere around eight or nine thousand feet, my twin carburetors gave out from the thinning air. I had to readjust the mixture screws to keep the engine going the rest of the way to the bare, treeless summit at 11,676 feet. Then, just as I crossed back down below the tree line on the downside of the Divide, I came around a curve, rode right into a pothole the size of a hot tub, and bounced out sideways, leaving me pinned under the bike. An adrenaline surge got me back on my feet and the bike upright. I discovered a few big abrasions on my limbs and right flank but was otherwise unhurt.

The front end of the bike was a mess. The headlight and directionals were smashed, the forks were slightly askew, and the handlebars out of true. But the engine started right up again, and the drivetrain functioned, and I was able to limp the rest of the way out — maybe another twenty miles — to the hippie hamlet of Nederland, a gateway back to the world of paved roads and hot showers. I'd been aiming to stop in Boulder to visit Roger, my childhood friend from Long Island, who was working as a carpenter there, framing houses, a few years after graduating from UCLA. I called from a rough bar in Nederland and he came to get me and my damaged bike in a pickup truck.

There was a Honda shop in Boulder and I was able to get parts to fix the bike. Having been incommunicado since leaving San Francisco, I checked in with Ginger Barber (a collect call). She was chirpy and cheerful but had no progress to report. My novel was out there getting read, she said. It'd only been a month . . . relax. A few days later, I had the bike fixed up and hit the road again.

Just east of Boulder, of course, one enters the Great Plains, and I was in for several more mind-numbing days of perfectly straight, level motoring on Interstate 70 across Colorado, Kansas, and Missouri. Without music or anything else in my head — try to imagine a world before iTunes and podcasts — I resumed spinning fantasies about my scintillating future, rolling in dough like Scrooge McDuck swimming among his moneybags, hanging out on movie sets, buying nice things, and living the life of an overnight sensation. I can't apologize for these philistine raptures, though I knew, even at the time, that's just what they were.

I got off the interstates for good at St. Louis and finally began to enjoy riding the bike for its own sake on the back roads of southern Illinois and Indiana — surprisingly lovely country — though I barely avoided a crash around New Liberty, Indiana, when a cocker spaniel tried to run under my wheels and, avoiding him, I nearly swerved into a Mennonite's horse-drawn buggy. (I must have smoked half a pack of Lark cigarettes before I was calm enough to mount up again.) I almost got into a fight gassing up at a combo café and filling station in Ezel, Kentucky, with some ruffians I caught fingering the panniers on my bike when I emerged from the bathroom — but, at that very moment, miraculously, a state police car pulled in to gas up and they backed off. After a night in Bluefield, West Virginia, I lazed up the sine-cosine curves of the beautiful Blue Ridge Parkway along the spine of the Appalachians. Eventually, I landed in Washington, DC, where I was welcome to rest up at a friend's house in Georgetown and take stock. I stayed for three months.

When I got hold of Ginger Barber again, she told me what a couple of editors who rejected the book had carped about and asked if I minded doing a rewrite before she sent it out again. She express-mailed me a Xerox of the manuscript. I borrowed my friend's typewriter and churned out a thorough rewrite pronto at the kitchen table. Around that time I also ran out of money. I got a job working at the café in the old National Portrait Gallery, washing dishes, boning-out boiled chickens for its famous chicken salad, and mopping the gallery floors at closing. It was a downer after being a magazine editor in a nice office, a harbinger of things to come. After a month of that, I passed the Virginia taxi driver test and started driving the day shift (6:00 a.m. to 6:00 p.m.) for the Arlington Yellow Cab company, grueling and boring. I stuck at it through the fall of 1975, waiting, waiting, waiting, expecting that any day I'd get the exhilarating letter or phone call that *Bagging Bigfoot* had landed safely at one of the grand old publishing houses — of which there were more than a dozen back then — and I'd have it made in the shade.

It was not to be. Instead, I got a phone call just before Christmas that Ginger Barber was, regretfully, giving up on my novel. She cut me loose, just like that. By that time I was living in a dreary rooming house off Dupont Circle, spending too much of my hard-earned cab fare money on one decent meal a day in a Chinese restaurant around the corner. My dream of instant riches died hard and fast. Washington, DC, had always been a mere stopover. The snow was flying. I decided to just get on with the rest of my plan and return to upstate New York.

HUNKERING DOWN

I arrived in Saratoga Springs in January 1976, by Greyhound bus, leaving my motorcycle chained to a cast-iron fence at my friend's house back in Georgetown. I'd been very happy in Saratoga those autumn months of 1974 just before *Rolling Stone* lured me out west. It seemed the perfect place to hunker down and continue my struggle to write publishable books. Within a few days I got a job as an "aide" in the mental health unit of the local hospital, on the three-to-eleven shift, which gave me most of the day to pursue my literary ambitions. (Kurt Vonnegut said, "Nobody can be intelligent for more than five hours a day.") I found a sweet little one-bedroom furnished apartment in a carriage house off a cozy alleyway. The job was easy and interesting but required no personal investment.

When the weather turned nice in April, I took the bus down to DC to bring my motorcycle back but, chained up right out there on the sidewalk, it had been pretty much wrecked by vandals who'd smashed the lights, cut the cables, and sliced up the seat — perhaps frustrated that they couldn't steal it. I gave it away to the boyfriend of a girl I knew there and rode the bus back upstate. There was a Suzuki motorcycle shop in Saratoga and right away I bought a brand-new GT-380 — then about $1,400 — on an installment loan arranged by the dealer. And so I settled in for the long haul.

I was deliriously happy in my new life as a starving bohemian in this charming, sturdy small town of about 29,000 people. In 1976 there was still a residual hippie community there, and many wannabe musicians orbiting around a little folk club that Bob Dylan had once played in before he got famous (Caffe Lena), and Skidmore College where you could go see free movies, and a lot of bars downtown (the drinking age was still eighteen in New York) with a mix of students and hippies and working people. I made a lot of friends in that milieu. I quickly built a nicely structured life. I arranged to have my boxed-up books and my old Smith-Corona portable typewriter shipped east from San Francisco. And I got right down to work.

I decided to put *Bagging Bigfoot* on the shelf and start another novel right away, an ambitious comic metafiction phantasmagoria set in Saratoga Springs in 1881 called *The Summer That President Garfield Got Shot*. Saratoga had a colorful history and I expected to be there a long time, so this was kind of a love letter to my adopted town. I got a lot of it written in the months ahead, but the plots and subplots spiraled out of my control and proved unresolvable. It never did get published, but I learned a lot about what I didn't know about writing fiction, so it was a worthwhile exercise, and writing comedy kept me in a cheerful mood as I persisted in my quest to produce a publishable book.

I lasted in the hospital job about a year. I was a good mental health aide, having been on the patient end myself not many years earlier, and sympathetic to lost souls. I had some useful experience to share with the people who came into the unit, and we aides spent way more time talking with and listening to them than their shrinks did. But I backtalked the lady who ran the unit about something and got canned.

After that I had many unserious jobs with little long-term responsibility, many of them in restaurants — bartending, waiting on tables, prep cook, line cook. I liked that world. It was very sociable. I liked the work, developed a lot of useful skills, and was pretty good at it. Plus, you never had to worry about where dinner would come from — even if it just meant grabbing a half-eaten veal cutlet off the busboy's tray. I stayed away from the cocaine that was rampant on the scene at the time, though I would publish a different Saratoga novel (*The Halloween Ball*) about that very scene in the 1980s.

In 1977, I put aside my crazy historical novel and dusted off the summer camp novel I'd composed in Cambridge way back in 1972. The manuscript had followed me everywhere since then. I gave it a brisk rewrite, sent it out a few times, and soon enough managed to land another young agent named Wendy Lipkind. She sold it to a young Doubleday editor named Whit Stillman, who would go on to a career directing quirky independent movies (*Metropolitan, Barcelona, The Last Days of Disco*).

A Long Career in Short

The Wampanaki Tales would be my first published book. It came out in 1979. (In those days, the period needed to prepare a book for publication ran more than year.) Once out, it attracted next to zero critical attention from reviewers. But Doubleday would sell the paperback license that netted me a few extra bucks, and the movie option would be sold for $1,500 and resold annually for twelve years thereafter to the man who invented the Steadicam. Doubleday's hardcover advance (on royalties) was $3,000, minus Wendy Lipkind's 10 percent. I received the first half on signing the contract and would get the rest when I met whatever rewrite obligations Doubleday required — a standard arrangement at the time. I spent most of the money right away on a first-rate Orvis bamboo fly rod and a color TV. They proved to be excellent investments.

Perhaps to compensate for my dreary boyhood in Manhattan, I became a fly-fishing nut. The region around Saratoga contained several first-class trout streams and it was a way of immersing myself in nature that had been so out of reach for me as a city kid. Between fly-fishing and motorcycling, I managed to act out in my twenties the teenage adventures I'd missed out on, and get all that out of my system. The color TV allowed me to get Red Sox ballgames, which satisfied my entertainment needs the nights I wasn't working. By 1978 I'd also moved into a third-floor, two-bedroom garret apartment in a magnificent circa 1900 mansion in the center of town, where, for the first few years, I had a series of roommates, young guys like myself getting their lives together, most of whom became good friends.

My romantic life in those years was purposely spotty and opportunistic. My chief commitment was to my career in literature. Besides, I barely made enough money to take a girl out on a proper date. Skidmore had been an all-women's college until a few years earlier and was still predominately women by a big margin. The bars were full of avid young ladies. And I made plenty of female friends in the community too. I had my share of casual hookups. But, turning thirty, I still had a very firm sense of avoiding any commitment that veered anywhere near matrimony.

My second published novel, *A Clown in the Moonlight*, was a dark comedy about a young college professor at a place like Bennington (not far from Saratoga) whose marriage was going down the drain. I had never been married, of course, and had never taught in a college, but the exercise was worthwhile in imagining lives a little bit outside my own experience. Wendy Lipkind didn't like it and dumped me as a client, but I was picked up by Russell Galen at Scott Meredith's agency. He sold that book to St. Martin's Press. It was a flop commercially but I kept on going, often starting a new project as soon as I'd finished the last one. I experienced a lot of what anyone in this line of work would construe as failure, but I did not surrender.

JHK 1985

In this first phase of my book-writing career, between 1975 and 1988, I would publish eight novels, and at the end of that cycle I was still waiting on tables. By some miracle I did not lose heart. I managed to finally get *Bagging Bigfoot* into print (Tor Books, 1987), though the publisher stupidly changed the title to *The Hunt*. It sank without a trace. Many of my friends thought I was already a success, getting so many books published before I was forty. But I wanted commercial success. I wanted to earn enough money from my books to stop doing shit jobs on the side, real money, enough to live well. And I wanted some recognition from the literature world. Oddly, by then I was known enough among the reading public to get letters from other young writers who wanted help and advice. What I told them will give you a feel for the psychological state I'd adopted as my own credo, given the experience I'd acquired as a professional writer.

I told them that the central reality of a career in the arts is that perseverance counts more than talent. It's so important that I will repeat it in boldface and italics: ***perseverance counts more than talent***. There it is. Now you, too, know a strange and enigmatic truth about real life. This was a hard truth for young, ambitious writers to accept. Many were astounded to learn I was still waiting on tables after publishing eight novels. I refused to feel sorry for myself. I actually felt some pride and gratitude walking out of a bistro after a night's work with a hundred bucks in my pocket. I was at least my own man. Writing books was not a game for squishy egos. I encountered many people with talent, some huge talents, who simply could not pick themselves up from rejection and try again. Some of them came to very unfortunate ends.

I told them a couple of other important things. 1) The only way you'll ever know whether the universe has asked for a given work you want to produce is to step up and get the job done. Some people never get the answer to that question, even after doing the job. Herman Melville's *Moby-Dick* flopped when it was published in 1851. By the time it caught on in the college curricula as the quintessential great American novel Herman was long gone.

Along the same lines I told them: 2) You work in a vacuum. Get used to it. Don't seek validation from friends and relatives. Don't ask them to read your work, especially loose manuscript pages, which are an utterly annoying pain in the ass to read (especially in bed). Relatives, parents in particular, will dread finding themselves depicted as characters in your book(s) and will hate you for it. Seek validation only in the literary marketplace.

I handed them a few other nuggets about things I was personally convinced about, such as: don't go to writers' workshops; don't pursue a master's degree in so-called creative writing; don't join coteries of writers because all you'll get there is condescension, envy, rancor, malice, and schadenfreude.

As my career continued, I was sold down the river by one publisher after another. Dumped. Hung out to dry. Just about every publishing calamity that could happen in that era happened to me. One editor got fired just before my book came out, making it an "orphan" that no one at the company cared about. Another editor was an alcoholic who lost the manuscript of *An Embarrassment of Riches* on the subway and was too embarrassed to tell my agent, but instead just delayed her decision on the book for three months — after which we pulled the book and sold it elsewhere. One imprint I signed a contract with (Dial Press) was put out of business by its parent, Doubleday, when I was at the start of a two-book contract. One of my paperbacks came out without being proofread, full of typos. Another came out with my name printed wrong on the top of every other page (*John* Howard Kunstler). But I hung in there. I was confident that eventually I would *break through*.

In 1984, going on thirty-six, I married a nice girl I'd been living with for three years. She was a Skidmore grad, managing a chain bookshop in the shopping mall outside town when we met. I was squeaking by on one book advance after another — they were getting a little bit larger, but not by much — with some movie option money in the mix. All that just barely allowed me to hold up my end of the marriage. I was also cranking out short stories for the "glossy" magazines. These were the twilight years of that literary form, as the magazine business was headed for extinction. But one night, while I was off waiting tables at a fancy joint outside town, my agent called my wife at home to say he'd sold two of my stories in one day — one to *Playboy* and one to *Cosmopolitan* — which improved my agent's morale, at least. I walked out of the restaurant that night. These days, there is next to zero market for short stories. It's a dead medium, except in the writing classes.

That marriage ended in 1987. We just weren't happy. I put all the money I'd ever saved (and some borrowed money) into a down payment on a charming but decrepit little house near the Hudson River, ten miles east of Saratoga. I'd acquired a stray dog named Chloe. I sold my last motorcycle — a Suzuki 400 twin, nice bike — and bought a beater pickup truck and a bicycle. I was back to waiting tables at a joint in Saratoga when novel number eight came out, *Thunder Island* (Bantam Books), about adolescents in a summer beach town on the east coast. I was madly churning out nonfiction magazine articles to pay the light bill. I felt like I'd reached the end of the road in literature. That was the nadir of my career to that point, but it also proved a turning point into Phase Two.

I got a phone call out of the blue from an editor at the *New York Times Sunday Magazine*, named James Atlas, who was a kind of low-grade literary celebrity in his own right (he'd published a big biography of the legendary poet Delmore Schwartz). Atlas had seen some pieces of mine around in the magazines and he asked me to do a story about the real estate development boom in Vermont, which was only a half hour drive from where I lived. Atlas had a summer house in Bennington.

His tribe of Ivy League elites who summered there feared a suburban development explosion that would wreck the little state's rural charm. I executed the article well enough and got several other assignments from Atlas about late-modernity's effect on the landscape and society. One was about a suburban housewife outside Bangor, Maine, who was shot by a deer hunter, another about the economic decline of the little Hudson River town I was living in, two decades after its half dozen factories had all shuttered.

I'd been thinking about the subject of how we occupied the landscape of America for a long time, and I pitched the *Times* a story about, shall we say, the ontology of American suburbia, with the working title: "Why Is America So Fucking Ugly?" I was given a green light to go ahead. I handed in the story some weeks later and it was rejected. Boo hoo. My agent had me convert it into a book proposal and he sold it pronto to Simon & Schuster. It took me three years to get the book written (including legwork and interviews), and it took S&S another year to get it out with the title *The Geography of Nowhere*. That was 1993. Michiko Kakutani gave it a positive review in the *Times*. It sold briskly. It got me into a groove. I published two sequels on the subject of urban design for a popular audience — *Home from Nowhere* (1996) and *The City in Mind* (2002) — and that propelled me into a lucrative lecture career. I was good at it, with my background in college theater. Audiences were hungry to hear someone articulate the problems with their everyday environment, which they sensed and suffered in but couldn't quite comprehend, since it was an immersive reality. I liked to describe suburbia to them as "entropy made visible." They got it.

Young Man Blues

I wasn't a blockbuster author but, in my forties, I was finally making some decent money and I enjoyed what I was writing and lecturing on. These nonfiction books of mine caught on in the graduate schools, boosting my sales, keeping them alive year after a year. My book advances went up into six figures. I could order anything I wanted from the L.L. Bean catalog, my chief marker of true success. I even overcame my fear of flying by sheer necessity, having to make airplane trips to shoot my mouth off onstage and pick up handsome honoraria for doing it. And it was quite a privilege to finally travel to many parts of the USA I'd never visited. I made hundreds of these trips and even some overseas to lecture in Germany, Sweden, Australia, New Zealand, and South Africa. I was invited to most of the Ivy League universities. I was taken seriously as a literary intellectual.

I got married and divorced two more times during those years, but produced no children from any marriage. My divorces were not punishing, just genteel breakups. I didn't regret not having children; I was accumulating a large family of books. As it happened, writing those books about the history and fate of suburbia, I was prompted to pay attention to the subject of the oil industry, as oil was the prime mover behind mass motoring, the animating device of suburban life.

By the late 1990s several senior geologists retired from the major oil companies and published their dark and secret thoughts about where things were going — the darkest being that the oil age was liable to end in the first half of the twenty-first century, probably sooner rather than later, and would probably entail something that resembled a collapse of industrial civilization as we knew it. One couldn't help but be impressed by the gravity of that, coming from serious scientists.

Around the very same time, the mid-1990s, the internet was gaining traction with the general public and chat forums were sprouting on it. Some of these chat rooms picked up on those ominous quandaries about oil and our ability to carry on an advanced technological society. The general theory of the energy decline was called "Peak Oil."

I'd noticed this chatter while I was still writing *The Geography of Nowhere*. I discussed the implications in that book's final chapters, and throughout both its sequels. Then, around 2002, I undertook a book about this predicted collapse of our way of life. My long-time agent, Russ Galen, dismissed it out of hand, said it was "too dark," and wouldn't entertain selling a proposal for it. I had to fire him. I couldn't get another agent interested. Simon & Schuster, my publishing home for three books, turned it down and released me like an over-the-hill ballplayer. I was out in the cold. So I picked my ass up off the floor and sold the proposal on my own.

I'd had some correspondence over the years with Morgan Entrekin, part owner and editor-in-chief of the independent publisher Grove Atlantic Books. He liked the proposal for the book I was calling *The Long Emergency*. He liked it enough to offer me a contract, which I negotiated myself. I also twisted his arm to publish the completed manuscript of a novel I'd managed to compose in the interstices of my nonfiction labors through those busy years — this was my Martha Stewart roman à clef, *Maggie Darling, a Modern Romance*. It was a comedy about a "media goddess of hearth and home" whose marriage was cracking up. It was a fine performance, I thought.

Maggie Darling came out in 2003. It was trashed in the *New York Times* by reviewer Janet Maslin, an old colleague from back in 1972 at the *Boston Phoenix* (where she reviewed movies after John Koch went to *The Globe*). Grove Atlantic marketed *Maggie Darling* less than enthusiastically; I suspect because Mr. Entrekin socialized in circles that included Martha Stewart herself — Ms. Stewart had just been indicted for insider stock trading — and he had gotten squeamish about my book. In any case, it was a commercial flop. On the other hand, *The Long Emergency*, which Grove Atlantic brought out enthusiastically in 2005, was a hit, my bestselling book ever.

Industrial civilization took its sweet time collapsing — I didn't call it the *long* emergency for nothing — but the book industry started unraveling in the years that followed. Ironically, I was busier than ever. After *The Long Emergency*, I wrote a series of four novels under the banner *World Made by Hand* (the title of the first book — the others are *The Witch of Hebron*, *A History of the Future*, and *The Harrows of Spring*). It was quite an opus, more than a thousand pages altogether. The novels depict life in a small town on the upper Hudson River following an economic collapse. They feature a large cast of characters who revolve from foreground to background and back again through all four books. I wanted to get the same message of *The Long Emergency* out in a form that readers could experience differently, to get the picture through their senses, to feel, hear, touch, taste, and smell that new disposition of things.

In between the first two of those novels, I pounded out another nonfiction book, *Too Much Magic: Wishful Thinking, Technology, and the Fate of the Nation*. After that, Grove Atlantic told me not to write any more fiction, and that was the end of my run (seven books) there. I immediately wrote a novel set on a hippie commune in Vermont in 1967–68, with a nineteen-year-old girl as the protagonist. Why? Because I wanted to. I called that novel *A Safe and Happy Place* (2017). By then, I'd acquired another agent. He told me it might take two years to find a publisher for it, so I self-published it on Amazon and then self-published six novellas about an eleven-year-old boy growing up in Manhattan —again, because I wanted to — and I considered those ventures in self-publishing well worth doing. By then, I had a website (www.kunstler.com) as a platform for selling my own books and I was putting out a blog of political / social commentary titled *Clusterfuck Nation*. I even wrote a third nonfiction book on the subject of collapse, *Living in the Long Emergency* (BenBella Books, 2019), at my agent's urging — to "keep [my] brand alive." The advance was measly. I got it done . . . because I am a professional.

Meanwhile, by the twenty-teen years, the book-selling industry was falling apart. The independent bookshops were dying because of Amazon dot com. The distributors had fewer places to distribute to. The whole book-reviewing apparatus had dissolved, along with the newspaper business, so the book-reading public had no way of learning about new books from people capable of evaluating them. I was not sanguine about the fate of the entire scaffold for presenting literature to society, or even the future of the book itself as a prime cultural artifact. It'd had a good run of several hundred years, but perhaps its run was over. The long-playing record had been dead for decades and, as I have noted, that was the art form of my generation. The CD was dead too now. Even the Hollywood assembly line of motions pictures was falling apart. Americans were not going to cinemas anymore. Video streaming was a new wild west of fourth-rate content.

Young Man Blues

My regular stream of substantial book advances was certainly over. In whatever was left of bigtime trade publishing, the advance money was all being funneled into books by former presidents and other media celebrities, with mere crumbs left over for everybody else. I had to find another way to make a living. I was fortunately able to *monetize* my blog, as we say now. That is, make enough money writing political commentary on the internet to live on. Luckily, my book readership came along to the blog. And that is where things stand as I prepare to turn seventy-five the year I am writing this. I am closer to the end of my career now than to the middle of it. I'm satisfied with how it turned out. Adolescence is behind me.

Final Family Notes

Across my adult years, really from the time I turned professional in my twenties, my relations with my mother and father were distant. I was geographically remote from New York City through all those years, but especially during my long starving bohemian period in Saratoga, in the 1970s and '80s, when all I had was a motorcycle, and I was not inclined to ride it two hundred miles at holiday time in icy weather to see them (and was too poor take the train). Besides, the city repelled me. I'd become allergic to it, to its scale and its manic bustle. Later, when I was married and had cars, I visited my mother, Muriel, in Manhattan a few times a year, with my wife for cushioning against my mother's tyrannical personality.

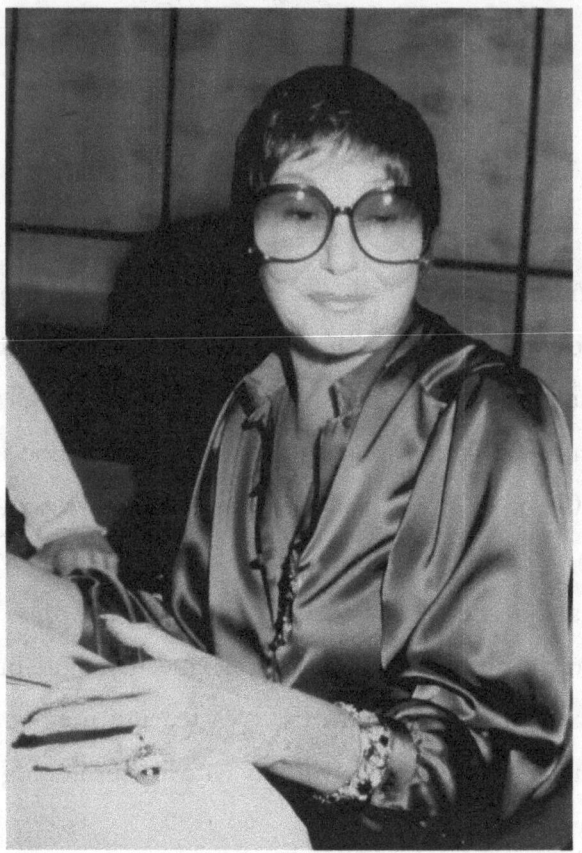

Muriel, 1992

My stepfather, Bernie Glaser, passed away in 1981 after a battle with lung cancer. He smoked Camel "straights" (unfiltered) ever since the war. (The year 1981 was when I quit smoking for good, too.) He'd had a tempering influence on my mother, and now he was gone. Muriel remained in their apartment on 68th Street. But our visits were always a travail. Her business, the stationery shop on Madison Avenue and 72nd Street, remained successful for the better part of another two decades. She'd had enough of marriage, though, by sixty, and she seemed comfortable alone. She had some old married friends and girlfriends to eat dinner out with and spent summers around her old coterie of gay boyfriends out on Fire Island, or in rented houses in Putnam County, just north of the city . . . "the country." She never discussed my books with me. I doubt she ever read them.

My father, Henry, broke up with my stepmother Pauline in the mid-1970s after twenty years of marriage. Both of them got married again eventually, my father to a woman named Judy whom I barely became acquainted with. Henry moved back into Manhattan after all those years in the Long Island suburbs, to an apartment on 57th Street. He worked in the diamond business until the bitter end. I met him for lunch near his office whenever I was in the city visiting Muriel, but we didn't have much to say to each other. I doubt he read any of my books either. We never talked about them.

In the mid-1990s, in her seventies, Muriel had enough of business and closed her shop. She couldn't sell the business because the lease was up and her low-rise building was slated for demolition to be replaced by a new apartment tower. She eventually had enough of New York City, too, though she'd spent her entire life there. Her friends were passing away, one by one. I was the only kin she could hope to depend on. She proposed to come upstate and live in Saratoga, where I could help care for her in her old age. I understood my obligation.

My then wife, Jennifer, and I found her a spacious apartment in the center of town, and eventually moved her into an even larger condo that we bought in a brand-new building one block from Saratoga's main street, Broadway, and all its attractions. In the late 1990s Saratoga entered a fabulous redevelopment cycle in which all the planning blunders of the postwar decades in the heart of town were being corrected with new buildings. It was one of the few small towns in the USA that was actually thriving.

Poor Muriel was desolate, though. Her few living friends were far away now, and she was unable to make any new ones upstate. Her haughty, imperious manner didn't help. She considered the locals hopeless rubes. With no one else at hand, she raged at me whenever I came to see her, or took her somewhere in a car or out to eat. Her old New York City doctor, a favorite with upper east side ladies of a certain age, had put her on the steroid prednisone many years earlier for muscle and joint pain, inflammation generally, and she never got off it.

I suppose it made her feel a lot better in the early going — that's why the doctors liked to prescribe it — but the side effects over time are awful and they were clearly catching up to my mother. She put on weight — a disaster for someone as vain as she was. It disordered her emotions. The last years of her life she was in a perpetual *'roid rage*, as the pro athletes call it, which probably also induced depression to go with the rage. I took to thinking of her as *Auntie Mame meets Rodan the Flying Reptile*. Whenever I stepped into her apartment, the first thing she said was, *I'm furious!* At what, Mom? *At the housekeeper . . . at George W. Bush . . . at the elevator taking too long . . .* She'd also been on a hormone replacement regimen at least since her fifties (in the 1970s). God knows how that interacted with the steroid she was on. Plus, she maintained her old habit of drinking a couple of scotches every evening. This aggravated her insomnia.

Her rages oddly plunged me back into some of my older emotional patterns and I began to suffer panic attacks after spending time in her company. Altogether, Muriel was in town about three years. Her only major medical emergency turned out to be her last. One night, in April 2001, she called after midnight complaining of trouble breathing. We lived only a block away and I went right over. It was obvious we had to get her to the hospital. The EMTs arrived and she was admitted. In a matter of hours, she was in the intensive care unit. She lingered there in a state of liminal consciousness for weeks. I read Dickens to her and she barely seemed to know I was there. The pulmonologist was frank about her prognosis. She'd smoked cigarettes since the 1930s. And prednisone had degraded all the tissues in her body, including her lungs, a condition the doctors call PPP, *piss poor protoplasm*. Eventually, she went into progressive organ failure, and on a night in May she passed on. She was eighty-one.

By a strange fate, I was informed by my father's wife Judy earlier that day that Henry had gone into emergency surgery for gallbladder cancer in New York City and died on the operating table at age eighty-four of heart failure. I told Judy that my mother was in extremis and I would not make it to Henry's funeral. I have never visited his grave, wherever it is in the city. Separated for forty-four years, Henry and Muriel passed on within hours of each other. Their deaths were merciful. Neither had to go through many years of abject decline nor arduous medical interventions. Both were mentally competent to the end. Their deaths were merciful to me as well — as I'd seen some of my friends' lives turn upside down with prolonged elder care.

Though she was completely nonreligious, I engaged the Saratoga rabbi to preside over her funeral. Her brother Buddy, the retired CIA spook, and his wife, Ina, flew up from Washington, and a handful of her old friends from the city managed to come too. A surprising number of my own friends showed up for the service. They'd met Muriel at parties and dinners we threw and found her charming and witty. She was that to them, I'm sure, just not so much when she was alone with me, capable of expressing only rage and fury.

We buried her in a peaceful rural cemetery near the Hudson River. I'm sure that never in her wildest dreams would she have imagined it to be her final resting place. After nearly year, in the Hebrew tradition, I arranged for a modest headstone to be placed on her grave. The inscription I ordered reads "Furious No More." Whatever you may think, it gave me tremendous satisfaction. Passing strangers will surely wonder about it. I've left instructions, when the time comes, to be planted in the same cemetery somewhere nearby. It's a tranquil, lovely place on a hill below the monument that commemorates the Battle of Saratoga, 1777. I've left instructions for my own epitaph: "Finally, a Good Night's Sleep."

The End

www.ingramcontent.com/pod-product-compliance
Lightning Source LLC
Chambersburg PA
CBHW011407070526
44586CB00022B/2585